Strange Attractors

WILEY SERIES IN COUPLES AND FAMILY DYNAMICS AND TREATMENT
Florence W. Kaslow, Series Editor

Treating the Changing Family: Handling Normative and Unusual Events
edited by Michele Harway

In-Laws: A Guide to Extended-Family Therapy
by Gloria Call Horsley

Handbook of Relational Diagnosis and Dysfunctional Family Patterns
edited by Florence W. Kaslow

Child-Centered Family Therapy
by Lucille L. Andreozzi

Strange Attractors: Chaos, Complexity, and the Art of Family Therapy
by Michael R. Bütz, Linda L. Chamberlain, and William G. McCown

Strange Attractors

Chaos, Complexity, and the
Art of Family Therapy

Michael R. Bütz
Linda L. Chamberlain
William G. McCown

John Wiley & Sons, Inc.

New York • Chichester • Brisbane • Toronto • Singapore • Weinheim

Copyright © 1997 by John Wiley & Sons, Inc.

Library of Congress Cataloging-in-Publication Data:

Bütz, Michael R.
    Strange attractors : chaos, complexity, and the art of family
therapy / Michael R. Bütz, Linda L. Chamberlain, William G. McCown.
        p.   cm. — (Wiley series in couples and family dynamics and
treatment)
    Includes index.
    ISBN 0-471-07951-0 (cloth : alk. paper)
    1. Family psychotherapy.   2. Chaotic behavior in systems.
I. Chamberlain, Linda L.   II. McCown, William George.   III. Title.
IV. Series.
RC488.5.B85   1996
616.89'156—dc20   96-16000

Printed in the United States of America

10 9 8 7 6 5 4 3 2 1

To my family, and the time it has taken for me to find a pattern amid the chaos of my father's death, as well as my deep gratitude to my lovely wife Shelli for her abiding support.

—*Michael*

To family, friends, colleagues, and students who have supported me in the writing of this book. A special thanks to Dr. Bill who brought so much order to my chaos and chaos to my order.

—*Linda*

To the families who assisted us in conceptualizing the dynamics described in this text.

—*Bill*

Series Preface

Our ability to form strong interpersonal bonds with romantic partners, children, parents, siblings, and other relations is one of the key characteristics that define our humanity. These coevolving relationships shape who we are, and what we become—they can be a source of great gratification, or tremendous pain. Yet, only in the mid-twentieth century did behavioral and social scientists really begin focusing on couples and family dynamics, and only in the past several decades have the theory and findings that emerged from those studies been used to develop effective therapeutic interventions for troubled couples and families.

We have made great progress in understanding the dynamics, structure, function, and interactional patterns of couples and families—and made tremendous strides in treatment. However, as we stand poised on the beginning of a new millennium, it seems quite clear that both intimate partnerships and family relationships are in a period of tremendous flux. Economic and sociopolitical factors are changing work patterns, parenting responsibilities, and relational dynamics. Modern medicine has helped lengthen the life span, giving rise to the need for transgenerational caretaking. Cohabitation, divorce, and remarriage are quite commonplace, and these social changes make it necessary for us to rethink and broaden our definition of what constitutes a family.

Thus, it is no longer enough simply to embrace the concept of the family as a system. In order to understand and effectively treat the evolving family, we must incorporate into our theoretical formulations, and therapeutic armamentarium, information derived from research and clinical practice on important emerging issues such as ethnicity, culture, religion, gender, sexual preference, family life cycle, socioeconomic status, education, physical and mental health, values, and belief systems.

The purpose of the Wiley Series in Couples and Family Dynamics and Treatment is to provide a forum for cutting-edge relational and family theory, practice, and research. Its scope is intended to be broad, diverse, and international. All books published in this series share a common mission—to reflect on the past, offer state-of-the-art information on the present, and speculate on, as well as attempt to shape, the future of the field.

FLORENCE W. KASLOW
Florida Couples and Family Institute
Duke University

Preface

What is chaos and complexity theory really? Well first of all, if our readers are confused about these terms, and the debate over them, we advise them to sit back and relax. *So is everyone else!* The list of the "informed confused" includes physicists, mathematicians, biologists, and neurologists and virtually anyone else attempting to use these terms. Each discipline tends to define these areas of study, as well as particular phenomena within the field, differently (Gleick, 1987; Goldstein, 1993, 1995). Our approach has been to find a palatable way of explaining these ideas to students and professionals in the mental health field. Based on our experience with presentations on this topic, we assume that most mental health practitioners do not have backgrounds in high-level mathematics or physics. Therefore, we attempt to instruct at two levels: The first is a conceptual introductory approach, as provided in Chapter 2; at the second level, we introduce technical applications in bits and pieces throughout the book. In addition, Chapter 11 presents an overview of such applications for interested readers. At times it has been difficult to simplify some of these highly technical ideas to make them conceptually more available to a general audience. We apologize if, at times, we offend those who are wedded to the more technical approach. We also apologize for occasionally being unable to describe nonlinear and chaotic processes in other than linear acumen. Here, Korzybski's call for better maps is certainly appreciated (1948). The issue of map and territory definitely applies to the next aspect of our discussion.

Each term—chaos, complexity, and the new physics—is an umbrella term under which a wide variety of conceptual models reside. For example, among other ideas, under chaos theory one finds dynamical systems theory, fractal geometry, and self-organization theory; under the new physics, one finds quantum theory and associated ideas that deviate from classical physics. Although each of these umbrella terms has its merits and ideas associated with it, we believe that the immense popularity of the term "chaos theory" has arisen from its mythological resonance (Bütz, 1995a; Bütz, Duran, & Tong, 1995; Bütz, Duran, Tong, & Tung, 1991). This set of ideas seemed to take hold with the popularization of Gleick's book *Chaos* (1987). Before that, most presentations in this area were reserved for scientific journals and academic discussions. The ideas really hadn't caught fire. James Yorke[1] (1975) got the right term—chaos— in his attempt to describe Lorenz's work (1963). Gleick ran with it. We believe the term resonated with a very deep mythological context, one might even say it has archetypal significance. Chaos theory, as a cluster of similar ideas, acquired its name because the dynamics observed engendered the primordial feeling of chaos in scientists attempting to describe what they were witnessing. These dynamics appeared to be completely random, which is how chaos is defined here in the West. However, according to the vast majority of indigenous mythological interpretations, chaos is only one aspect of a holistic process for forming a new, unknowable order. The use of chaos in myth indeed parallels its use in today's science (Briggs & Peat, 1989). While we will also use complexity theory and the new physics in our descriptions, it appears that the use of the term chaos theory has "stirred the pot" most vigorously.

It is our intention and hope that this book will speak to family therapists from broadly different theoretical backgrounds. While illustrating our perspective, we will address many of the theoretical works that have functioned as touchstones in family therapy for decades. In our theory and practice, we attempt to walk back and forth across the lines of what have been termed pure approaches (Haley, 1987; Jurek, Maier, Sandgren, Tall, & Searight, 1989; Norcross & Prochaska, 1982; Russell, Olson, Sprenkle, & Atilano, 1983) and integrated approaches (Aradi & Kaslow, 1987; Case & Robinson, 1990; Kaslow, 1986; Lebow, 1987). And, from our attempts to tread this path, there are inconsistencies. In fact, we actually disagree with one another on certain points. We view this as a positive, however, since rigid adherence would limit our view and reduce the number of opinions available. As Kauffman points out (1995), diversity increases the complexity of social systems and their ability to adapt. Using the theories previously described, and others, as different elements of a complex stew, we have worked toward providing a holistic conceptualization of theory and practice that together yield new ideas and techniques on working with families.

---

[1] Prigogine has also indicated that the first known use of the term *chaos* in relationship to this type of phenomenon was given by Kupemann in 1932 (Staff, 1992).

These new areas of science suggest techniques for family therapists, and in our opinion, new techniques that may be "strange attractors" in the colloquial sense as the title of this book implies. Chaos, complexity, the new physics, and family therapy may well be strange, or even odd things, to be attracted to one another. Although this is true in some ways, in many it is not. As we will describe in Chapter 1, systemic family therapy was born out of the search for new ideas about the origins of maladaptive, even pathological, behavior. Along the way, researchers discovered that patients have families[2] and that looking to ideas from the philosophy of science might tell us more about communication. Central notions in family therapy were inspired by this type of synthesis between therapists and scientists. Ideas such as the double bind and feedback loops were applied fruitfully to familial communication, and a field was born. Chaos, complexity, and the new physics represent science today, as well as some aspects of science that were left untapped for the past hundred years.

Out of these three models, chaos theory has been the one most frequently applied in family therapy to date. As we will argue in the pages to follow, whether or not chaos theory has provided "new techniques" in the past decade or more remains to be seen. Pioneers in this effort such as Dell and Goolishian (1981), Elkaïm (1981), Hoffman (1981), and Minuchin & Fishman (1981) all suggested new techniques and conceptualizations. Identifying pioneers in this area has been difficult because investigators have often used a piece of these theories here and there, and have used titles for their works such as "Order through Fluctuation" or "Non-equilibrium, Chance and Change" or simply not indicated they were describing chaotic dynamics. At times, this has been an embarrassing process of omission. Nevertheless, ideas about the use of chaos theory in family therapy have been entertained for over a decade. Throughout the remainder of this book, we will be suggesting what has worked, what will not work, and what may work. For example, it was originally thought that using certain models from chaos theory would enable professionals to diagram a family's process better (Elkaïm, 1981). It was discovered, however, that this is only useful in a retrospective fashion (Elkaïm, Goldbeter, & Goldbeter-Merinfeld, 1987). This was similar to meteorology's dismay at Lorenz's "sensitive dependence on initial conditions" (1963), in which he described dynamics so sensitive and complex that a variable as tiny as a butterfly in a weather system could completely alter the system over

---

[2] A distinction Richardson made (1948).

time. Thus, meteorologists had to settle for forecasts that would be accurate for a couple of days, maybe, and they gave up their attempts to extend forecasts years into the future.

Another suggestion was that chaos theory would be suitable for describing family dynamics in an analogous fashion. This has indeed been the case, and we make use of it here, but it falls short of the "physics envy" position many social scientists yearn to appease. Consequently, this approach often meets with criticisms that users cannot predict and control behavior, and that "this is not empirical." However, many aspects of chaos theory, to borrow from Levy (1992, p. 110), spit in the face of empiricism as unstable systems over time can neither be predicted nor controlled. In addition, we have come to understand that in the past several years scientists have had a difficult time agreeing about when they actually have found "chaos." While certain measures exist that are generally agreed on, many more questions exist about measuring its presence. In Chapter 11, the final chapter of this book, we will discuss these highly technical arguments regarding data collection and a host of new ideas about measuring change in systems. Other scientific disciplines we have mentioned are less affected by these problems, since complexity theory is so new and the new physics (quantum theory and related nonclassical ideas) has been developing since the beginning of this century. To place this synthesis in perspective, we choose analogical descriptions for this book, not only to reflect the tenuous nature of measuring chaos at this time but also to focus on what the scientific method is all about. The scientific method does not outline measuring phenomena in a haphazard manner. Instead, one must build hypotheses, and then build a theory that can be tested out through measurement. This is our focus here, and analogy best serves our need to build theory as well as comment on the state of the field.

The text begins with a brief history of systemic family therapy and describes how ideas there were inspired by new developments in science. The emphasis is on how new scientific theory was used in family therapy to lead toward new conceptualizations, techniques, and perhaps support for existing techniques. Chapter 2 introduces the reader to ideas in chaos theory, complexity theory, and the new physics with a brief contextual history. Here, we have provided theoretical constructs that may serve as landmarks as we discuss these theories and family therapy. In Chapters 3 and 4, we look at central ideas in chaos, complexity, and the new physics; we will revisit the "theoretical constructs" discussed in Chapter 2 and begin our journey through case material illustrating those constructs.

Chapters 5, 6, 7, 8, and 9 offer more complex formulations of various theoretical constructs with specific recommendations for practice. We emphasize the idea of stability in these chapters, and explain how stability offers a two-way mirror for therapists to conceptualize their cases: Is there enough complexity, enough chaos, or not enough? At the end of our path, we emphasize caution in therapy, and the ethics of practice. Chapter 10 contains our ideas about ethics as well as approximations about the future of family therapy. We hope you will find this a worthwhile journey.

M.R.B.
L.L.C.
W.G.M.

Acknowledgments

A S WITH ANY endeavor, there are those who often anonymously have set the stage for others. Ours is no exception. Tom Masters is a soft-spoken, even-tempered man who went about the task of attempting to organize the first conference on chaos theory for the social sciences. Only a select few answered the call for papers, and the conference was canceled due to the lack of interest. But, out of that initial failure, Tom began to assemble what eventually was called the "Chaos in praxis network." There, one could find others interested in chaos theory, their field of study and specific topic of interest. Out of this network grew the publication *The Social Dynamicist,* which Tom edited, and the Society for Chaos Theory in Psychology, founded by Larry Vandervert, Fred Abraham, and Alan Combs. *The Social Dynamicist* was a very valuable publication as it served as one of the first forums for those of us attempting to apply chaos theory to the social sciences. The society was important for similar reasons and, in addition, the inaugural conference in San Francisco was where, unwittingly, all three of us met. At the following year's conference, Tom Levine asked the three of us to present together on a panel. There, he admitted interest that exceeded knowledge and gave us the floor, without fully realizing that at this time we may have all been similarly lacking in qualifications. Later that day, Bill invited Michael and Linda to join him to speak at a symposium at the American Psychological Association the next day, where although somewhat flustered by the crowd, we came to understand each other's ideas more fully. Therefore, we would like to thank Tom Masters, Larry Vandervert, Fred Abraham, Alan Combs, and Tom Levine for fostering an environment where we could come together. Also, we wish to thank Divisions, 1, 3, 12, 16, 17, 20, 24, 26, 29, 37, 42, 45, and especially 43, Family Psychology, for sponsoring our presentations at the American Psychological Association National Convention for the past five years. This has been an immensely generous and useful forum.

We also owe thanks to those who have reviewed our work and offered the right balance of both support and constructive criticism. Prominent among these individuals are Eduardo Duran, Bruce Francis, Tom Masters, Robert Morgan, Robin Robertson, and Ben Tong.

There are also many who have provided professional and personal support over the past several years that we would like to thank: Eduardo Duran, Peter Dybwad, Kim and Terry Faulkner, The Fenton Family, Karen Huang, Julia Lewis, Robert Morgan, Richard Recor, Robin Robertson, the Takata families, Ben Tong, May Tung, Bill Vlach, Carlos and Ann Wagner, and the Society for Chaos in Psychology and the Life Sciences.

Michael Bütz wishes to specifically acknowledge the support received at Cornerstone Behavioral Health and Mountain Regional Services, Inc. from John Holderegger, Kim Faulkner, Cay Cox, Linda Bennet, Cloyd Cornia, Wendy Slagowski, John Knopf, and Sue Regnier. Without this support for more academic pursuits this book would have never been realized.

Linda Chamberlain wishes to acknowledge Marty Dubin and Justin Schulz for their encouragement in pursuing this area, her students at the University of Denver whose interest and enthusiasm are so infectious, Shelly Smith-Acuña, Debra Anderson, Cindy Jew, Jon Richard, Arlene Green, and the Denver "Chaos Club."

William McCown wishes to acknowledge the long-time collaboration of Judith Johnson. Previous research regarding family therapy and nonlinear dynamics was generously supported by the late Mrs. J. B. Lesley. Luciano L'Abate, Alan Summers, and Bob Abouee deserve a tremendous degree of thanks for their ideas and inspiration.

Last, and most importantly, our thanks to our editor, Kelly Franklin, who had the foresight, patience, and courage to seek out a text of this nature and follow it through to the end with us.

Contents

PART ONE   SENSITIVITY TO INITIAL CONDITIONS

1 Warning, Objects Behind the Mirror May Be More
   Complex Than They Appear   3
2 A Walk Through the Canyon   21

PART TWO   FAMILIES . . . COMPLEX TERRAIN

3 Into the "Phrase Space"   55
4 The Eerie Beauty of Strange Attractors   67

PART THREE   CATCHING THE BUTTERFLY—
             CHAOS IN THERAPY

5 In the Eye of the Storm   85
6 Fractals and Forks in the Road   93
7 At the Turning Point   117
8 Trying to Unscramble the Eggs   149
9 The Critical Moment   172

PART FOUR   NO PREDICTABLE PERIOD

10 From Chaos to Order, or . . . From Order to Chaos   193
11 Epigram: Measuring Change in Chaotic Systems,
    Problems with Modeling, and the Need for
    Case Studies   219

References   233

Author Index   251

Subject Index   257

PART ONE

SENSITIVITY TO INITIAL CONDITIONS

Warning, Objects Behind the Mirror May Be More Complex Than They Appear

The law of chaos is the law of ideas,
of improvisations and seasons of belief.
                              —Wallace Stevens (1982, p. 255)

A CENTRAL QUEST for psychologists and other social scientists is to understand what constitutes the process of change in human beings. Regardless of theoretical orientation, the question of how to influence and produce differences in human behavior is a fundamental concern of clinical research and theory. Perhaps all sciences can be thought of as orbiting around this search for the conditions or variables that create transformations in a "subject," be it a weather pattern, an atomic particle, a virus, or even a human being.

Scientific research has long relied on the linear paradigm of cause and effect that forms the basis for lawful, orderly, and predictable change. The search for the "x's" that produce the "y's" has guided science for the past century. In many areas of scientific inquiry, however, a new paradigm has begun to challenge the Newtonian laws of an orderly, predictable universe. Chaos theory, and related fields such as nonlinear systems dynamics have stirred scientific study in almost every discipline during the past two decades. Questions arising from some of the "blanks" in our scientific understanding of the interaction between elements in a given system have resulted in a rethinking of how the world operates. The expression "chaos theory," is an umbrella under which researchers have categorized a wide variety of new scientific theory. The central focus shared by this new set of theories is the notion that while certain phenomena appear to be chaotic, or random, they are actually part of a larger coherent process that results in adaptive transformation. James Yorke coined the expression *chaos theory* in attempting to describe nonlinear dynamics to other scientists. The term resonated with these professionals, who having focused on linear phenomena, experienced nonlinear phenomena as chaos too.

"Complexity" is a term that is often used alongside chaos theory, and often confused with it. We view complexity as part of chaos theory, and as descriptive of systems at the edge of moving into chaotic dynamics. These systems are open and have "complex" interactions with the environment and within themselves, but they are not so open as to become chaotic. They are still in a stable state of existence. The implications of these new ideas are vast, almost mind numbing in the leap they make from classical modes of thought where the emphasis is on linearity.

This new epistemology is being examined in disciplines as diverse as economics, meteorology, mathematics, biology, physics, medicine, and anthropology. The examination of chaos in systems breaks across the lines that separate scientific disciplines. Because it is a science that addresses the global nature of systems, "it has brought together thinkers from fields that had been widely separated" (Gleick, 1987, p. 5).

Since the beginning of the linear paradigm's influence on scientific inquiry, certain assumptions about nature have been maintained—that orderly structures and immutable laws operate to maintain order. Our new science, the science of chaos and complexity, is based on the vastly different premise that *nature is disorderly*, and that pattern and order are generated by scientific inquiry. One of the significant shifts that is at the heart of chaos theory, and began in quantum physics, is the introduction of the observer into the observed. By rejecting the notions that our presence does not alter the environment and that the universe operates predictably, we open our eyes to see that *"order" is chaos in nature*.

As Thomas H. Leahey (1987, p. 25) notes in his text on the history of psychology, psychologists have long suffered from a peculiar malady known as "physics envy." Throughout psychology's relatively short history, the major theorists have attempted to model psychology's epistemology after developments in the science of physics. The linear paradigm laid the foundation for a cause-effect, lawfully ordered epistemology in all sciences including psychology. Change, in the Newtonian paradigm, is a predictable, law governed, orderly process that offers a consistent outcome from a given set of circumstances.

The belief in cause and effect is the cornerstone of empirical research in all scientific endeavors. Experiments are designed to define and delineate a cause or stimulus that will provide a predictable effect or response. Bohm and Peat (1987) describe the purpose of empiricism in physics as "to produce formulae that will correctly predict the results of experiments" (p. 5). As a result, empiricists believe in a Newtonian universe which operates according to a set of comprehensive, immutable laws that "unfailingly govern all phenomena." The search for this kind of universal theory of human development, personality, and behavioral change has been the ultimate goal of many researchers and theorists in the mental health field.

The theory of the universe as the ultimate machine was widely accepted during the formative years of the science of psychology and other fields that address human change. Behaviorism followed suit, and the paradigms of classical and operant conditioning largely defined human behavior as a mechanistic process that could be predicted and controlled with a clear enough understanding of the relationship between a stimulus and a response. Mechanistic science emphasizes stability, order, uniformity, and homeostasis. Its goal is to provide a systematic means for acting on the world, for predicting and modifying the course of natural processes, and for conceiving devices that can harness and exploit the forces of nature. But as Waldrop (1992) notes, "Predictions are nice, if you can make them. But the essence of science lies in explanation, laying bare the fundamental mechanisms of nature" (p. 39). And, therefore, the goal is not necessarily analogous to the political slogan of manifest destiny that served to conquer much of North America.

The basis for scientific inquiry and understanding began to shift early in this century when physicists like Bohr and Heisenberg, as well as others whom we will describe later, delivered evidence that challenged the universal harmony of Newton's paradigm (Herbert, 1985, p. 199). Concepts derived from quantum theory emerged, introducing the observer back into the system, and set the stage for profound changes to occur in the sciences. Although it presented a clear challenge to Newtonian laws, the epistemology of even Einstein's physics (1954) was still largely deterministic and decidedly mechanistic. As he once said, "I cannot believe God plays dice with the universe." For Einstein, the use of probabilities was unacceptable given the goal of achieving a "complete" deterministic description of the world. As Alvin Toffler notes in his introduction to Prigogine and Stengers', *Order out of Chaos* (1984), "Today, however, the Age of the Machine is screeching to a halt . . . the decline of the industrial age forces us to confront the painful limitations of the machine model of reality" (p. xiii).

What are the implications of this new outlook for the dynamics of change in human systems? This first chapter will clarify how hypotheses generated by science have influenced our perceptions and understanding of family dynamics. Once we have established this foothold, our focus will shift to how chaos theory and other related scientific pursuits are beginning to influence family therapy. In Chapter 2, we will go into a comfortable level of detail, we hope, in sharing the basic concepts of chaos theory to a degree that will facilitate the explanations of family dynamics in the remainder of this book.

SYSTEMIC FAMILY THERAPY: MOVING TOWARD A PARADIGM OF FLUID COMMUNICATION

The discussion of order is often couched in terms of information. This is of particular value for the discussion of self-organization because the general paradigma [sic] embraces not only material structures, but also mental structures , such as ideas, concepts or visions. (Erich Jantsch, 1980, p. 50)

In comparison with individually based therapies, family therapy is a relatively new field in the history of psychological treatment. Family therapy developed between the 1940s and the 1960s. Since that time, three primary modalities have emerged: structural, strategic, and systemic. Our focus here will be on a systemic orientation to family therapy, with specific attention to aspects of its evolution. From our point of view, "systemic" family therapy is distinct in recognizing communication as vital to the adaptation of the self-determined system we have come to know collectively as a family. Our emphasis here begins at the midline of strategic family therapy and extends toward the outer bounds of the systemic viewpoint. During the development of systemic family therapy, five paradigm shifts have been influenced by theories in the "hard sciences." It appears that the fifth paradigm shift has been constellating for more than a decade with the aid of ideas found in chaos theory. Bearing this in mind, we will begin with a brief history of family therapy and then move on to address each of the five paradigms.

FAMILY THERAPY IN THE BEGINNING

The field of family therapy emerged between 1940 and 1960 in many places and from several disciplinary orientations at roughly the same time. Because of the multiple places from which family therapy emerged, there are contending "founders" of the movement including Ackerman (1938), Richardson (1948), and Bell (Broderick & Schrader, 1981). These theorists made connections that today some may feel are obvious—such as that *Patients Have Families* (Richardson, 1948). At the time, however, their observations were considered revolutionary. While these theorists were pioneers in family therapy, much of their work still favored their own training in either psychoanalysis or medicine. What has come to be uniquely the domain of systemic family therapy was first developed by Bateson's group in Palo Alto in 1952.

In redefining the reference point of therapy by focusing on specific dynamics that occur in familial communication, Gregory Bateson and his group Don Jackson, Jay Haley, and John Weakland (1956) created a new model for therapy whose kernel was the "double bind" hypothesis. Essential in formulating this new orientation were the group's inquiries into the ideas of logic and structure which were cited frequently: Whitehead and Russell's work on the theory of logical types (1910/1964) and Korzybski's work on "map territories" in *Science and Sanity* (1948). The double binds (Bateson et al., 1956) that the group spoke of were created when members of a family "tangled" these logical types. They mapped territories to the point where the client was in a no-win situation; as some say: "Damned if you do, and damned if you don't." As a result, communication in the family was also tangled to the point where it was often unintelligible—particularly the client's attempts to express him- or herself. The group focused on a three-party type of interaction to uncover this pattern, and at the same time Haley emphasized what was truly unique about the "schizophrenogenic" family (1959). He found that the two primary ingredients that made the family of an individual diagnosed with schizophrenia unique were first, the lack of affirmation in communication, and second, the lack of leadership in these families. Other theorists were working on their projects at this time as well, but it appears historically that Bateson's group was the most influential.

At the same time, theorists such as Lidz (1957), Bowen (1960) and Whitaker (1958) were doing work with similar families to develop their own theoretical models. Family theorists of the time did not work in isolation, and referenced one another often in their essays. Bowen's work, which started in 1954 , is a good example of theorists' endeavors outside the Palo Alto group. His work focused on the idea of "emotional divorce" between parents, who remained aloof and disconnected from one another. Bowen cited Hill's work, which hypothesized that it takes three generations to produce a child manifesting schizophrenic behavior. He also recognized the idea of "peace at any price," which was connected to the notion that the parents had a difficult time with anxiety. This type of behavior seemed to also correspond with the parents' aloof and emotionally distant behavior. Bowen's work, like that of Lidz and Whitaker, was unique, and at the same time similar to Bateson's group in that its primary focus was on communication patterns within the family.

Family therapy seemed to come into its own with the establishment of the journal *Family Process,* which called for works from many disciplines to build theory on "broader interactional and transactional events in the relations among people" (Haley, 1962). Most notably, the journal acknowledged the omission of the family in theory devoted mainly to the individual or the social community.

Obviously, family therapists such as Laing, Minuchin, and Satir, to mention but a few, also made a significant impact during the early years of family therapy that followed the establishment of the journal *Family Process.* Still, among these pioneers, it was Bateson and his group, Haley, Jackson, and Weakland, who seemed to derive what became uniquely systemic family therapy with their emphasis on communication, and later cybernetics. It is here that we are able to see the first two paradigms in systemic family therapy. The first is the metacommunicative tangle theory, the double bind. The second was based on Wiener's cybernetic theory (1961), which was first addressed in Bateson's group, but later brought to its full power with the Milan group's work (Selvini-Palazzoli, Boscolo, Cecchin, & Prata, 1978).

THE FIRST PARADIGM: DOUBLE BIND

In an early essay Bateson (1955) stated that "human verbal communication can operate and always does operate at many contrasting levels of abstraction." Also in this essay, he advanced the idea of metalinguistic and metacommunicative messages, describing their importance through the implicit messages in communication. Using monkeys at play as an example, he described how the implicit message may be different from the explicit behavior observed, in that while the monkeys seem to be in "combat," there is the implicit message, "This is play." With these ideas as a base, Bateson discussed frames and paradoxes as possible problems in psychopathology, and psychotic behavior in particular, where the individual is unable to recognize metaphors and interprets them literally. In this article, Bateson made especially noteworthy mention of two works outside what some may consider as the "normal" realm of study in the social sciences: Whitehead and Russell's *Principia Mathematica* (1910/1964), and Korzybski's *Science and Sanity* (1948).

Whitehead and Russell's theory of logical types (1910/1964) may be summarized by discussing the "vicious-circle principle." The authors define vicious circles as questions that "arise from supposing that a collection of objects may contain members which can only be defined by means of the collection as a whole" (p. 55). What the whole series of arguments in this essay seem to communicate is that an all-inclusive total set has subsets or apparent variables that fit the set better or worse than others, and as such they do not exactly fit the "whole." Whitehead and Russell argue that these situations in logic are better described by a hierarchy because in each instance there is *ambiguity* at a certain point in a "set." In a similar manner, Korzybski (1948) also discusses the problems inherent in defining structure. In his chapter on structure from *Science and Sanity*, he makes three essential points in discussing structure: (a) no object occurs in isolation, but belongs to a collection of relations; (b) language is only a map of structure; and (c) relations occur in a multidimensional order. Applying these points, Korzybski describes language as a map that guides and inspires scientific theory. He argues that the linguistic map is not necessarily the same as the territory itself; that, in fact, it is an effort at representing the territory, but its accuracy and detail can and should be questioned. Consequently, Korzybski contends that to build more accurate linguistic maps, we must develop better theory for greater precision.

Bateson and his group then applied these ideas to metacommunicative tangles in a way that clarified troublesome family dynamics. Leading up to the paper on the double bind, Bateson (1955) gave a talk[1] in which he made the point of redefining "ego weakness" in schizophrenia as an inability to interpret signals that define what type of message a message is meant to be. He stated that a person diagnosed with schizophrenia finds him- or herself in a "metacommunicative tangle" created

---

[1] As Bateson indicates in this book: "This is the edited version of a talk, 'How the Deviant Sees His Society,' given May, 1955 at the Conference on the Epidemiology of Mental Health held at Brighton, Utah."

by playing multiple logical types[2] against each other in the traumatic situation. As a result, the person is unable to distinguish a "message-identifying signal," and consequently is ill-suited to discriminate between reality and fantasy. What followed this talk was the group's seminal paper on the double bind.

The double bind, which is now so well known (Bateson et al., 1956), was described as "a situation in which no matter what a person does, he can't win." The authors hypothesize that a person caught in a double bind may develop schizophrenic symptoms. This was in essence the sequence that led to the first systemic paradigm with a basis in hard science. By building on the ideas of the vicious-circle principle and map-territory ambiguities, Bateson and his group were able to derive an extremely useful model of family interactions. Family communication, seen from this perspective, allowed therapists to view these complicated living systems we call families with some reference point to assist them. It seems this was one of the first steps systemic family therapy had to make. The second step, or the second paradigm that followed this first step, is not nearly so simple to describe. Consequently, we will simply admit that an entire book could be written about cybernetic theory's use in family therapy, and try instead to point the reader to what seems to be its beginning, and toward what appears to be its best use.

THE SECOND PARADIGM: A TOTALITY THAT AUTOCORRECTS

In an article that shortly followed the introduction of the double bind, Haley (1959) pointed to the use of cybernetic theory (Wiener, 1961) as a better language to discuss family systems. A great deal of work on this topic followed Haley's article discussing cybernetic theory and family therapy "The Family of the Schizophrenic: A Model System" (1959). A treatment of this work encompasses too many articles and books to cover historically with any degree of clarity here. Nevertheless, this theory continues to occupy a central position in contemporary family therapy literature (Dell, 1986; Steinglass, 1984; White, 1986). For that reason, we will attempt to provide a brief overview of the main tenets of this approach. Cybernetic theory's best use seemed to come from the work of Mara Selvini-Palazzoli, Luigi Boscolo, Gianfranco Cecchin, and Giuliana Prata,

---

[2] Whitehead and Russell's work, 1910.

frequently termed the "Milan group" (Selvini-Palazzoli, 1970; Selvini-Palazzoli, Boscolo, Cecchin, & Prata 1978, 1980). What was especially inviting about this system's approach was their evenhanded treatment of family members (MacKinnon & Miller, 1985, p. 83). This group seemed to emerge fully on the scene of family therapy with the publication of *Paradox and Counterparadox* (1978). In this book, they outline their method of doing systems work, while in a later article they clarified the practicality of their method (1980).

Basic to their ideas is the notion of feedback,[3] which is a central concept in cybernetic theory. The Milan group states it this way: "The family is a self-regulating system which controls itself according to rules formed over a period of time through a process of trial and error" (Selvini-Palazzoli et al., 1978, p. 3). This statement in itself is nothing particularly new (Bateson, 1972), but the method that this group used to attend to what is labeled as "pathological behavior" was indeed new. The method is the key here because in the Milan system of approaching family difficulties we find no emphasis on pathology, but instead on troublesome rules for feedback in the family system and symptoms that represent systemwide attempts at adaptation.

In its study, the Milan group used a team approach to work with families in a noninvasive manner. Typically, a male and a female therapist were behind a one-way mirror, while another male and female therapy team were in the room with the family. There are many more details in their method that for brevity we must omit here, but essentially what happened is that the team as a whole (four members) would make hypotheses about the presenting family's troublesome rules, and then during the session each team would form new hypotheses or elaborate on the original hypothesis formed by the larger team.[4] Toward the end of the session, the team with the family would leave to join the team behind the mirror.[5] There they would discuss their hypotheses, and formulate an intervention. Up to this point, they would have made no intervention; the therapists in the room were only asking questions to gain more information. This intervention is also unique in that by design it does not attribute bad or good to any part of the system.

---

[3] In their early reference to feedback they cite Watzlawick, Beavin, and Jackson (1967), as well as Rabkin (1972) (Selvini-Palazzoli et al., 1978, pp. 3–4).

[4] In the case of the therapists in the room, this hypothesizing would be in their own minds, while behind the mirror the other team was free to discuss these hypothesises aloud.

[5] This approach was an offshoot of Minuchin and Haley's coaching technique developed in the late 1960s and early 1970s (Broderick & Schrader, 1981, p. 29).

Instead, the intervention *positively connotes* or *prescribes* behavior observed. As the group states it:

> Dysfunctional families are in fact regularly, especially in moments of crisis, prone to . . . the distribution of such stereotyped labels as "bad," "sick," "weak," "inefficient," "carrier of hereditary or social taints," etc. *Therefore, the primary function of the positive connotation of all the observable behaviors of the group is that of permitting the therapists access to the systemic model.* (Selvini-Palazzoli et al., 1978, p. 56)

Finally, they saw the system as having three fundamental characteristics:

> (1) *Totality* (the system is largely independent of the elements which make it up); (2) *autocorrective capacity* (and therefore the tendency toward homeostasis); (3) *capacity for transformation.* (Selvini-Palazzoli et al., 1978, p. 56)

In this unique approach, what we see is that the Milan group had faith in the system's ability to "autocorrect" if only the team could find the correct trigger to change the rules of the system. And, rather than jump in willy-nilly to evoke change immediately, they observed the system for a long while before offering an intervention. Even this interaction was constructed to be in concert with the harmony already existing within the family. *Therefore, we see the second shift in family therapy—respect for the family's own unique harmony as a totality.*

Where Bateson and his group introduced therapists to families as metacommunicative wholes in the first paradigm, this in itself does not convey a respect for the family as a totality or as an autocorrective system. Under the first paradigm, it was still within reason to attempt various types of intervention not aimed at positively connoting all the observable behaviors of the family. The Milan group directed family therapists to respect the uniqueness of a family system, and incorporate it into their recommendations for change. This congruence and respect are what seem to be the most unique aspects in the Milan group's approach to systemic theory.

What the observant reader may have noticed is the overlap to general systems theory (Bertalanffy, 1968) in the Milan group's third fundamental characteristic. This is the capacity to transform. It is one of the hallmarks of general systems theory, which for us is an advance over cybernetic ideas. In fact, their use of both cybernetic theory and general systems theory may have fostered the unique aspects of the Milan group's approach, allowing them a decided advantage over previous uses of cybernetic theory in family therapy.

THE THIRD PARADIGM: AN OPEN SYSTEM
WITH TRANSFORMATIVE STATES

Before the advent of general systems theory, it was still conceivable to think of organisms as machines. We know machines can communicate. In fact, in this age we refer to our computers as "talking to each other." There are also autocorrective machines that are able to make use of feedback, and may be seen as totalities. Arguably, one of the most primitive cybernetic mechanisms is the thermostat in the home that regulates temperature. Still, we would not refer to a computer or a heating system as "transforming." "Transformation" is a partial or whole change in composition or structure. In this instance, moreover, we are referring to an entity that is self-transformative. Machines are able to transform, but only by our intervention, whereas caterpillars transform into butterflies by themselves. We could also add to this dimension the argument of self-aware transformation. Perhaps a caterpillar cannot approach this type of existence? Since we know of no one who speaks caterpillar, with the possible exception of Dr. Dolittle, we cannot know the answer to this question. Besides, this argument is not as ridiculous as it might seem because the two theories we are comparing are at the heart of the artificial life debate (Levy, 1992). Without the ability to transform, humans become robots, and without self-awareness they may or may not be equivalent to caterpillars.

Bertalanffy's general systems theory reorganizes autocorrective totalities into irreversible transforming systems.[6] He makes clear the distinctions between his theory and Weiner's cybernetics:

> Systems theory also is frequently identified with cybernetics and control theory. This again is incorrect. Cybernetics, as the theory of control mechanisms in technology and nature are founded on the concepts of information and feedback, is but a part of a general theory of systems; cybernetic systems are a special case, however important, of systems showing self-regulation. (1968, p. 17)

What we have then is an open system[7] that is dominated by two main states, "homeostatic tendency on one hand, and the capacity for transformation on the other" (Selvini-Palazzoli et al., 1978, p. 4). Or, do we? Again, we must distinguish between mechanistic language and organic language:

---

[6] This is a major component in the criteria Prigogine and Stengers use to distinguish their theories also (1984).

[7] This is no minor point, as it is the crux of the difference.

> Concepts and models of equilibrium, homeostasis, adjustment, etc., are
> suitable for the maintenance of systems, but inadequate for phenomena of
> change, differentiation, evolution, negentropy, production of improbable
> states, creativity, building-up of tensions, self-realization, emergence, etc.
> (Bertalanffy, 1968, p. 23)

Bertalanffy introduced and prefers the term "steady state" to describe
periods of stability. In our discussion, we will use this term since it better
describes organic processes: "It is presently clearer to refer to the *steady
state* or *stability* of a system" (Watzlawick, Beavin, & Jackson, 1967, p. 146).
Bertalanffy's ideas are entirely unique in contrast to models offered earlier, and as such the use of his ideas in family therapy were also. One
might see the Milan Group as the bridge between the mechanistic and the
organismic viewpoints whereby they made use of both cybernetics and
general systems theory.

   Auerswald (1985) nicely introduces what general systems theory is able
to provide family therapy by comparing several therapeutic paradigms
with one another through a description of his interventions with a client:

> It is probable that the *medical* helpers at the time of Rose's first hospitaliza-
> tion concluded that their treatment had produced "change" in Rose. My
> *paradoxical* prescription did produce "change" in the family and in Rose's
> behavior—albeit limited and temporary. But not until I had completed my
> ecological exploration did I find the intervention that produced a *transform,*
> not a change [italics added]. (p. 12)

Intrinsic to the whole notion of transformation is that the system is open,
not closed. Like the emphasis of many theorists on feedback in cybernetic
theory (Barry, 1972, among others), the sticking point in general systems
theory was the openness of the system. While emphasized by a number of
early theorists (Bowen, 1978; Minuchin, 1974; Minuchin et al., 1975), this
distinction had already made (Watzlawick, Beavin, & Jackson 1967) the
virtues of an open systems approach and general systems theory strikingly clear. They ascribed to a Bertalanffian position, in which open systems possess certain "properties:" wholeness, nonsummativity, feedback,
and equifinality (1967, pp. 123–129). These properties were key, since
they laid the groundwork to discuss transformation: "There are important simultaneous factors of change in operation, and a model of family
interaction must incorporate these and other principles into a more complex configuration" (1967, pp. 146–147). Once the therapist incorporates
the notion that organisms are open systems which transform, it becomes
clear that the life of such a system is a "Game Without End" (Watzlawick,
Beavin, & Jackson, 1967, p. 232).

The introduction of this paradigm produced new conceptualizations (Mostwin, 1974), applications in which technical aspects were synthesized (Boerop, 1975), and eventually a general systems perspective was applied to areas as pragmatic as rural mental health (Bagarozzi, 1982). Still, this approach was not without criticism (Ackerman, 1972) and some needed corrections:

> When faced with the complexity and chaos which is present in actually doing family therapy, the therapist may seek a position as observer or systems analyst in an effort to try to bring some order to the confusion he sees. (Murray, 1975, p. 188)

In tracking the complexity of the theory and the process at hand, therapists could lose perspective, forgetting they were dealing with people. Engaging in both complex conceptualizations of family dynamics and attending to a client's interpersonal needs is a bit like stepping on a banana peel and a piece of ice at the same time. If the therapist attends to the banana peel, slipping on the ice becomes an ever more possible outcome, but in attending to the ice, the therapist becomes aware immediately of the slippery peel under the other foot. This uncertain and disorienting feeling is nowhere more apparent than in our next paradigm.

THE FOURTH PARADIGM: AUTOPOIESIS

The idea of *autopoiesis*, as described by Maturana and Varela (Maturana, 1980; Maturana & Varela, 1987; Varela, 1989) has gained a good deal of attention over the past decade. Autopoiesis means that "living beings are characterized in that, literally, they are continually self-producing" (Maturana, 1980, p. 46). This position was most clearly advanced by Paul Dell (1985, 1986, 1987), who asserted that Maturana and Varela's idea of autopoiesis, and associated theories, could be used as a "biological foundation for the social sciences" (1985). This position offered a number of useful ideas extended from Bateson's work, in which his ideas on cybernetic theory gained renewed attention. Dell maintained that the missing pieces to Bateson's epistemological puzzle lay in autopoietic theory. He emphasized epistemology's differential usage, the errors that arose from its misuse, and the "impossibility of objectivity" (1985). Dell also illustrated that while many therapists believe that change is multidetermined and circular, they construct their reality of the family as a linear process (1986). Many important ideas were brought forward by this integration, only a few of which were mentioned here. His perspective has also been roundly criticized (Fendanzo, 1983) as "epistobabble" (Coyne, 1982), "hegemonic" (Erickson, 1988) and contradictory. "Maturana's own doctrine is exempted from the relativistic strictures it lays down for the rest of us" (Held & Pols, 1987a, p. 467; Held & Pols, 1987b). Basic to most criticisms are that autopoietic theory reifies a closed system's cybernetic perspective (Constantine, 1989; Erickson, 1988) and reduces the human condition to mere biology without fully addressing language or social systems (Mahoney, 1991). Nevertheless, it is important not to throw the "baby out with the bathwater." Michael Mahoney (1991, p. 395) articulates a position quite close to our own in pointing out valuable aspects of autopoietic theory:

- Significance of systemic integrity basic to the survival of living systems.
- Self-referential nature of all adaptation and knowing.
- Plasticity of learning.
- Whole-being embodiment of knowing.
- Rejection of rationalist objectivism.
- Emphasis on language (and symbols) as an important medium of human interaction.
- The reappraisal of traditional distinctions between subject and object.

There are still questions to be answered about the contribution of this fourth paradigm. In refocusing on Batesonian cybernetics did we also lose track of the open system's transformative paradigm? Or, did the field simply integrate the two? In a rather pithy, but quite astute three-page commentary, Larry Constantine (1989) succinctly described the underlying technical systemic problems in family therapy and leaves us with this thought: "Neither knowledge nor skills necessarily disempowers families. It's all in how they are used." So, the question is, did this emphasis survive?

THE FIFTH PARADIGM: SELF-ORGANIZATION AND CHAOS THEORY

At the more general systems level, a system in crisis may be best defined as a system under such a high degree of environmental stress that both the system's ability to adapt through a process of growth and differentiation and its ability to maintain its steady state are overwhelmed, resulting in a disorganization of the system.

Following such disorganization, the system will reorganize itself, but the potential for change is much greater in the reorganizing system than had the crisis not occurred. Thus, the potential exists that the system will be more functional after crisis than before. (Halpern, Canale, Bant, & Bellamy, 1979, p. 89)

The tenets of this approach come close to a generalized full description of self-organization. It was stunning to come across this integrated model that so closely resembles self-organization theory. Others with knowledge of the emerging paradigm described the theory in different ways. Dell and Goolishian (1981) indicated that integrating this paradigm might be a "traumatic step for our Western minds" (p. 177). And, there has been an increase in Asian or Eastern thought popping up in the literature to perhaps assist: "This constant "motion" of things was not seen as simply chaotic or random. On the contrary, the Taoists firmly believed that this ceaseless process of change followed certain understandable and eternal principles" (Jordan, 1985). Surely, Western minds will find this ceaseless process unfamiliar, and Chapter 2 outlines the major tenets of this fifth paradigm. Therefore, we advise the novice reader to sit back and soak in the ideas outlined here in the fifth paradigm on the first read, and perhaps return to them after having read Chapter 2 for a more vivid understanding of the potential meaning of this paradigm.

Where Dell and Goolishian took a more epistemological introductory view to this paradigm, as did Minuchin and Fishman in many ways (1981), Elkaïm (1981) moved toward application:

In our method of work we try to spot and then block the behavior feedback loops that lead the family to a dead-end. We let the families test, through trial and error, other interaction loops while we remain open to the appearing and to the proliferation of unusual material apparently external to our field. (p. 293)

Ultimately, Hoffman (1981) fully connoted what the integration of self-organization theory would mean: "What I believe we are witnessing is the emergence of a second generation of family therapists clearly distinguishable from the first . . . not content with just a change in etiology" (p. 345). There, she also lists the challenges that the second generation will face in terms of applying theory to practice:

- Emphasize circular rather than linear thinking.
- Change from the idea of causation to a concept that is nearer that of "fit."
- Add positive to the usual negative interpretations.
- Legitimize time and irreversibility.

- Accept the concept of unpredictability.
- Give up the notion of the therapist as a force.
- Give up the traditional idea of resistance.
- Favor instability over equilibrium.
- Replace homeostasis with coherence, a balance internal to itself and external to its environment. (pp. 346–348)

We believe the second generation Hoffman foretold includes individuals from the first generation who focused on self-organization (Elkaïm, Goldbeter, & Goldbeter-Merinfeld, 1987; Goolishian & Anderson, 1987). In the six years that followed its introduction, these theorists gained insights about what had now come to be known as *chaos theory.*

Consistent with what Hoffman termed her "benchmarks," Harold Goolishian and Harlene Anderson (1987) criticize "empirically objective, cybernetically layered, prediction and control of human behavior" (pp. 530–533). Instead, their emphasis was on "the development of coevolving languages of coordinated exchange" and on therapists as "simply a participant manager" (p. 533). In kind, Mony Elkaïm, Albert Goldbeter, and Edith Goldbeter-Merinfeld (1987) emphasize "discontinuous change in behavior," and "time evolution of a given family system" (p. 22). And, still others (Kaplan & Kaplan, 1987) amplify these ideas: "A system as it exists at any moment is not its history but its current structure as evolved to this point in time" (p. 563). Statements that carry a similar message were also found in a number of articles appearing in the *Australian and New Zealand Journal of Family Therapy.* There we have found three attempts to address what appears to be the paradigm shift we are currently witnessing: "Co-evolving with Anorectic Families" (Gibney, 1987); "Epistemology and Constructivism" (McLeod, 1988); and "Chaos: A Challenge to Refine Systems Theory" (Stevens, 1991).

In all of the preceeding articles, chaos theory is given central importance. These authors are part of a new synthesis in systemic therapy, based on the tenets of self-organization theory. The fifth paradigm blossoms to cast a much wider shadow by describing the transformational process of open systems as nonlinear, chaotic, and self-organizing.

This begins with Gibney's pragmatic article (1987) in which he reviews some of the primary work with anorectic families, and then moves on to describe coevolving with families by mentioning Bateson (1979) and Jantsch (Briggs & Peat, 1984). While emphasizing the coevolution that occurs between therapist and family, he seems to make his true case known in the following statement:

The families in their original form had entered in the process of therapy and at a critical point, had seemingly stepped up to a more differentiated form and consequently more differentiated behavior. But how to describe theoretically this change at some critical point? The work of Ilya Prigogine provides an elegant metaphor. (Gibney, 1987, p. 78)

He then frames Prigogine's work in this manner:

By necessity, the system needs to become more complex to move into a more stable condition and yet there are many directions in which it could move. After the singular moment, the new order is established and becomes highly resistant to further fluctuation.[8] (Gibney, 1987, p. 79)

Gibney goes on to elaborate how this perspective allows us to view various forms of family therapy differently as well as to interpret familial behavior in a more integrative framework. His views may be summarized in the following statement:

I no longer see them in form terms as "anorectic families," but rather in process terms as families in transition and at this stage of transition, anorexia is a metaphor for the necessity to step to a new level of functioning. (Gibney, 1987, p. 80)

An article that followed Gibney's was McLeod's (1988) "Epistemology and Constructivism." McLeod's work focuses less on therapy and more on introducing family therapists to several contemporary theorists, among them Bateson, Prigogine, and Maturana. In his discussion of Prigogine, he points mainly to the role of extreme perturbations in higher order creative change and describes how difficult dissipative structures[9] may be to change by listing the examples of an alcoholic, a toxic couple, and a problematic family. In addressing creative ability in humans, he cites Prigogine's work (1986) on electrical activity in the brain: "Biological evolution, he suggests, may be the history of dynamic instability, "which is also the basic ingredient of human creativity" (McLeod 1988, p. 11). This leads us to the work of Stevens (1991).

---

[8] Part of this quote comes from Briggs & Peat (1984, p. 181). Jantsch, cited earlier, has written an excellent book entitled *The Self-Organizing Universe* (1980) that may in part explain the confusion of autopoiesis with self-organization theory. In this book, Jantsch takes autopoiesis and combines it with Prigogine's ideas on self-organization advancing the concept well beyond Maturana & Varela's use of it originally. This is also addressed to some extent in Briggs & Peat (1984, pp. 184–203).
[9] Technical terms such as perturbations and dissipative structures will be defined in greater detail in Chapter 2 and 11.

Stevens' work (1991) is by his own admission tentative. He simply points to possible connections between the models found in chaos theory and patterns one finds in a family therapy context. Stevens offers this as a possible connection:

> Strange attractors describe the way a dynamic system settles down to a simpler set of motions. This might be a helpful concept for therapy. Even in the most chaotic of family situations there may be organizing principles. This may be seen in regular consequences. Such factors as alcohol abuse, reckless driving, violent outbursts, sexual demands and tears may be in some way organizing. Predictability may seem minimal but on careful examination such "attractors" may draw behavior into an overall pattern. (Stevens, 1991, p. 24)

What is common to all these explanations is the idea that we are beyond simply autocorrective or cybernetic systems; we are onto self-organizing systems (Prigogine & Stengers, 1984) that evolve in parallel lines to general systems theory's steady and transformative states. Prigogine's description of self-organizing systems better explains Bertalanffy's transformative state. "Self-organization" is what occurs in a system as it emerges from a chaotic period in a transformational state. This new organization then becomes the new steady state.

Families presenting for therapy seem to be asking for a "hand up" to a higher order of systemic existence, a more adaptive form. In short, if we return them to their previous steady state, assuming this is possible, we may be doing them a horrible disservice. Conversely, as one of us have indicated (McCown, 1992), families may also wish to return to a steady state after a critical moment and/or a bifurcation.[10] We must evaluate what stage of development the family is at before we intervene. As Gibney (1987) indicates, we coevolve with our families as they attempt to self-organize at a higher, more complex level of existence. This may indeed frighten both clinicians and the families they work with, but the clinician must evaluate what is being requested: return to a steady state or guidance through transformational chaos (Bütz 1992a). This key question, and the techniques chaos theory suggests for treatment of the family, will be discussed in detail in the remainder of this book.

---

[10] Ibid.

CHAPTER 2

A Walk Through the Canyon

We have as a basis of physical description dynamical systems which have chaotic behavior, that on the macroscopic level, on the social level, and so on, that you have this variety of behavior that you observe. And that is what I would like to call the unifying role of chaos . . . the basis of our microscopic description threatens the structure of physics.

—Ilya Prigogine[1]

MANY 'SCIENTISTS are working to construct an epistemology based on a concept of reality that instead of being intrinsically orderly, stable, and equilibrial, is seething with spontaneous change, irregularity, disorder, and chaos.[2] This began roughly one hundred years ago when a number of ideas began to emerge that would call into question the classic laws of physics. Still, it would not be until 60 to 70 years later that a quirky, eccentric group of scientific ideas would evolve into an entire paradigm for viewing complex behavior. Remarkably, in approximately the time it took for Einstein's special theory of relativity to be widely accepted, chaos theory has made the transition from a fringe movement to an orthodox, mainstream science (Beltrami, 1993; Moon, 1992). Indeed, some commentators have argued that chaos theory

---

[1] Stated in an interview with *The Chaos Networker* asking him about his work (Staff, 1992).
[2] At different points in the text, we provide more technical descriptions. As will be apparent in this chapter, the definition for chaos depends on who is providing the definition—it is still a point of contention. The preceding description is about as generic as we are able to provide at this point.

represents the third great scientific revolution of this century, a scientific innovation of the same magnitude as relativity theory and quantum mechanics (Vandervert, 1992).

Ten years ago, chaos theory was thought of by many mathematicians, physicists, engineers, and other scientists, as at worst a fad. Others saw it as an arcane set of pseudotheories with limited applicability to much in the real world. Today, however, ideas about chaos are more respectable and have become mainstream (Goldstein, 1995). Undergraduate physics curricula include entire courses on chaos (Tufurilla, 1994). The concept of nonlinear dynamics, so integral to the study of chaos theory, is now making its way into introductory physics textbooks (Davies, 1989). What appeared to be a passing fad just a few years ago is now a well-established and routinely applied science.

Part of the confusion regarding when chaos became "legitimate" rests with the theorists and researchers themselves. Chaos theorists are a diverse, perhaps even motley lot. No one single name can be said to be primarily responsible for chaos theory. Contributions have been made from economists, mathematicians, engineers, theoretical physicists, biologists, meteorologists, computer scientists, and an occasional psychologist. These are groups that hardly talk to one another in the scientific enterprise, let alone discuss with other disciplines what may simply turn out to be a fad. In fact, a hodgepodge bunch of unconventional graduate students, unfettered by commitments to traditional interpretations of data, were among the most prominent early "chaoticians." The immensely popular book *Chaos* (1987) by the *New York Times* science writer James Gleick helped bring to international attention the work of these disparate theorists, operating with common assumptions, but in almost incompatible worlds. Other texts aimed at a popular audience followed, which also described the pioneering efforts of these scientists as well as related theories; for example, John Briggs and F. David Peat's *Looking Glass Universe* (1984) and *Turbulent Mirror* (1989), Steven Levy's *Artificial Life* (1992), and M. Mitchell Waldrop's *Complexity* (1992). Other works anticipated these ideas, as in David Bohm's *Wholeness and the Implicate Order* (1980) or Fritjof Capra's *The Turning Point* (1983). Some chaos theorists, like most scientists, are a cantankerous bunch, and historical accounts of this nascent field in these volumes necessarily excluded some pioneers and certainly bruised some egos.

There are probably as many definitions of chaos as there are chaoticians. Even James Gleick (1987) had a difficult time marshaling a coherent definition. Instead, late in the book (pp. 305–307) he lists the opinions of Phillip Holmes, Hao Bai-Lin, H. Bruce Stewart, Roderick V. Jensen, James Crutchfield, Joseph Ford, John Hubbard, and Arthur Winfree. As one might expect, each had a unique idea about how to define chaos. We would like to add a few definitions to this list:

> Allgood and Yorke (1977) define chaos as a trajectory that is exponentially unstable and neither periodic or asymptotically periodic.

That is, it oscillates irregularly without settling down.

> Pure novelty, that is to say, uniqueness, does not contain any information; it stands for chaos. Pure confirmation does not bring anything new; it stands for stagnation or death. (Jantsch, 1980, p. 51)

This means that systems cycle somewhere between the two extremes of pure novelty and stagnation, just as complexity theory has been briefly described earlier. There needs to be just enough of "this and that" (Levy, 1992, pp. 109–110).

> Prigogine uses the word *chaos* in two distinct, though sometimes inter-changeable ways. There is the passive chaos of equilibrium and maximum entropy, where the elements are so intimately mixed that no organization exists. This is the "equilibrium thermal chaos" of the eventual lukewarm universe predicted by Clausius. But the second kind of chaos is active, hot, and energetic—a "far-from-equilibrium turbulent chaos." (Briggs & Peat, 1989, p. 136)

Hence, there is utter disorganization and death, or the type of chaos we are attempting to describe which is energetic and organizing.

> **Chaos** originally used by the Greeks to describe the limitless void, it is now used to describe unpredictable and apparently random structures. (Davies, 1989, p. 494)

As mentioned earlier in this text, a parallel can be drawn to consider how scientists experienced these types of phenomenon and how they subsequently described it. The quote here by Davies nicely illustrates this point.

> Baker and Gollub (1990, p. 1) describe chaotic dynamics where a small initial difference results in a measurement error, this error "grows *exponentially* in

time, so that the state of the system is essentially unknown after a very short time."

This definition is closely tied to the concept of sensitive dependence on initial conditions or Lorenz's "butterfly effect," which the reader should look for later in this chapter. In shorthand, this means that a variable as tiny as a butterfly in a weather system might, by its very motion, destabilize a weather system enough to contribute to an increase in instability. In time, the fluctuations may become chaotic.

Devaney (1992) defines a function as chaotic if it has sensitive dependence on initial conditions, it is topologically transitive, and periodic points are dense.

In other words, it is unpredictable, indecomposable, and yet contains regularity.

Under the right circumstances, the slightest uncertainty can grow until the system's future becomes utterly unpredictable—or, in a word, chaotic. . . . Eventually, the sequence would become so complex that the drops would seem to come at random—again, chaos. (Waldrop, 1992, p. 66)

Thus, there are a considerable number of opinions on what is scientific "chaos." Sifting through all these definitions, we can attribute certain key characteristics to chaos or chaotic systems: Initial differences result in errors that grow exponentially over time; the system is complex, appears random, is unpredictable and is in an essential state for transformation. These characteristics add dimension and scope to the cursory definition we offered at the beginning of Chapter 1. Combining these characteristics with our brief definition in Chapter 1, we are now able to offer this partial definition: *Chaos theory, as an umbrella term, describes a holistic process of adaptive transformation, where, over time, small instabilities may result in complex behavior, that may eventually appear random and is experienced as chaos by those accustomed to linear science.* Though lengthy, this definition describes a process that begins with instability and ends with adaptive transformation. Chaos, lies somewhere between these two points, and explaining where that point "is," and how these systems evolve will be the focus of the remainder of this chapter.

Despite the variety of definitions previously listed, these theorists do seem to agree on some common theoretical descriptions of phenomena housed under chaos theory. The following are a few commonly encountered terms associated with these phenomena, to an extent stripped of their mathematical preciseness for the purpose of explanation, and placed in an order that may give the reader a general feeling of the unfolding process being described:

Attractor [paraphrased here for clarity]—a place where trajectories converge (Baker & Gollub, 1990, p. 20). In essence, an attractor, for all the fancy language used to describe it, is basically what it sounds like. The sun is one big attractor for our solar system.

Sensitivity to Initial Conditions—the butterfly effect; vast, sweeping changes are the result of minute primary differences (see also Baker & Gollub, 1990).

Perturbation—introduction or deletion of energy or information to or from a system resulting in a change in state of equilibrium (see also Davies, 1989).

Point Attractor—common point or state to which a system moves after perturbation from a wide variety of starting positions; they "seem to attract trajectories" (Briggs & Peat, 1989, p. 36).

Bifurcation—the branching, splitting, evolution of dynamics within a system; a process by which a dynamic equilibrium changes to a new equilibrium; it typically occurs when a system is moving from linear behavior to nonlinearity, although many nonlinear systems may appear to behave linearly for a time. Some have referred to it as a fork in the road (Coveney & Highfield, 1990, p. 360).

Nonlinear—circular, repetitive, interacting, nondirectional process of a system or "getting more than you bargained for" (Coveney & Highfield, 1990, p. 363).

Period-Doubling Route to Chaos—"The time it took for the system to oscillate back to its starting point doubled at certain critical values of the equation." Then, for example, "after several period-doubling cycles, the insect population in his model varied randomly, just like real insect populations, showing no predictable period for return to its original state"—chaos (Briggs & Peat, 1989, p. 60).

Chaos—an erratic, nonprobabilistic, nonperiodic state or process that is not predictable, yet may be understandable through the analysis of previous evolutions (Chubb, 1990).

Strange Attractor—associated with chaotic dynamics, the position or set of boundary conditions to which a system gravitates as it moves from order to disorder where it is able to "pierce every arbitrarily small region in the attractive space" (Abraham, Abraham, & Shaw, 1990, p. V–3).

Self-Organizing—the spontaneous emergence of order out of chaos reflecting the capacity of all living systems to "generate their own new forms from inner guidelines" (Loye & Eisler, 1987, p. 56).

Despite our paring down, the definitions are still pretty technical and may engender in people a desire to run screaming from wherever they are reading this text—perhaps onto a freeway or into an open field. If you are experiencing this reaction, do not go into a frenzy quite yet, as we are about to bring some order into the chaos of describing chaotic phenomena. We have shared just this taste of how technical and jargon-laden this field actually is, and how far apart even sister disciplines such as mathematics and physics are from one another, to illustrate how much more technical this field actually is than the descriptions we will offer here.

THE BIG PICTURE, AND A WALK THROUGH THE CANYON

Speaking less technically, let's take a look at the big picture—the entire process described by chaos theory. The key to all of the ideas in chaos theory is the concept of *instability*. Truly random behavior, or stochastic behavior as some prefer to call it to impress people, has no stability whatsoever. It is random! Chaos may look like a random process, but it is not. It is an unstable state a system moves through in order to transform. Chaos, in essence, is a system's attempt to adapt. Greatly simplifying the matter, the system is looking all over the place for the solution to new environmental demands. It is looking far and near because it does not have in its repertoire a solution for this particular problem, or set of problems. Thus, the system's behavior deviates from its stable pattern, or steady state. It looks unstable during this process, it may even look random. This is where terms like sensitivity to initial conditions and point attractors come into play. The initial conditions are what we know about all the variables interacting with the system at a certain time. They are so important because a change that seems as slight as the flapping of a butterfly's wings in a weather system might leave us with no idea of how the system will behave over time. This depends on how stable the system is to begin with. If a family system's initial conditions are like nitroglycerin, we would use a very different intervention than if their initial conditions were more like a large slab of granite. Stability is the key. A point attractor connotes a relatively stable system (see Figure 2.1), where with each perturbation, or change in the environment, the system returns to its previous steady state.

A point attractor is a little like running into a skunk while hiking in a canyon—moving off the trail for a bit will probably solve the problem. Its not necessary to climb the canyon wall to escape it. Attractors, therefore, may be thought of, at least metaphorically, as similar to a hiker walking through a canyon. For instance, running into a bear in the same situation, however, is an entirely different story. Climbing up the canyon wall, and into the next canyon may almost be second nature. And the trail? Faced with a bear in one's path, the trail seems a small consideration. This is where concepts like bifurcations, nonlinearity, and a period-doubling route to chaos are useful.

A bifurcation indicates that the perturbation the system has encountered is more on the level of say a bear, than a skunk. It is so strong that the system finds itself unable to adapt to it, and so it deviates substantially from its usual stability or steady state. This may be where it begins to behave in a nonlinear fashion with no perceptible purpose in movement. In this condition, our hiker may want to stay near or on the trail, but with the bear there, his path deviates in what is perceived as a nondirectional manner. He may vacillate in his direction between going part way up the

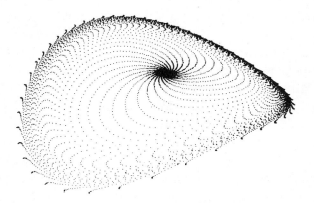

Figure 2.1 A Fixed Point Attractor. This is an attractor whose dynamics represent a system's movement toward rest. All movement in this type of system is attracted to a fixed point where it comes to rest, that is, until something might perturb it at a later time. From *Strange Attractors: Creating Patterns in Chaos* by Julian C. Sprott (New York: M&T Books, 1993). Copyright © 1993 by Julian C. Sprott. Reprinted by permission of Henry Holt and Co., Inc.

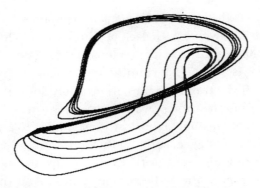

Figure 2.2   A Cyclic, or Limit Cycle Attractor. This attractor is a bit more exotic than most used in texts describing chaotic dynamics. Still, it represents something akin to a steady state, where a system with these types of dynamics is resistant to change. In this chase, the system's movement is beyond rest, as in the fixed point attractor, but it also does not vary in any dramatic sense—its dynamics are cyclic. From *Strange Attractors: Creating Patterns in Chaos* by Julian C. Sprott (New York: M&T Books, 1993). Copyright © 1993 by Julian C. Sprott. Reprinted by permission of Henry Holt and Co., Inc.

canyon wall and hedging back toward the trail as in Figure 2.2. After the hiker has made several attempts to return to the trail, the bear might begin to growl loudly sending the hiker up the wall of the canyon or around in circles in terror. Let's say, he cannot get up one side of the canyon wall and attempts scaling the other, and still he is unable to get out of the canyon. From afar, we witness him going back and forth across this small canyon attempting to find a way around the bear. This is where a period-doubling route to chaos applies because he has tried to return to the trail, his steady state, and being unable to do so he wanders wildly about the canyon looking for a way around the bear. This is chaos, deterministic, but apparently random. Let's say we cannot see the bear, and atop the canyon wall, we watch this poor man running willy-nilly all over the canyon. Our first assumption would be that he is mad or a bit manic. In reality, his pattern of behavior may make sense, but viewing his behavior from above without seeing the bear it is difficult for us to detect any method to his movements.

This is where the concept of the strange attractor is useful; it is a pattern, of say footprints, that marks the movement of a system as it attempts to adapt to new environmental demands like our bear. But, this pattern is chaotic, and represents our hiker's conundrum. He does not want to lose track of the trail and become lost in the wilderness, but at the same time he does not want to get eaten, mauled, or violated in some way by the bear. If we were to trace the path of his footprints as in Figure 2.3, the pattern he makes across the canyon demonstrates his dilemma. There is a pattern though, a deterministic one, bent on solving the situation. This deterministic, chaotic pattern is a strange attractor. Identifying modeling patterns such as strange attractors is one of the primary methods for detecting the presence of chaos in systems.

What we call *phase portraits* are three-dimensional representations of the movement of a system. Phase portraits visually depict the movement a system makes from its initial conditions to some point in time. Typically, when researchers use modeling techniques for their data, they are hoping to find a pattern similar to the strange attractor in phase space. Researchers in this field usually feel that they have found "chaos" in a system when their data in three-dimensional space form a strange attractor. This is not random behavior because it has a pattern, even though it is difficult to detect. The pattern is one where a system searches for a solution to a strong perturbation in the environment. The bear and the path are both points in the attractor pattern; the bear creating fluctuations in

Figure 2.3 The Well-Known Strange Attractor. As is immediately evident, its dynamics are more complex than any of the attractors previously described. Still, there is pattern to this portrait that tells us it is not random behavior. While the system's movement varies wildly, we are able to see that there is a certain determinism, like our hiker movements. But, this determinism is not like a limit cycle attractor that centers around the same behavior over and over. There is a wide variation here that indicates a system's "search," we might say, for a new solution to a novel situation. From *Strange Attractors: Creating Patterns in Chaos* by Julian C. Sprott (New York: M&T Books, 1993). Copyright © 1993 by Julian C. Sprott. Reprinted by permission of Henry Holt and Co., Inc.

the pattern, the path creating stability. The hiker can neither fluctuate to wildly and thus become lost; nor can he stay entirely on the path and thus become lunch for the bear.

At this point, our hiker has found another trail skirting the top of the canyon that will both keep him in sight of the original trail and far enough away from the bear to feel safe. We could say that his erratic behavior has organized. He has adapted to the circumstance. This is where self-organization comes into the picture. A system is said to have self-organized when it adapts to the perturbations that destabilized it enough to induce chaos as depicted in Figure 2.4. While the true essence of self-organization is quite a bit more complex, this will do as an introductory explanation. We will revisit self-organization a number of times in this book, each time adding more detail in order to provide a full understanding of this very important concept.

So our big picture is a process, a walk through our metaphorical canyon, where each concept describes a distinct period in the system's transformation toward a more adaptive stability or steady state.

Again, stability or instability is the key to understanding this process. Chaos theory, greatly abbreviated here for clarity, was not understood

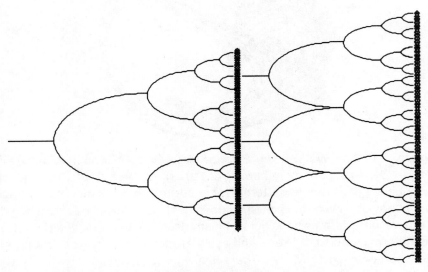

Figure 2.4 Stability and Bifurcation. The horizontal lines represent a form of stability, with forks representing bifurcations, and vertical lines indicating chaos. Note that subsequent to chaos, at least graphically here, the stability is more complex as the system self-organized.

overnight but evolved as a set of theories and concepts over the past hundred years. Each scientist contributed a piece to the process. In the pages to follow, we will describe the paradigm of chaos theory by addressing its history: We will explore its implications for behavioral science and reductionism and elucidate theoretical constructs that will serve as landmarks in this new world. In each case, we have tried to make this meal palatable without the bitter and spicy extremes of techno jargon that fill this field.

THE FIELD'S BRIEF HISTORY . . . OR A BRIEF HISTORY OF THE FIELD?

Much of the mathematics of chaos theory, or of nonlinear dynamical systems theory as some prefer to call it, have been known for quite some time. Sophia Kovalevskaya, Europe's first woman to become a professor of mathematics, provided a mathematical definition of dynamical instability in 1889 (Percival, 1993), thus laying the foundation for the scientific study of complexity. Her compatriot, Aleksandra Lyapunov, expanded this definition and developed a measure that bears his name, the Lyapunov exponent. This exponent is used to measure the degree to which a system is sensitive to initial conditions and is now frequently employed in nonlinear research.

At the turn of the century, the French mathematician Henry Poincaré offered a mathematical proof that the behavior of very simple systems could be complex and in fact, quite literally unpredictable, even if their entire histories were known in advance (Cvitanovic, 1984). Scientists embarked on this piece of research to find "the answer" to what was termed "the three-body problem." Three bodies were in fact three planets in motion near one another, and despite Newton's contention that the universe worked like a clock, no one could quite figure out the course these three planets would take. Two planets, sure they knew the answer, regular motions like a clock, which Newton had predicted. But, three planets told a different story. As noted earlier, Poincaré found the answer to this equation—no answer! The behavior of three planets in motion around one another was unpredictable; it was nonlinear. The motion of those planets could only be approximated and their movement bears little resemblance to Newton's clocklike matrix. In fact, this is where the fabric of Newton's universe began to unravel. In 1928, Balth van der Pol, a Dutch engineer, developed a practical mathematical model for oscillating electronics based on Poincaré's dynamic topology, providing the first application of what is now known as chaos theory.

Poincaré's model was very complex, and attempting to work out the math of it with only pencil and paper calculations nearly drove him mad. Only since the advent of the high-speed computer have researchers possessed the technical capacity to fully explore the implications of the nonlinearity Poincaré found in his data.

A discovery relevant to this goal was made by Edward Lorenz, a meteorological researcher at the Massachusetts Institute of Technology, who was studying weather patterns by creating models in his computer (Gleick, 1987). Accidentally, Lorenz found that when he changed the input of an equation by a mathematically infinitesimal degree, his computer produced results that varied much more widely than would be expected (1963). This infinitesimal degree is what we are taught to do regularly (e.g., rounding to the second decimal point). This tiny difference in the original situation magnified itself enormously over time. Lorenz postulated that apparent turbulence in nature could be partly explained by what he termed "sensitive dependence on initial conditions" (Gleick, 1987). He called this type of dependence the butterfly effect, based on the metaphor that weather in New York, for example, could eventually be changed by a perturbation as minute as the flapping of a butterfly's wings in China. What has been described as the butterfly effect is now widely evoked to explain natural limits on our ability to accurately predict the weather.

Mitchell Feigenbaum, working at Cornell University, found that in a surprisingly large number of natural systems, a sequence existed of order followed by turbulence eventually resulting in a new state of stable predictability (Loye & Eisler, 1987). By entering values repeatedly into a formula, he discovered that within diverse systems that appeared chaotic and random, certain predictable patterns of order emerged. Feigenbaum then predicted that at a critical point, when an ordered system begins to break down into chaos, a consistent sequence of period-doubling transitions would be observed. This so-called period-doubling route to chaos was thereafter observed experimentally by various investigators, including the French physicist Albert Libchaber and his coworkers. Feigenbaum went on to calculate a numerical constant that governs the doubling process (Feigenbaum's number) and showed that his results were applicable to a wide range of chaotic systems (1978, 1979). In fact, an infinite number of possible routes to chaos can be described, several of which are "universal," or broadly applicable, in the sense of obeying proportionality laws that do not depend on details of the physical system.

In 1971, a Belgian physicist, David Ruelle, and a Dutch mathematician, Floris Takens, together predicted that the transition to chaotic turbulence in a moving fluid would take place at a well-defined critical value of the fluid's velocity (or some other important factor controlling the fluid's behavior). They predicted that this transition to turbulence would occur after the system had developed oscillations with at least three distinct frequencies. Experiments with rotating fluid flows conducted by American physicists Jerry Gollub and Harry Swinney in the mid-1970s supported these predictions. An exceptional discussion of the role of chaos in modern life is available in the highly readable book by Ruelle (1991).

By the late 1970s, scientists from many disciplines were beginning to investigate chaos. Biologists and ecologists such as Robert May looked at seemingly unpredictable changes in global populations of plants and animals (1976). Mathematicians like James Yorke (1975), Benoit Mandelbrot (1977) and Gregory Chaitin (1988) focused on the stages of chaos and disorder that all mathematical, physical, and natural systems seemed to move toward. More complex still is the work of the Belgian scientist and Nobel laureate Ilya Prigogine, whose interest initially was in a class of chemical reactions that seem to violate the second law of thermodynamics. Prigogine (1971, 1982; see also Elkaïm, Prigogine, Stengers, & Denenbourg, 1982; Prigogine & Stengers, 1984; Staff, 1992) discusses the idea that order comes out of chaos in the form of feedback loops within a system. He believes that this order is a state of self-generated dynamics and has done much to advance the mathematical models applicable to such systems. Prigogine's notion that chaotic systems have the innate capacity to "self-organize" from this feedback remains one of the most controversial but exciting aspects of chaos theory. Again, self-organization is said to occur once a system has moved through chaos and attained a new order.

Chaos theory, a modern development in mathematics and science, provides a framework for understanding irregular erratic fluctuations in nature. Chaotic systems are found in many fields of science and engineering. Many bodies in the solar system, for example, have already been determined to exhibit chaotic orbits as Poincaré predicted, and evidence of chaotic behavior has also been found in the pulsations of variable stars. Evidence of chaos occurs in models and experiments describing convection and mixing in fluids, in wave motion, in oscillating chemical reactions, and in electrical currents in semiconductors. Many examples of the wide applicability of chaotic models exist. Chaotic processes have been found in the irregularity of a dripping faucet, the flow of eddies in a stream of water, turbulence in the air, the pattern of smoke rising, and the spread of epidemics and forest fires (Crutchfield, Farmer, Packard, & Shaw, 1986; Tufillaro, Abbott, & Reilly, 1992). Other researchers studied systems within living organisms and found patterns that imitated the nonlinear dynamics found elsewhere.

Similar patterns were found in cellular development, animal physiological systems, direction and pattern of plant growth, infant motor development, and even brain anatomy. It is found in the dynamics of animal populations, and of medical disorders such as heart arrhythmias and epileptic seizures. Chaos theory has also been applied to problems in population ecology. A classic paper by May (1976) fruitfully elucidated an extremely simple model from chaos theory. Stephen Jay Gould (1980), a paleontologist, has expanded the theory of evolution by providing an alternative to the Darwinian theory of gradual, sequential change. Alan Garfinkel (1983) and Leon Glass and Michael Mackey (1988) have begun examining the relationship of chaos to human physiology, medicine, and the dynamics of disease. Many of the problems that medical researchers, psychologists, and sociologists have struggled with through the ages are now coming under the scrutiny of chaos theory (Hall, 1991).

Not only did the dynamics of these systems resemble the chaotic global models of physical properties and mathematical and physical laws, but they all seemed to be in a constant state of flux (Rapp, 1987). This flux followed the now somewhat familiar pattern of order to chaos and back again to order. Noteworthy is that this return to order does not connote the same old order. This is a new, more adaptive order, a new organization. Regardless of the domain involved, the same kinds of processes occur repeatedly, across different media, time frames, and size scales. Chaos has now been discovered at many levels of measurement, from the macrolevel of movements of bodies in the solar system to the microlevel of the movement of wave particles in the quantum world (Moon, 1992). Given the paradigm's unnerving ability to explain historically stubborn problems, how has chaos theory been received by the larger scientific community? Moreover, when a worldview has been established in the context that linear is "real" and nonlinear basically does not exist, what is the effect? How are the shock waves dealt with, and what will all this mean for fields like psychology and other behavioral sciences?

IS THIS REALITY?

The response of the scientific community to theories of chaos and nonlinear process certainly demonstrates Kuhn's theory of the advancement of scientific thought. As Kuhn (1970/1962) describes, "Because it demands large-scale paradigm destruction and major shifts in the problems and techniques of normal science, the emergence of new theories is generally preceded by a period of pronounced professional insecurity" (pp. 67–68).

The shaken advocates of empiricism have been challenged from several directions. Beginning over 60 years ago, quantum theory challenged our ability even to "guess at the true nature of the world" (Appleyard, 1993, p. 144). If observed phenomena are affected by the act of observation, can there really be an independent empirical reality? If reality can behave differently in varying circumstances then how are we to achieve the goal of predictability? Even statistics are essentially an admission of our inability to capture causality and absolute order. Chaos theory defines systems as inherently complex and prone to a type of chaotic disorder and, therefore, potentially unknowable. "Complexity will always overwhelm any system" (Appleyard, 1993, p. 155) which effectively prevents reducing phenomena to a deterministic, cause-and-effect system of unvarying equations. This, in addition to related ideas such as quantum theory, is the message of chaos theory.

The revolutionary paradigms of chaos in systems are not based on a linear progression in the accumulation of more data to confirm hypotheses that have been the basis of empirical science—commonly called logical positivism. Instead, it involves a major shift in perspective that provides a very different frame of reference on which to construct reality. Gleick (1987) states, "Where chaos begins, classical science stops" (p. 3). Physics and other sciences are undergoing a theoretical shift that has the makings of a Kuhnian "revolution" in how we perceive our universe. And, unlike paradigms that are raised to the fore simply by political power (Kuhn, 1991; McNally, 1992), these ideas are occupying center stage due to the heuristic potential of the concepts. As researchers in the other sciences continue to expand the theory of chaos in systems, we can begin to recognize the implications for social sciences such as psychology.

FROM ORDER TO CHAOS IN PSYCHOLOGICAL THEORY

At this point in development, psychology, unlike physics, still seems secure in its sense of the dynamics of human behavior primarily formulated since the 1930s by behaviorists and empiricists despite the field's continued fragmentation (Bütz, 1992b; Cahan & White, 1992; Hornstein, 1992; Leahey, 1992). Although the theory is incomplete, there is still a sense from the standpoint of logical positivism that the application of traditional scientific method will eventually fill the gaps in the paradigm.

Human behavior will thus prove to be predictable, lawful, and amenable to change through the systematic application of a set of relatively standard practices and techniques in psychological theory and practice. Bateson offered the following critique of behavioral scientists over two decades ago:

> Many investigators, particularly in the behavioral sciences, seem to believe that scientific advance is predominantly inductive . . . they believe that progress is made by study of the "raw" data, leading to new heuristic concepts. Gradually (they believe) the heuristic concepts will be corrected and improved until . . . they are worthy of a place in the list of fundamentals. About fifty years of work in which thousands of clever men [sic] have had their share have, in fact, produced a rich crop of several hundred heuristic concepts, but . . . scarcely a single principle worthy of a place in the list of fundamentals. (1972, p. xix)

Certainly the question of whether psychology can be a "true" science has been debated almost since its formation as a separate discipline. Perhaps the dilemma is not so much whether psychology is a science, but whether psychology has found or created an appropriate model from which to pursue, gather, and process information. The vantage point from which psychologists have attempted to observe human phenomena may have constricted our ability to develop a more comprehensive understanding of behavior and the process of change in human beings. Many an empirical scientist may debate that social science has simply not been rigorous enough; our techniques have not met the challenge presented by the complexity of human behavior. The paradox of classical science is inescapable in psychological research when researchers attempt to classify complex behavior by assigning a one or a two to it, or at best, plugging these digits into a multivariate formula. Essentially, empiricism's dilemma for psychology is that it provides an extraordinarily effective way of understanding the world by pretending that we do not exist.

ACCORDING TO BEHAVIORAL SCIENCE, DO WE EXIST?

Psychology, for much of the past three decades, has increasingly become a reductionistic science. Empirical research in psychology has sought to break down patterns of behavior into the lowest common elements and thereby establish a set of universal "rules." Typically, this is referred to as the law of parsimony. In traditional science, the way to explain observable events is to impose an ordered, linear logic to their occurrence and their relationships to each other. The scientific method of problem solving that we now use most of the time has been developed over centuries. The technique is well known: The researcher defines a specific question that she or he deems interesting and worthy of attention, comes up with several solutions to the dilemma, chooses one solution, applies it to the problem, and, finally, analyzes the effectiveness of the chosen method through observance of validating data. If such data are found, the solution, now in the form of a hypothesis, is supported. Technically, a better description of the process is that the "null hypothesis" is rejected. If unique mathematical solutions can be developed to assist in this process, all the better.

While there is tremendous scientific and financial prestige associated with being the first to predict novel findings, there is also disrepute attached to publicly stating predictions that are not verified by the scientific community at large. In this manner, science has more or less successfully policed itself, ferreting out potential frauds, solipsists, and charlatans, and just plain accidents and randomness in the data that inevitably occur.

Perhaps the traditional scientific method is an appropriate technique for most types of science. Since Galileo, it was recognized that the major goal of traditional science is to offer discrete laws as explanations for a vast quantity of events and observations. Indeed, this is how we intuitively are led to believe that "good" sciences advance. Reduction from the many to the few and from the general to the specific has been science's approach toward making sense out of human life and the surrounding universe. Consequently, what will be repeatable; for example, the orbital frequencies in Halley's Comet, is worthy of inquiry. This is because reasonable hypotheses can be tested through observation and can be potentially refuted. This method of scientific inquiry, outlined in the classic text by Cohen (1932), generally works quite well. Because of this, it has been retained for future use and refined over time. If the hypothesis proves ineffective, the scientist discards it and starts over again at Step 1. Obviously, there is more room for subjectivity than researchers might admit. The notion of what constitutes appropriate criteria of rejection of solutions has been one of the more fascinating areas in the philosophy and sociology of science.

The historical goal of psychology and other behavioral sciences was to follow this pattern. It can be thought of as the attempt to describe, to organize, and ultimately to predict the phenomena of nature by use of the traditional scientific method. Since Francis Bacon, perhaps even since Aristotle, the focus of such efforts has primarily been toward delineating cause-and-effect relationships among repeatable patterns and constructing mathematical models to simplify them. In fact, the hallmark of the entire scientific framework has been that researchers justify their conclusions through claiming novel predictions about the world. Then, through the process of discovering these predictions, theories are "validated." The process is open and subjected to scrutiny because the physical world does not change. Replications are performed primarily by the scientist's peers. An entire enterprise is built on this process of replication, generally with the most esteemed scientists performing the critical experiments and less eminent colleagues (and graduate students) attempting to duplicate these findings.

Problems occur, however, when we discuss data with phenomena that do not repeat themselves. History—not withstanding occasional trends that are subject to much speculation—may be an example. The scientific analysis of social unrest is yet another (Tolstoy, 1869/1982). It is much easier to avoid a rigorous explanation of facets of phenomena that are essentially unrepeatable, especially since traditional science has learned to lump all its ignorance into the omnibus terms "measurement error, randomness" or worst of all "bad data."

In many cases, "bad data" are simply thrown out to support one's findings, or phenomena are held out as too complex to study, or "statistical magic" as well as some embellishment turn poor studies into publishable or even seminal studies. These extreme measures generally involve problems about the prediction of complex systems with diverse components. One might say these studies are "linearized"; nonlinear behaviors are extracted and our picture of whomever we were studying has been digitized. The mathematics of predicting the behavior of such systems becomes quite formative. To "solve" such a problem, we engage in what is known as a "linear approximation," attempting to force complex relationships into much more manageable mathematics. The schedules of reinforcement that every first-year undergraduate psychology student learns is an example from psychology. A more impressive example from physics is the turbulence of fluids, a very important problem that was avoided by many major theorists because it did not lend itself to neat, linear formulations involving replicable patterns. In psychology, a similar omission has occurred in studies involving microbehavioral units (such as why you may be chewing your pencil while you read this text). These "oddities" are removed from the data set.

In traditional science, the concept of prediction depends on assumptions involving the mathematical linearity of the data, applied through a logical and sequential process. Where data do not fit linear models, they are "transformed" into approximate linear theories. This methodology developed through time by means of a natural selection process. It has flourished for so long, compared with other worldviews, such as animism, simply because it works quite well. Scientific knowledge regarding regularity makes our computers function and our bridges carry our cars (well, with the exception of the Tacoma Narrows bridge). The underlying principles that allow these miracles are based on application of traditional scientific methods that have been developed over centuries. Because they are so replicable, they may be trusted. In fact, the physics involved in constructing a suspension bridge is hardly beyond that capable of being mastered by the first-year college student. Yet, as psychologists attempt to transfer an empirical model to the study of more complex human behaviors, the constraints of a reductionistic approach to describing phenomena become painfully apparent. Simply note all the areas that are missing from behavioral science's list of successes. So, do we exist? Well, yes and no. As we have discussed, data that do not fit the "assumptions" of the scientific enterprise are either linearized successfully, or thrown out as "bad data," or too complex for serious study. We propose, according to behavioral sciences list of successes, that in the classic sense of the word, we do exist but only in our simplest form. The more complex, seemingly ineffiable conditions of human existence, therefore do not exist—at least according to the classical scientific model.

REDUCTIONISM: A PROBLEM?

Reductionism in science has led us to focus on discrete aspects of a problem or question, even when they are clearly embedded in a broader context. One of the problems inherent in reductionistic empiricism is that scientists may fail to notice unforeseen negative consequences that cannot always be dealt with in terms of a fragmentary mode of thought. Those consequences spread into the whole context and may eventually create problems that are worse than the initial conditions. As Hunter, Hoffnung, & Ferhold, (1988) note, "Reductionistic assumptions can be especially intimidating when they are presented in the vocabulary of science and hence are invested (by association) with various claims to rationality, neutrality, and irreducible truth" (p. 331).

Sperry (1988), in his article on the new "mentalist" paradigm states:

> Long-trusted principles in neuroscience and behaviorist doctrine had proclaimed a full account of brain function and behavior to be possible in strictly objective physiochemical and physiological terms. . . . These principles, which always had seemed to be airtight and irrefutable, were discovered to have a logical flaw or shortcoming and to be outweighed by a new "emergent interactionist" reasoning with wide application throughout nature. (p. 607)

Sperry goes on to note that current and future psychological theories are less likely to be atomistic, reductionistic, and mechanistic, and more contextual, subjective, and humanistic. Consequently, outside the areas of psychological study already noted, there is a vast accumulation of "data" and a variety of hypotheses, but no universal principles to explain even simple human behaviors. It may be said that behavioral science did not bother to notice that the larger society of science had introduced Heisenberg's "uncertainty principle" into the mix early in this century (1958).

SHIFTING PARADIGMS: THE NEW "LAWS" OF SCIENCE

Chaos and nonlinear systems offer an alternative model for observation and understanding in psychology. In order to consider this paradigm, traditional concepts of science must be altered. Prigogine and Stengers (1984) note:

> [Traditional] science is based on the discovery of a new and specific form of communication with nature-that is, on the conviction that nature responds to experimental interrogation. . . . the scientific method is applicable only by virtue of the astonishing points of agreement between preconceived models and experimental results. (p. 5)

For example, certain immutable "laws" have already come under strong criticism. Newton believed his laws of planetary motion were universal, as did many who followed his ideas. And yet, Newton's clocklike laws only worked for two planets, and not three or more. The "truths" that one derives about phenomena are determined by the observer's approach to understanding the world.

In the traditional paradigm of science, experimentation establishes an artificial dialogue with nature due to the experimenter's requirement of controlled inspection of discrete samples of behavior. It is a reductionistic procedure which separates that activity or behavior in question out of the environment and then subjects certain elements to empirical tests. This artificial arrangement (the element of study separated from it's environment) may be replicable, deterministic, and reversible. Still, it is well known in behavioral science that laboratory research often does not generalize to the larger world (Kerlinger, 1986), this is so because nature and living systems contain essential elements of uniqueness, randomness, and irreversibility. What differentiates the theorists in the new science is that they "jump from the paradigm of things to the paradigm of pattern" (Keeney, 1983, p. 95). To be irritating, we might attach the label of "laws" to certain central ideas from the "new physics," as it is sometimes called, or as we describe it—chaos theory. Laws of science in this paradigm are "thought laws" and not "natural laws." The laws are generated by our perception of phenomena, not by the phenomena itself. However, this new thought form enlists our cooperation to establish equally new rules in describing our ideas. Inspired by Poincaré's willingness to only approximate certain behavior, it is our contention that the furthest one may go is to describe a hypothesis that by consensus has greater heuristic potential than others. This is called a theory. The life of a theory, in our view, depends on future generations recognizing a more comprehensive set of ideas that assimilate what was once our generation's "grand theory." To call it a law in our view is simple narcissism. We will use the term *theoretical construct*[3] to describe the rubrics of this position where laws no longer exist.

THEORETICAL CONSTRUCT 1: OBJECTIVITY

In the new science model, the subject being observed (be it a plant, star, or human being) is no longer the passive substance described in the mechanistic worldview. Instead, spontaneous activity and interaction with the observer occur. As Appleyard (1993, p. 191) asserts, "Science was everything we could logically know of the world, but it could not include ourselves." Thus, the observer is introduced into the pattern, operation, and function of the system. This is one of the first "theoretical constructs" of

---

[3] We use the term *construct*, because this is the world as we see it. Ideas are in essence constructions to explain the world in which we participate.

the new science: There is no purely objective observer. For example, in physics, so long as a quantum system is not being observed, its wave function evolves deterministically. However, when the system is inspected by an observer, the wave function suddenly jumps. "The system is . . . capable of changing with time in two completely different ways: one when nobody is looking and one when it is being observed" (Davies, 1988, p. 168). Maturana and Varela (1987) also note that there are systems that change when they are observed, such that the "mere attempt by an observer to predict their structural course removes them from the realm of . . . predictions" (p. 123).

In one of Bateson's metalogues (1972), he describes scientific objectivity in the following manner:

DAUGHTER: What does "objective" mean?
FATHER: Well. It means that you look very hard at those things which you choose to look at.
DAUGHTER: That sounds right. But how do the objective people choose which things they will be objective about?
FATHER: Well. They choose those things about which it is easy to be objective. . . .
DAUGHTER: So it's a subjective choice?
FATHER: Oh, yes. All experience is subjective.
DAUGHTER: But it's human and subjective. They decide which bits of animal behavior to be objective about by consulting human subjective experience. . . .
FATHER: Yes—but they do try to be not human. (p. 47)

Prigogine and Stenger (1984) also emphasize that our perception and description of reality are always a construction of our intellect. As Watzlawick (1984) notes, *objectivists are inventors who think they are discoverers because they do not recognize their own inventions when they come across them.* Consequently, the myth of a simple, passive world that gives itself to objective, "scientific" observation must be abandoned. Facts and scientific data are created in the act of observation.

THEORETICAL CONSTRUCT 2: IRREVERSIBILITY

A long-standing challenge in physics grew out of the second law of thermodynamics (concerning entropy), which introduced the elements of time and irreversibility. Entropy has been popularly thought of as the measure of disorder in a system. The idea is you have a system, a closed system typically, full of different elements. As these different elements interact they are used up, and the waste from these interactions creates disorder; something like manure within a closed horse stall where there is plenty of hay. The death of this system happens when all the elements of the system are used up, and it's full of disorder (manure). There's no more hay, and well, the horse cannot be found either—at least quickly. This is maximum entropy or death, and is the cause for some scientists to run around saying that the universe is dying.

One problem is that in the strictest sense of the word, there are no known closed systems in the universe. So, the "machine" of nature is unable to function unchanged through time as an open system, and the longer it runs the more it ebbs and flows adapting to different phenomena. Thus, there is an irreversible process that depends on the direction of time. Once an element of the universe has been used, it cannot simply return to its previous form; it has become part of something else. Newtonian physics had postulated that the laws of nature served to maintain equilibrium and that irreversible processes (such as the buildup of disorder) were nuisances or aberrations in a naturally lawful, stable, and orderly universe. But these irreversible, spontaneous processes are at the center of interest in the study of chaos and nonlinear systems. Systems in nature are historically determined since they are changed by the passage of time. Natural systems collect information over time that is stored and exerts an effect on both their current and future activity. Therefore, it is impossible in a natural system to "start over again" or return to a baseline. Time, as we know it today, cannot be reversed, nor can the inevitable changes that occur over time. Simply put, you can't unscramble an egg.

THEORETICAL CONSTRUCT 3: COMPLEXITY

Prigogine and Stengers (1984) takes the equation of the second law of thermodynamics one step further with their hypothesis:

> In far-from-equilibrium conditions we may have transformation from disorder . . . into order. New dynamic states of matter may originate, states that reflect the interaction of a given system with its surroundings. (p. 12)

Along with entropy, another direction of time exists, equally fundamental and undeniable. Although entropy is an irreversible process, it does not lead only to the deterioration or destruction of a system. This is only for closed systems. From the increasing complexity in an open system, organization can occur that maintains an order with its own energy. The system must continue to interact in original ways either within itself (between different elements) or with the environment. This reaction of a system away from maximal entropy may be described as "complexity" (Corcoran, 1992; Kauffman, 1991, 1995; Waldrop, 1992). Davies (1988) writes, "The universe is progressing—through the steady growth of structure, organization and complexity—to ever more developed and elaborate states of matter and energy" (p. 20). It is this theoretical construct, "complexity," that describes the maintenance of order at the edge of chaos.

Transformations between randomness and simple, regular orders are intimately related to the index of entropy in a system. Platt (1970) describes the sudden changes of structure in natural (e.g., biological, evolutionary, and political) systems as the formation of larger integrated systems resulting from the chaos or malfunctioning of subsystems in the organism or organization. When we move away from equilibrium states to far-from-equilibrium conditions (an increased index of entropy or period-doubling), we move away from the repetitive and the universal to the specific and the unique. The folks at the Santa Fe Institute have been pondering the tremendous amount of a system's energy that is required to navigate chaos, and instead believe that the easier road is complexity where equally valid forms of organization may emerge.

Before his arrival there, Stuart Kauffman (1991) discussed what he called *antichaos,* that described self-organizations, but in his view entering chaos is not necessarily the next step. Instead, life evolves most freely at the "edge of chaos." A system exists on this edge of chaos turning back to its steady state following multiple adaptations as in Figure 2.5. He believes this is so because:

> Organisms lack the momentum to develop explosively into a new breed; supracritical communities expand so rapidly that they consume all their available food and die off. At the edge of chaos, however, mutation and innovation occur." (Kauffman in Corcoran, 1992, p. 20)

Many systems may adapt to a new environmental demand by navigating chaos, but expend so much energy that the system has no energy left for negotiating other adaptations. By maintaining itself at the edge of chaos, the system's energy requirements are more reasonable, and at the same time the complexity generated there is sufficient to make "just good

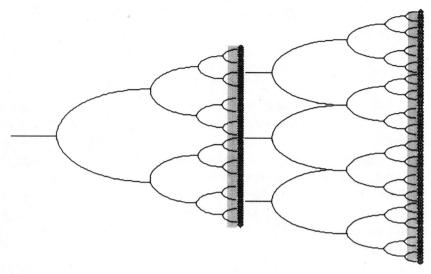

Figure 2.5 Stability and Bifurcation with Complexity. As in Figure 2.4, the horizontal lines represent a form of stability, with forks representing bifurcations, and vertical lines indicating chaos. Note that subsequent to chaos, at least graphically here, the stability is more complex as the system self-organized. But, here, the shaded vertical lines represent complexity and this complexity does not imply the movement of the system on through chaos necessarily. Rather, a sort of vacillation or hovering at the edge of chaos as a form of adaptation.

enough adaptations" (Sulis, 1995). In these statements is the idea that a system must move from a previously ordered, yet maladaptive state, to a more flexible adaptive state (Kauffman, 1995).

Put simply, this third "theoretical construct" of complexity in previously integrated systems states that the more complex a system is, the more likely it is that a spontaneous organization will occur which establishes a different, more adaptive, order. Change of this type does not occur as a mechanism returns the system to its previous steady state (a reversal of the disorganization or a return to equilibrium), but as a means of moving the system to an entirely different level of organization. Equilibrium, is a part of the change process, not an endpoint or "goal" of a system. Change is not controlled or imposed by a source outside the system. Rather, it is the interaction of the elements in the system or their interaction with the environment which generate a different structure. Life and consciousness are emergent properties generated by complexity.

THEORETICAL CONSTRUCT 4:   ORGANISMS ARE NOT MACHINES

We have mentioned that "you can't unscramble an egg," and that equilibrium is not an endpoint; it is only part of the change process. What these statements have in common is that they assume that organisms are progressive additive structures. They adapt to their environment through the use of complex or chaotic behaviors that stretch the parameters of a system's behavior. This is unlike a machine such as an automobile, which will fly apart if it behaves in such a manner. Moreover, engineers strive for homeostasis and/or stability as a central tendency. Such machines are reversible because a person needs only to replace a "bad" part to make it function "like new again." While many have contributed to the distinction between how machines operate and how organisms exist, Bertalanffy's work (1968) has been the guiding force in this area. The basic constructs of steady state and transformative state set the framework for our discussion.

A steady state has often been labeled homeostasis or equilibrium, the seemingly central tendency of an organism. However, both terms connote an endpoint, a desire for this state. A steady state is just a stop along the way as a system evolves. It adapts to certain conditions in the environment, and when this happens it achieves a steady state. Typically, the environment changes in some way, and our steady state cannot be maintained. Thus, it becomes maladaptive. Some new form must be achieved, and to do so, the system must adapt—"transform." This is where the transformative state comes into play.

The constructs in chaos theory really begin where the steady state leaves off, because of the manner in which organic systems transform. An automobile is unable to transform its basic structure and function to adapt to a new situation in the environment. Organic systems are able to adapt in this way. Moreover, mechanistic systems are typically designed to be robust within a set of parameters for their operation. They are able to last for "three years or thirty thousand miles." An organic system's steady states may last three years, or only for the blink of an eye, or be destabilized by something as small as a butterfly. So, a person is not an automobile, and an automobile is not a person because an automobile does not evolve and adapt as do people or other organisms.

THEORETICAL CONSTRUCT 5: THE BUTTERFLY EFFECT

Another important concept in chaos theory is that even a minute difference in any element of the environment may drastically alter the whole structure and behavior of an organic system over time. "Tiny differences in input could quickly become overwhelming differences in output—a phenomenon given the name 'sensitive dependence on initial conditions'" (Gleick, 1987, p. 8). As described earlier, Lorenz (1963) labeled this phenomenon in meteorology the "butterfly effect," which states that "a butterfly stirring the air today in Peking can transform storm systems next month in New York" (Gleick, 1987, p. 8, see Figure 2.6).

It is not a simple linear concept that the butterfly caused the storm; the theory is not based on a cause-effect model. Rather, the "butterfly effect" describes the importance that even infinitesimal elements of a system exert in influencing and changing the structure of the entire system. As already noted, a system is more vulnerable to spontaneous transformation when it is far-from-equilibrium. At that point, the imbalance that precedes structural change can be pushed to a critical moment or bifurcation by even the most "inconsequential" aspect, member, or part of the system. Bohm and Peat (1987) hypothesize that a "subtle perceptive response to the environment" could give rise to new kinds of active information in a system. This would dispose the subject(s) to enter a "state of 'free play,' in which new totalities of structure are proposed" (p. 203). In

Figure 2.6　The Butterfly Effect.

evolutionary theory, Gould (1980) proposes that "small changes early in embryology accumulate through growth to yield profound differences among adults" (p. 192). Therefore, "any tiny change that looks meaningful a long time ago sends history cascading off in another direction" (Batten, 1988, p. 16). Prigogine and Stengers (1984) maintain, "In far-from-equilibrium conditions we find that very small perturbations or fluctuations can become amplified into gigantic, structure-breaking waves" (p. xvii). This paradigm of the nature of change in systems provokes interesting questions for the dynamics of change in human systems.

THEORETICAL CONSTRUCT 6: CRITICAL MOMENTS AND/OR BIFURCATIONS

This theoretical construct of chaos postulates that when fluctuations (within any element of the system or its environment) force an existing system into a far-from-equilibrium condition and threaten its structure, it approaches a critical moment or bifurcation. At this moment, where a transformative state may start, it is impossible to predict in advance how the system will change or reorganize. Briggs and Peat (1989, p. 143) describe it in this manner: "The system undergoing a flux is, in effect, being offered a 'choice of orders.'" It is produced by an event as small as the proverbial Dutchboy's finger in the dike, or a butterfly in a weather system as we have discussed. Over time, this small event can achieve a magnitude that may change the entire character of the system. Once this path is chosen and the system reorganizes, a steady state takes over again until the next far-from-equilibrium point is reached. "Systems can undergo sudden transitions to new self-maintaining arrangements which will in turn be stable for a long time" (Platt, 1970, p. 2). The science of chaos does not rule out the deterministic paradigm. Rather, the two paradigms coexist as inseparable parts of any system. The critical moment or the bifurcation is the point of fluctuation between a steady state and chaos. As Prigogine and Stengers (1984, p. 167) indicate, "Bifurcation . . . occurs when we push a system beyond the threshold of stability."

THEORETICAL CONSTRUCT 7: "SELF-ORGANIZATION OUT OF CHAOS"

Following critical moments, a system starts to move down a path that may lead to a transformative state. At this point during the system's life one can only approximate how the path will unfold (Bohm, 1980), and once the system enters chaos, approximation is also lost. Prediction of the system's behavior is useless at this point because the system's behavior appears random to the observer. In fact, it is ordered, but so complex and multiply determined it appears to be random. This is chaos. If our system were a machine, this would be "bad" because it is likely that it would fly apart. On the other hand, our system is organic and so we are aware that this behavior is just part of a transformative state.

What is chaos that we should be mindful of it? Ford (1989, p. 351) tells us to "regard the source of chaos as missing information, for chaos is what humans (cavemen and modern) observe when they lack the information to perceive the underlying order." In many cases, chaos is there to push the system beyond its steady state parameters to enable it to glean new information. Once the system has "found the missing piece of the puzzle," a spontaneous new steady state "self-organizes" out of chaos. Self-organization is exactly as it sounds—a system using what Prigogine and Stengers (1984), like Jantsch (1980), speculatively refer to as a "collective mind" (p. 186) to organize itself. It is self-determined, and once this organization is chosen, Prigogine and Stengers (1984, p. 176) say, "Life becomes as predictable as . . . a falling stone."

THEORETICAL CONSTRUCT 8: "PUNCTUATED EQUILIBRIA"

Scientists who follow chaos theory predicate that "leaps," "jumps," and "spontaneity" are representative of the process of change as opposed to an ordered, step-at-a-time process. Families, like other complex systems, do not change in gradual increments, but in discontinuous leaps. Stephen Jay Gould (1980) has argued against Darwin's slow, orderly evolutionary process and proposed that there is equally convincing evidence for cataclysmic change in the evolution of species. He proposes a theory that is based on "sudden appearance" in which species do not arise gradually through minute changes in their ancestors, but appear all at once and fully organized or formed as a different species (p. 182). Gould has referred to this as "punctuated equilibria" in evolution and natural history.

The theory suggests that change in systems occurs in leaps following a gradual accumulation of stresses that a system resists until it reaches a breaking point. The more stressed or farther from equilibrium a system moves, the greater its perception of differences in the external world. When the system is at equilibrium, it is blind because its functioning is not threatened and there is no demand for adaptation. Complex systems in a steady state are highly resistant to change. The further the system moves from equilibrium, however, the more susceptible it becomes to small fluctuations or bifurcations (an abrupt change in behavior). When a system is conflicted or dysfunctional, this does not necessarily lead to disaster or dissolution. Instead, it may indicate that pressure is mounting that will push the system to leap to a more complex integration.

THEORETICAL CONSTRUCT 9: UNPREDICTABILITY

According to this new scientific theory, the empirical goals of predicting and controlling change are illusions fostered by the artificial nature of the experimental dialogue science has relied on for its examination of phenomena. The search for the Grand Unifying Theory in psychology relies on the assumption that human behavior is predictable. Does abandoning an empirically based science require an admission that a comprehensive explanatory theory is unattainable? According to this model, an all-encompassing theory that can control and predict how a system will change is an impossibility. In linear relationships, equations are solvable; there is predictability and stability. Time is considered reversible, such that the system can be taken apart and put back together again without assuming that the elements have been changed in the interim. In the system of mathematics, a 3 is a 3 is a 3 and its value is not affected by the passage of time. This factor is crucial to empirical science. Experimental science relies on replicability and predictability to establish validity. Natural systems cannot be "solved" and cannot be understood in isolation from their context. Three rabbits (assuming that at least one is of a different sex than the other two) will not be three rabbits for very long. Replicability becomes problematic due to the irreversibility of time. All natural systems change through the passage of time such that they cannot be taken apart and put back together in the same way. Changes implicit in the passage of time include maturation and aging in all life forms. Also, elements are not equivalent across systems or subsystems. "Nonlinearity means that the act of playing the game has a way of changing the rules" (Gleick, 1987, p. 24).

Platt (1970) states, "It is not at all clear whether self-structuring hierarchical jumps of this kind can be to any appreciable degree anticipated or guided" (p. 47). The unpredictability of change in systems makes calculation and empirical investigation difficult, but also creates a richness and potential for higher levels of organization. Determinism can offer some predictions for how a system maintains at a steady state, but not how, when, or what will begin the process of disequilibrium or the structure of the new order that will result from disturbance in a system. As Auerswald

(1987) points out, "'New science' formed a basis for a new set of rules that could be used to define a universal reality" (p. 323). But it is a reality in which predictability, equilibrium, reversibility, control, and dualism (separation of events into cause and effect, stimulus and response and/or individual and environment) are no longer the central elements. As recent developments in nonlinear systems dynamics have demonstrated, it is often impossible to accurately predict the effects of an outside intervention on a nonlinear, multidimensional system. This is especially true when the system is undergoing a transitional phase of instability, a period when it is most vulnerable to slight perturbations (Abraham, Abraham, & Shaw, 1990). Although we may speak probalistically about the behavior of such systems, chaos theory demonstrates that it is not feasible to precisely predict the functioning of complex nonlinear systems. The more unstable the system is, the more variable the effects of our intervention may be on systemic functioning and the less accurate our predictions regarding the system's future behavior.

During our journey into the world of chaos theory, we will find that discussions will be led by concepts that focus on holistic and coevolutionary paths. These paths will be full of butterflies, bifurcations, and self-organizations that all go hand in hand with this new theory of development. We will provide more of these new ideas here and there that will act as landmarks along this path we will take together.

PART TWO

FAMILIES . . .
COMPLEX TERRAIN

CHAPTER 3

Into the "Phrase Space"

It also has some trying implications for therapists, let alone their clients, who may not take kindly to the message: Come in and I will get you out of this state of anxiety, nervousness, depression you are in and make you unstable again.
—Lynn Hoffman (1981, p. 348)

TO BEGIN our discussion of chaos theory and family systems, one of the first questions that may arise is, "What does chaos theory do that cybernetics and general systems theory do not do?" As stated earlier, on purely a systems level, cybernetic theory addresses mechanistic systems (Wiener, 1961), and these insights were adapted to family therapy (Haley, 1959). This presented a kind of mechanistic feedback orientation to working with families: It advanced family systems theorizing about the way families communicate moving beyond Korzybski's map territory (1948) and Russell's logical types (Whitehead & Russell, 1964/1910), but it did not address organic systems, such as a family. General systems theory (Bertalanffy, 1968) explains the evolution of organic systems, described in terms of a *steady state* and a *transformative state*. While the steady state may be viewed as a more flowing version of homeostasis,[1] the transformative state is not so clearly described. For brevity, one might say that a system has a state it "tends toward," which is where homeostasis has been so overused, and misused. When the system moves

---

[1] More specifically, homeostasis is a systems general tendency, whereas a steady state describes organisms and is an advance over that concept where one system can move from one steady state to a more adaptive steady state via traversing a transformative state.

away from its "steady state" in order to adapt, it is said to be in a transformative state. What chaos theory, and specifically self-organization
theory, describes in greater detail is the transformative state of general
systems theory.

What is chaos in the human condition? This topic has been addressed
in an earlier work (Bütz, 1992a), and was speculatively described as a
state of overwhelming anxiety. This definition for chaos in the human
condition might also hold for a family system. In that article, chaos was
described as a precursor to a more adaptive higher order, a more complex
level of growth than had previously been obtained. Perhaps the most applicable model of how this process of transformation works may be explained by utilizing Ilya Prigogine's self-organization theory (1971, 1982;
Prigogine & Stengers, 1984).

SELF-ORGANIZATION AND STABILITY

In Prigogine's view of self-organization theory, for which he won a Nobel
prize in 1977, we see roughly five main states: a steady state, a bifurcation,
a bifurcation cascade or period-doubling route to chaos, chaos, and self-
organization. In examining the models we have discussed, one fundamental idea is stability of the system, whether it is a family system, a biological
system, or some other system. These five stages in Prigogine's theory of
self-organization describe various levels of stability. And, as described in
Chapters 1 and 2, out of severe instability, or chaos, an underlying order
often will emerge. The system's chaotic behavior is, in fact, adaptive and,
in part, there to increase the system's parameters of behavior.

A "SYSTEM'S" ATTEMPT TO ADAPT

As a system attempts to understand[2] how to adapt to these perturbing or
destabilizing agents, it seeks solutions beyond its previous parameters. It
does not behave in the manner that it usually does. The system behaves in
an apparently random fashion, doing "this or that," with no discernible
goal or direction. Once the system has found some sort of solution (perhaps a new piece of information), it begins to self-organize toward a new,
more complex and adaptive steady state. All the constituent elements of
that system appear to cooperatively organize to a new stable level of a

---

[2] This would be generally considered an anthropomorphism but expresses the process
unfolding here.

system's existence. This new stability, this new steady state, isn't like the old one though. It may look like the earlier steady state, but it is a more complex and adaptive state. This new organization is an adaptation that can respond to these new perturbations and/or destabilizing agents in the system's environment. This new level of organization may be seen as emerging from the system's ability to move beyond its previous parameters of existence. Crucial is the system's ability to gain new information that allows it to adapt. The key element here is new information found through chaotic behavior that allows the system to become more complex and more adaptive in the face of novel situations or stimuli.

MECHANISTIC AND ORGANIC SYSTEMS—INTERVENTIONS FOR DIFFERENT FAMILIES

Prigogine's work fully describes the transformative state of an open organic system's evolution and connotes chaos, or what may be experienced as chaos, as a positive state for the system. This differs from Wiener's idea (1961) of cybernetics, because cybernetics is based on a mechanistic idea of feedback inside a closed system. Cybernetics has been a key element in many family systems theories including Haley's work (1959) and that of the Milan group (Selvini-Palazzoli et al., 1978). Since families are open and organic, and not machines (as in Theoretical Construct 4, organisms are not machines), the focus of this chapter, this book in fact, will deal with families from this perspective. This brings us to an integration of chaos dynamics and models of family therapy.

The three main traditions in family therapy are structural interventions, strategic interventions, and systemic interventions. Since different families require different types of interventions (McCown, 1992), self-organization is not necessarily the goal of each. Also, some families are in need of interventions at the structural level, where the component parts of the system need to be reorganized. On the other hand, higher functioning families may be able to respond to systemic interventions. Moreover, each family has its own form of stability (Olson, Sprenkle, & Russell, 1979; Russell & Candyce, 1979). While some families may need to self-organize out of chaos, others that are too rigid may need nudging toward a chaotic state in order to adapt better. Accordingly, we encourage readers to keep in mind the family's developmental level of functioning before making interventions based on the perspectives offered here. Part Three of this text will elaborate on how to determine where a family might be in relation to the transition from stability to chaos.

THE FAMILY: WHAT DOES IT LOOK LIKE?

What is a family? What does a family look like developmentally? These are questions that family therapists have struggled with for decades now. As new scientific paradigms are introduced, clinicians incorporate information to develop new perspectives on the family.

One of the first questions to confront is, Where are the family's boundaries? Do we consider a family as part of an individual? Do we consider a family a piece of a larger community? What is the particular boundary that constitutes a family? In the literature, it has been indicated that a family boundary is in actuality drawn by the cultural definition of a family (McGoldrick, Pearce, & Giordan, 1982). In Native American cultures, the family can be very large with an emphasis on extended family members (Duran, 1990; Duran & Duran, 1995). In modern Euro-American culture, at least for the past several decades, the family has been described as a nuclear unit, indicating two parents, with their offspring. More recently, the definition of the family has been challenged when considering single-parent families and blended families (Carter & McGoldrick, 1988; Goldstein, 1986; Morawetz & Walker, 1984). Still, given all these considerations what does a family look like from a chaotician's standpoint?

A number of family chaoticians have commented similarly with regard to boundaries. We will first consider what chaotic system's structural boundaries look like. McLeod has this to say on boundaries from a structural perspective:

> Dissipative structures are paradoxical and are stabilized by their "flowing." If they are subjected to extreme perturbations they produce an escape to a "higher order" and move the universe "from being to becoming." The older idea that the universe is running down is no longer thought to be useful and its development is now believed to be ongoing. (McLeod, 1988, p. 11)

Dissipative structures[3] were the "workhorse" entities that Prigogine used to conceptualize self-organization. McLeod describes an open system that will not "run down" unless it is cut off from new sources of energy or information. Consistent with our somewhat cryptic description of Prigogine's work in this chapter, the system moves from *being* in the steady state to *becoming* in the transformative state. One type of boundary

---

[3]States of matter arising through bifurcation when a system is driven away from the state of thermodynamic equilibrium by external constraints exceeding a critical value (Davies, 1989, p. 495).

is described in terms of movement through these states. When we think of a family we need to ask whether what we call a *movement boundary,* is steady or transformative, since knowing this would lead us to entirely different interventions. This is where it becomes difficult, if not impossible, to account for a family's behavior in a linear fashion because one would assume constant relative stability. The idea of a movement boundary connotes both a steady and transformative state, and the fluid, adaptive transitions between the two.

In contrast to the movement boundary, there are limits to how much a system can change. Even in chaos, the racial characteristics of a family will not change. What we will call a *phenotypic boundary* is that a man will still be a man and a woman will still be a woman. Since these two boundaries exist, where do we look for conditions that bring about change in a family system?

THE FLUIDITY OF BOUNDARIES

Admittedly, the map may never describe the territory (Korzybski, 1948), but we are able to know more about the territory with better maps. Also, we may take for granted that truly defining a family is an impossibility with only words and theories. Still, we may be helpful in the attempt to do so. First, we must realize that at times families are like quicksilver, they are fluid in their being. So we must ask what connotes the family aside from the fact that they change, and have phenotypic characteristics that do not change because of their genotype. Chubb has this to say about families:

> From my point of view, what people do is the system. Social systems are processes. The notion of social systems as process assumes that there are patterns of interactions that persist over time—my family, their one night stand, the rolling catholic church—without treating them as independent organisms. (1990, p. 172)

Chubb's comments aptly reiterate the concerns that were stated earlier. Is the family an "it," a "process," a "thing"? How do we talk about families? Chubb admonishes, "Don't turn a process into a thing. What does it mean for therapy if you don't turn a process into a thing?" (1990, p. 173). The developmental sequence that Chubb describes is fluid, not static. The question then becomes how does one describe a fluid system that consists of individuals and social interactions? We would like to remember Chamberlain's comments (1993) on *strange attractors in patterns of family interaction:*

Instead of "phase space,"[4] I think of relationships as existing in "phrase space." Phrase space is the pattern of communication that establishes both problems and solutions in families. . . . to begin mapping the phrase space in a problematic relationship, the clinician needs to equally examine what is being said and what is not being said. To break the immobility and collapse of a family system, there must be a solution point established that the members can revolve around which is as compelling to them as the problem point.

By describing phrase space, Chamberlain is connoting a verbal boundary of sorts that focuses our attention to the abstract communication boundaries of a system. When we deal with such fluid concepts, *phrase space* is one way to describe a family's boundaries in terms of information. How information is communicated in the family system is at the crux of our description of boundaries. In his book *Artificial Life*, Levy describes the importance of information in systems: "Living organisms use information in order to rebuild themselves, in order to locate food, in order to maintain themselves by retaining internal structure . . . the structure itself is information" (1992, p. 108).

The fluidity of a family's becoming seems to be based on how information flows or is communicated within the family. Taking note of the earlier descriptions about change in open organic systems perhaps we may view communication patterns as steady, bifurcated, chaotic, or self-organizing. It appears that when an unstable system has been in need of a crucial piece of information and this piece of information is received and integrated, we may begin to observe this family system self-organizing out of chaos. Therefore, in concert with the idea of phrase space we propose that there are *information boundaries*.

Among the early family therapists to cover this ground, Dell and Goolishian (1981) had this to say: "Systems suddenly organize themselves, and, equally suddenly, make this continuous shift from one coherent order to another" (p. 175). Gibney (1987, p. 80) appears to describe anorexia as a chaotic transformative period where a family lacks the information necessary to adapt to its current environment. To step up to new environmental demands, the family requires more information. The fluidity of the system appears to be based around a boundary of *information, both*

---

[4] Phase space is roughly a three-dimensional portrait of a systems behavior, more technically "a space whose coordinates are given by the set of independent variables characterizing the state of a dynamical system" (Davies, 1989, p. 500).

emotional (Redington & Reidbord, 1992; Reidbord & Redington, 1992) *and intellectual* (Rapp et al., 1989; Skarda & Freeman, 1987). The therapist seems to act as an additional source of information that the family seeks out.[5]

THE THERAPIST, INFLUENCE TO WHAT DEGREE?

As therapists, "We may be simply a butterfly in the metaphorical weather system of the family" as Chamberlain has pointed out (1993). To what degree do we influence family dynamics? If we are butterflies in their familial weather system, do we play a significant role? After all, the modal amount of family therapy is one session, with the mean being three sessions, and yet there is a wide degree of variation around these points. How much real influence do we have? We propose as little or as much as the family allows us. The key is openness to new information. Some ideas in chaos theory may assist us in describing how to gauge this influence. We have already established that a family is an open system that has steady and transformative states. The essential consideration is how stable is the system is to begin with?

The concept "sensitive dependence on initial conditions" addresses the issue of stability. This is a classic concept in chaos theory, and well worth revisiting here. As the reader might recall, Lorenz was in the process of replicating weather patterns using one of the early digital computers in 1961. This weather replication seemed to match patterns that existed in nature. Each pattern started with an initial set of conditions, contained in a six-decimal place code (e.g., .506127). One day in 1961, Lorenz took a shortcut in attempting to replicate a pattern by inputting only a three-decimal place code (e.g., .506). He assumed that this would not affect the weather pattern in any significant or deleterious manner. However, when he returned to the room, he found a weather pattern had evolved bearing little resemblance to the previous weather patterns created before by this simple six-digit code. As stated in Chapter 2, and reiterated here for greater clarity, what Lorenz discovered is jokingly called the *butterfly effect* because the variable Lorenz had omitted was as tiny as a butterfly in a weather system. Technically, the butterfly effect was called "sensitive dependence on initial conditions," meaning that the initial conditions, inputs, or variables

---

[5] Or in other cases, where therapy may be mandated by government institutions.

are terribly important and sensitive. In this case, Lorenz changed the initial conditions by losing information from the set (e.g., the digits .000127). Without this information, the initial conditions evolved to a point where they were entirely different, and as a result, the weather patterns were also. For example, a weather system may be so sensitive that a butterfly flapping its wings in Salt Lake City, Utah, may influence the development of a hailstorm two days later in Denver, Colorado, as the system moves east.

Noting that something as small as a butterfly can have a tremendous effect on an unstable weather system, we came to appreciate the importance of minute variables. Open systems not only can move from chaos to a more adaptive new order, but can be unstable enough for a small variable to completely change their behavior over time. As one might guess, the most unstable period of a system's behavior is during a chaotic period, and this is when the system is the most open to effects from external sources. We can conceptualize that families behave in a similar manner. As we have used the metaphor of a butterfly several times, it seems helpful to provide an example of this effect in families. The Milan group has pointed out that the act of simply gathering information may be intervention enough (Selvini-Palazzoli et al., 1980). The act of questioning a family may engender enough novelty to influence transformation.

Therefore, it depends on the system's level of stability, its movement boundary, to determine the degree the therapist influences a family system. How do therapists affect systems? We have briefly described interventions for differentially functioning families, but the sheer presence of a therapist may also be influential.

CONTAINING

In the psychodynamic school, the therapist and therapy itself have been referred to as a "container." Integral to the psychodynamic conceptualization of the container is what is contained: This is typically anxiety. Perhaps one approach to working with a family is to contain its chaos for an hour or two a week so the system is free to explore more possible solutions to its problems. To a certain degree, support for this type of containment issue is offered in an article titled "Mastering Chaos," which appeared in *Scientific American*. In that article, Ditto and Pecora (1993) described "synchronized chaos." They have this to say about it: "The trick is to find those substances that react to a chaotic signal in a stable way" (p. 81). In other words, the chaotic system is coupled (we use this word timidly, since much of the chaos theory terminology is still being debated at this time [Goldstein, 1993, 1995]) with a stable system, and it in turn settles down in a respect. It seems that a stable system contains some of the chaos of the chaotic system. Goerner (1992) offered the example of how cuckoo clocks couple and synchronize once they are put on a wall in proximity. In Native American traditions, the healing practices that are described by Duran and Duran (1995) emphasize that the healer must be approaching the situation from a balanced place. The purpose is to assist the client, or in this case, the family, by offering stability to the frame of therapy—being stable when the client or clients are unstable. Conversely, when systems are too rigid, other therapists (Whitaker, Laing) seem to indicate the therapist must move into a chaotic condition. In either case, as therapists contain a family's experience and determine the level of intervention necessary, they will need to monitor their own experience in response to the system's movement boundary.

THE CLINICIAN'S ROLE

Clinicians, while resourceful, have no tools except themselves to work with their clients. Becoming an instrument of change—as either a butterfly or a fellow cuckoo clock in the system—is tied to the therapist's training and self-knowledge. In psychodynamic theory, Reik (1948) provides a wonderful guide titled *Listening with the Third Ear.* A therapist learns to pay attention to:

> those inner voices with more attention than to what "Reason" tells about the unconscious; to be very aware of what is said inside himself, and to shut his ear to the noises of adult wisdom, well considered opinion, conscious judgment. The night reveals to the wanderer things that are hidden by day. (pp. 146–147)

Carl Whitaker would have agreed (1989) since he indicated that knowing himself and his reactions to a family are important, if not vital, to his therapeutic approach:

> Another factor that is important in your growth as a professional is developing an increasing access to your free associations, to your images, to your fantasies, to your own craziness. (p. 222)

Through attending to ourselves as an instrument and developing those capacities through our training, supervision, and hopefully our own psychotherapy, how do we assess the effectiveness of this process?

HOW MUCH CHANGE IS ENOUGH:
IS IT COMPLEXITY?

Elkaïm (1981) offers these comments: "Family members reach a state where they consider that their exchanges with the external world have come to a satisfactory level for themselves" (p. 296). Elkaïm's statement may be taken to mean that a family knows when the members have adapted enough to a new environmental demand. This connotes a difference from earlier more predetermined models of a "normal" family's change process. The family, like a timid child who wants to swim, wandering in and out of the water on the pool steps, may be ambivalent about how deep they wish to get into their issues. Attending to the family's own sense of completion is often difficult. We may want more change than the family members feel prepared to accommodate.

A spectrum of interactions exists as a family dances in a fluid interchange between the individual and the community. For healthy functioning to occur, this dance can be neither too rigid nor too chaotic, which is reflected in Levy's description of life forms in *Artificial Life* (1992):

> This completely decisive property of complexity, that there exists a critical size below which the process of synthesis is degenerative, but above which the phenomenon of synthesis, if properly arranged, can become explosive. . . . In other words, a key ingredient of life. (p. 110)

There needs to be a balance of complexity and here we see the therapist involved in the process of determining whether the "movement" of the family has reached a "healthy" level. This process is terribly subjective, and an issue of debate both from within the field and outside the field. The therapist may have a difficult time knowing if family functioning has reached a healthy level, since the therapist coevolves with this process as Gibney (1987) and others have pointed out. Here lies the danger of being "sucked in," rather than being therapeutic. We will still coevolve, but there is a difference between being enmeshed and effective. It is the therapist's job to determine in consultation with the family, when a new level of adaptive health has been reached. Subtly, Chamberlain has indicated (1993, August) how to assess this issue at the outset of the therapeutic process.

> My suggestion to clinicians would be to begin by examining where the information or energy in the family has collapsed. What issue or problem appears to pull the family like a vortex and limit the flexibility and mobility of the system.

The question then becomes, "Has this impasse been resolved satisfactorily?" How do we actually measure whether change has taken place to a mutually acceptable degree?

MEASURING CHANGE

The issue becomes (a) how to view a family and (b) how to measure or describe change in the family. As we described in Chapter 11, psychologists who are chaoticians use phase portraits. We look to Freeman (1991; Skarda & Freeman, 1987), Rapp (Rapp et al., 1989; Rapp, Jiménez-Montano, Langs, Thomson, & Mees, 1991), and more recently Redington and Reidbord (1992, Reidbord & Redington, 1992) for their work on phase portraits during change. Where Freeman and Rapp focus on EEG patterns taken from the brain, Reidbord and Redington focus on cardiac rhythms. These have been relatively accepted methods in measuring change in systems, but Rapp (1993) had noted that "earlier indications of human chaos in physiological data might have been spurious" (p. 89). Earlier, Elkaïm, Goldbeter, and Goldbeter-Merinfeld (1987) mentioned another problem:

> At the same time, however, the purpose of analyzing the model remains conceptual rather than therapeutical: Even if such an ambition were nurtured, the specific analysis would come *too late* to be used in the course of the therapy session. (p. 34)

Finally, Elkaïm in a roundtable discussion with Prigogine and others (1982) states the problem as modeling boundary changes (this is paraphrased due to the length of the citation), "In modeling complex behavior we either find what we are looking for, or become lost if you draw a map as complex as the territory it depicts" (p. 63). So it seems that in measuring change we must use caution and realize that at this stage we use such models retrospectively, rather than prospectively, unless we consider symbolic material (Bütz, 1992a, 1993a, 1993b, 1995a, 1995b). There it may be possible to gauge the magnitude and direction of the change process. Still, this formulation is in its infancy, and like the phase portrait approach should be undertaken with considerable caution.

In this chapter, we have focused on how family dynamics would look through a chaotician's lens, and what may be useful ways to consider intervention. Two boundaries were identified that are useful in describing the family's process, *movement* and *information*. Although these boundaries have been addressed by others, this interpretation is unique due to the attention on self-organization. Measuring what constitutes change is still a mutually determined process that defies useful quantification (Barton, 1994). Finally, considering the movement and information in family systems, we may be able to understand them in phrase space in the therapeutic session, which does not lend itself to static descriptions that have so long underestimated the complexity of those interactions.

CHAPTER 4

The Eerie Beauty of
Strange Attractors

Strange attractors describe the way that a dynamic system settles
down to a simpler set of motions . . . even in the most chaotic of
family situations there may be an organizing principle . . .
predictability may seem minimal, but on careful examination
such "attractors" may draw behavior into an overall pattern.
—Bruce Stevens (1991, p. 24)

AN INTRODUCTION TO
THE STRANGE ATTRACTOR

The first encounter with a "strange attractor" pattern can create both a
sense of intuitive recognition and cognitive confusion. The intricate, beautiful portraits of strange attractors decorate the covers of many books on
chaos theory including this one. The symmetry of nature exposes itself in
the convoluted twists and loops of the attractor—an interplay of convergence and departure that depicts so much of the dynamics seen in natural systems. There is a holographic quality to the depictions of strange
attractor patterns. One can see that there is something orderly and patterned, but there is also an intricacy that is the product of persistently
novel behavior in the system. No two loops of the attractor are exact replicas; although there is convergence, there is no overlap or repetition (see
Figure 4.1).

In their book *Turbulent Mirror* (1989), Briggs and Peat define strange
attractors as the turbulence that breaks up orderly systems and causes

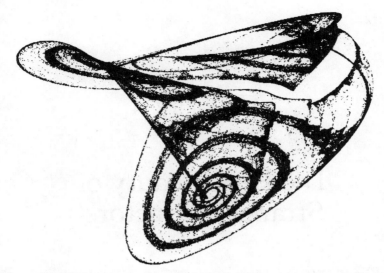

Figure 4.1 A Particularly Beautiful Example of a Strange Attractor. From *Strange Attractors: Creating Patterns in Chaos* by Julian C. Sprott (New York: M&T Books, 1993). Copyright © 1993 by Julian C. Sprott. Reprinted by permission of Henry Holt and Co., Inc.

disorder to boil across our landscape. They eloquently describe attractors as "creatures that live in a curious abstract place called 'phase space'" (p. 31), a concept explored in Chapter 2. They are beasts that exist at the juncture between turbulence and order. The metaphor of a "bowl of spaghetti" is Casti's (1992) way of providing a visual image of a strange attractor:

> Each strand of spaghetti in the bowl is one part of the strange attractor, the spaghetti sauce ensuring that no two strands ever quite make direct contact. Yet on each strand there is some point that is as close as we like to any other strand, some strands even closing back on themselves to become periodic orbits. (p. 29)

Strange attractors began their existence as descriptions for phenomena like smoke rising from a cigarette with patterned swirls and flooding water finding its point of ebb and flow. The "strange" aspect of the attractor is related to the dynamics of the systems they depict which are neither static nor periodically repeating. Strange attractor patterns are fantastic, complex maps that capture the interplay between stability and change in systems. Particularly intriguing attractors and an excellent description of how to render them may be found in Sprott's (1993) *Strange*

Attractors, Creating Patterns in Chaos. In looking at the images developed using mathematics to map chaotic systems, there is an eerie beauty and symmetry in the basic structure of nature that is strikingly rich and profoundly lovely. Strange attractor patterns, when the data points are mapped, often resemble a complicated sign for infinity. David Ruelle, a mathematician, becomes poetic when describing strange attractors:

> I have not (yet) spoken of the esthetic appeal of strange attractors. These systems of curves, these clouds of points, suggest sometimes fireworks or galaxies, sometimes strange and disquieting vegetal proliferations. A realm lies here to be explored and harmonies to be discovered. (1980, p. 126)

Essentially, a strange attractor is the process that unfolds through the complex interactions between elements in a system. Strange attractors can be thought of as an idealized state toward which an unpredictable or dynamical system is attracted. Although they are the most complicated type of attractor, they are the most common found in biological and natural systems. Part of the "strangeness" of this type of attractor is that they combine two contradictory effects. They are attractors because trajectories converge onto them, yet they are also sensitive to initial conditions, which means that trajectories that were initially close together diverge. It is through a pattern of folding and stretching that the structure of the strange attractor emerges. Although diagrams and illustrations make strange attractors appear to be objects, they are the reflections of the ebb and flow of life that exists only in the interplay of behavior among elements of a natural, living, evolving system.

As discussed in Chapter 3, boundaries exist that limit the behavior of a system. For example, phenotypic boundaries prohibit the spontaneous, natural transformation of brown eyes to blue (at least without the technical assistance of colored contact lenses). Although chaotic systems vacillate erratically, they stay within a particular range or norm. Strange attractors are the foundation for the hidden order in natural systems. Each variation of the pattern that occurs creates some unique experience for the members of the system. While there is often similarity, no one orbit in the pattern repeats the entirety of any other orbit. Although there is apparent order in the pattern, the system is chaotic because there is never an exact repetition in any of the orbits around the attractor points.

Unlike mechanical systems, natural systems thrive on variety and diversity. In nature, an exact replication of behavior often leads to disaster. For example, if a fish were to visit exactly the same place at precisely the same time every day to feed, it wouldn't take long for a predator to predict that appearance and make a catch. There are, of course, certain parameters to the fish's behavior. It is not likely to leave the lake to feed on land, and most fish prefer to feed at certain times of the day. There are boundaries to the behavior, but within those boundaries exist infinite variations. This phenomenon is inherent in systems that function according to chaotic principles: They may appear ordered over time and with the accumulation of a great deal of data, but are unpredictable from moment to moment. Chaos is a science of pattern, not predictability.

Strange attractors function like magnets that constrain variables, behaviors, or events within a certain range. A simple definition is that an attractor simply is what it sounds like, something that attracts this or that (we will present a more complex, technical definition of attractor dynamics in Chapter 6). Strange attractors are nonlinear and fractal in nature, which differentiates them from other types of attractors such as higher and lower frequency oscillations (as described in Chapter 2).

Another factor related to strange attractors is that they exist in a mysterious place called "phase space." Phase space, which was introduced briefly in Chapter 2, is a mathematical term that allows physicists to visualize many numbers simultaneously.

> They take the situation of the system at an instant as a point in what they call a "phase space" so that in phase space the complete state of knowledge about a dynamical system at a single instant in time collapses to a point. (Albert, 1990, p. 109)

In mathematics, "space" can have a number of different interpretations. It is usually used to define a territory of interest or to group data in some way that determines certain boundaries. In chaos theory, phase space is the territory in which strange attractors live. The dynamic nature of chaotic phenomena creates a map of data points that becomes manifest as the system periodically cycles through chaotic and orderly phases. The strange attractor becomes a historical map of the evolution in the system.

The concept of phase space is one of the most powerful inventions of contemporary science (Gleick, 1987). It provides a way of mapping information by turning data points into pictures that take every bit of essential information from a system; scientists can abstract information and create flexible road maps to all the possibilities for the behavior of the system. All of the information about a complicated system can be stored in any point in the phase space. Empty spaces on the map indicate areas in which the system does not venture, changes in the direction of the loop indicate changes in behavior, and the pattern of loops shows periodicity and the limits of the system.

HUMAN BEHAVIOR AND
STRANGE ATTRACTORS

Strange attractor dynamics have been used to examine several different human phenomena including changes in patients' mental states during psychotherapy (Pendick, 1993), daily mood fluctuations (Hannah, 1990, 1991), personality dynamics (Middleton & DiBello, 1990; Middleton, Fireman, DiBello, 1991), and the psychotherapy process (Lonie, 1995; Perna, 1995). The use of strange attractor dynamics to study human behavior patterns and extract some sense of organization and order is clearly increasing. Experienced family therapists have an intuitive sense that even in the most chaotic families, organizing principles exert some limitations on the interactions between family members. These principles can be based on religious beliefs, cultural norms, family "myths," values, and other concepts that establish some type of boundary for behavior. For example, despite repeated, hostile arguments, physical violence will never occur in some relationships. That particular expression of anger lies outside the realm of the attractor that organizes how those in the relationship express their dissatisfaction and frustration with each other. These patterns of organizing principles, or behaviors, constitute the strange attractors in families and provide stability when the family is in danger of moving outside the limits. Although some chronically problematic families appear to be in perpetual states of chaos, there are boundaries and identifiable themes or repetitive interactions that lead to the heart of the strange attractor.

In Paul Pearsall's book *Ten Laws of Lasting Love* (1992), he employs the concept of strange attractors in the following manner. He describes love as the product of two individual "strange attractors" drawn to each other to make windows through the chaos of living. His hypothesis is that many couples view life's chaos as an obstacle in their quest for self-fulfillment, and for them, the necessary turmoil of life is a barrier. They attempt to avoid disruption or change and maintain a fragile "sameness." In couples who have reached the level of "high monogamy," however, chaos is a necessary and natural aspect of life. Periodic chaos allows for fluctuation and uncertainty, which is the foundation for transformation and growth. These times of instability are as necessary to maintain the life of relationships as they are to maintain any other form of life. Unbroken stability in living systems is one way to define death. In the paradigm of chaos theory, the pattern of interaction between people is a living entity built of the coming together and moving apart that is the heartbeat of relationships.

The use of the term "attraction" to describe what draws us to others certainly echoes the sense of being pulled toward something in the other person that feels inevitable and powerful. Concepts in psychological theory about the "disowned" or "lost" self that we seek out in our partner are maps of the territory of the strange attractor in relationships. Gampel (1990) writes: "When we are drawn to another—perhaps as being drawn to another attractor—with great intensity, we transform as we fall in love and risk the dissolution of our boundaries in the merger."

In Gampel's view, the pull of the strange attractor is the familiar conflict between solitude and intimacy in a relationship. The need for distance (focus on the self) and the need for closeness (focus on the other) between people is a constantly changing dynamic in any relationship. If we were to map fluctuations in these levels of need between two people, it is highly likely that the familiar pattern of a strange attractor would evolve.

How, when, and why each individual will shift toward the attractor point of self or the attractor point of other is unpredictable in the immediate future. Over time, however, patterns will emerge. This level of unpredictability is simply the nature of complex interactive systems, not a lack of refinement in our therapeutic talents. When a therapist stops being surprised by a family's behavior, the therapy and/or the family are stuck. It is chaos at work when it appears certain that a couple will break apart over some crisis, yet they come to the following session describing a greater level of intimacy as a result of that event. Over time, a watchful therapist can begin to decipher certain patterns that organize the relationship.

Patterns of violence in families offer an example of attractor dynamics in motion. In the book *Madness, Chaos and Violence* (1991), Brendler, Silver, Haber, and Sargent describe phases in the patterns of violence in families. They define the first phase as "madness," which is the introduction of the therapist to the passion, frenzy, and patterns of behavior that define the problem in the family. The second phase, "chaos," is escalation of disorder, disorientation, and turmoil as the family is unsuccessful in dealing with the "problem." The third phase, "violence," encompasses the struggle to develop new patterns. The "violence" in the therapy involves the therapist's "relentless attack on the family's destructive patterns" (p. 24). The fourth phase is transformation and beyond; the effective use of therapy to move the system past the previous destructive outcome. The emergence of new limits and boundaries for the family's behavior indicates the creation of a new strange attractor in the system. The attractor pattern is moved from problem and violence (as solution) to problem and alternative solutions through therapy. Complexity or chaos are necessary phases preceding transformation.

The interplay of individual needs and the needs of the relationship sometimes flows smoothly, and sometimes is turbulent and chaotic. For example, following his mother's death, a man may need more nurturing and support from his partner; he may need more closeness to adjust to the loss at the same time that his partner is experiencing a greater need for separateness to focus on opportunities in her career. The flow between the amount of closeness and separateness that each person requires at any given point in time may be very different, and it may be difficult to negotiate with each other from the basis of what is most needed for the sake of the relationship. This also contributes to the inherent unpredictability of human relationships. The interaction of diverse attractors at different levels of organization gives us the richness and diversity seen both in strange attractor patterns and in family relationships.

In the realm of human relationships, even the most basic, two-person relationship includes the two as a couple, each as individual, and each as a product of his or her family and social experience. In the case of a couple, there is not just the conflict between the partners with regard to intimacy and distance, but also within each person from one moment to the next. The desire for greater closeness or separateness is experienced and expressed on both an individual and relational level and is further complicated by the unremitting influence of environmental factors that enter the pattern. The richness of pattern in family systems is an outcome of the chaotic patterns of interaction that occur both between and within individuals. As Chubb (1990, p. 172) observed,

> The fact that chaotic interactions occur between individuals while other interactions, nonlinear and therefore also chaotic, are occurring within the organisms, adds an extra measure of complexity to the study of social systems.

Multiple levels of nonlinear processes unfold constantly and simultaneously even in the simplest of relationships.

To map a strange attractor, we can conceive relationships as being maintained through the movement of energy between the two attractor points of fear and love. The crucial communications between parties in intimate relationships are the diverse and dichotomous expressions of fear or love, of closeness or distance, of desire or despair. These are the most basic organizing principles in any human interaction. Through our expression and acceptance of these dual aspects of our own and our partner's inner and relational life, intimacy is created and sustained. In the process of relating to another over time, we weave the fabric of separateness and togetherness into the complex tapestry of intimacy. Part of the stretching and folding of the strange attractor is a response to the intensity of each of those needs within each person, given his or her background, personality, and expectations of the relationship. The sensitive dependence on initial conditions that is part of the creation of the attractor lies within each person's history on one level and within the history of the relationship at another level.

The repeated patterns of holding and letting go, of pulling together and pushing apart, create the rhythm and vitality of intimacy. When we risk the dissolution of our individual identity in intimate relationships, arguments are destined to ensue, with the result that the boundaries defining identity are regained in the solitude that emerges from distance and distress. Intimate relationships generally reverberate between these two limiting conditions. Perhaps the definitive strange attractor pattern in relationships is the fluctuation between fear (loss of the other) and love (loss of self). The strange attractor reflects the complex interaction of these elements within and between individuals.

A WALK IN "PHRASE SPACE"

Relationships can be conceived as existing in "phrase space" instead of "phase space." Language and communication are the life breath of human systems. It is through language that transformation occurs in both individuals and families. The concept that change can occur through the exchange of thoughts is a basic assumption of psychotherapy. The reality of a relationship lies largely in the symbolic, linguistically established definitions of roles, rules, history, meaning, purpose, and direction that members share. Phrase space can be defined as the boundary of language and communication that organizes relationships. It emerges from the patterns of communication between individuals that establish and maintain both problems and solutions in their relationship. Certain boundaries constrain a system's behavior, and the phrase space in which a relationship exists is also held within certain parameters. For example, in some bilingual families, one language is used when speaking of emotional experience while another is used to discuss business matters. This provides some structure and pattern to communication within the family and also serves as a boundary to those outside the family who do not speak both languages.

Through prudent attention to both what is and what is not being communicated in the family, the clinician can begin to map the phrase space. The basic task becomes moving energy (thoughts, time, attention, dialogue) from the established attractor point of the problem to an equally engaging attractor point of a possible solution or alternative. The importance of understanding the problem point in the attractor is that the solution point must be at least as intriguing, stimulating and compelling as the established conflict. In order to pull sufficient energy from the problem, the alternative must appear at least as attractive or more so than the current pattern. An additional challenge is that the problem attractor may be defined very differently by each individual in the system. This is where the information boundary we have discussed is so important because understanding the metaphor each member of the relationship has established leads both the clinician and the couple to greater appreciation of what is missing. The initial task of the therapist then is to seek either a unifying theme or an understanding of how the diverse definitions interrelate. Incomplete or ill-defined attractor patterns, and the interventions based on them, will likely be rejected by the family. The work of therapy is to identify, establish, and create with the family opportunities for experiencing a new attractor that will allow the family to transform. Then, the therapist must introduce the concept to the family in a way that pulls them toward new understandings and patterns of interaction. The new attractor is created by using language to redefine, create new meaning, increase confusion, and challenge the existing patterns that define the family.

Relationships can be thought of as an intricate dance that people create over time. No two steps are ever exactly the same, and there are differences at times in tempo and position. As the dance is contained to a greater extent by the boundaries of the relationship or within therapy, the pattern of moving around each other and the sense of where the next turn will lead generally become more and more predictable. There is some sense of order although there is no way to know exactly where the couple will be five steps from now. Adjustments are constantly being made to maintain the dance; sometimes moving closer, sometimes apart, one partner leading, then the other. It is easy to observe familiar partners using signals—a certain look, a touch on the arm, saying the partner's name with a certain inflection—these are symbols that maintain the bound-aries of the dance.

Many things can cause dancers to falter. There are forces within each person and external events that interrupt the flow of this relational movement. Either party can take a different step at any time and change the entire pattern. The music can stop or suddenly speed up and leave the dancers tangled in trying to keep up. The established order is gone, toes are stepped on, momentum is slowed or quickened, and there is the threat that the dancers will be unable to continue. Learning new steps in a relationship occurs in the phrase space between the partners. Because the music, that external element by which the dance is defined, does change, the steps must be constantly redefined and altered. The dance of romance and seduction is very different from the dance of raising young children. The established patterns of interchange, the timing and nature of approaches and responses, the meanings attached to behaviors, and the established expectations are endlessly challenged and changed.

Many family therapists already embrace the knowledge that change in relationships is most likely to emerge when something unpredictable happens to the system and some new information or opportunities be-come apparent. The unforeseen accidents, surprises, losses, detours, and miracles that occur allow enough deviation in the pattern for new possi-bilities to evolve. Uncertainty, confusion, spontaneity, and creativity are vital ingredients in the evolution of relationships. How unbearable it would be to have only one song to dance to through a lifetime together.

MAPPING THE STRANGE ATTRACTOR
IN FAMILY THERAPY

Commonly, families seek therapy when the fluctuation in the patterns around attractor points becomes too erratic, out of synch, or far-from-equilibrium.* Entering therapy becomes a way to establish a new strange attractor point that can restore order to the increasingly chaotic interac-tions in the system. The act of engaging a therapist is itself a means of adding greater complexity to the family's interactions. Now, another per-son will be party to the family's theories, feelings, and hopes. The family, at least those members who are invested in change, establish an agreement

---

*This is not to say that we do not also see families in therapy where there is limited fluc-tuation, and rigidity. We will discuss families that are "stuck" in this manner later in the book, most focally in Chapter 8.

to bring in an agent (represented by the therapist) of stability and positive change. Dell and Goolishian (1981) note:

> . . . as the system becomes sufficiently nonequilibrium and approaches instability, a variety of different paths become available to the system. Which path is "chosen" is determined randomly by the particular fluctuation that is amplified to the critical value—that is, "order through fluctuation." (p. 179)

Entering therapy is one possible means of restoring order in the midst of chaos. At least some members of the system believe or hope that treatment will change something in the patterns that have developed.

By using the strange attractor model, we can hypothesize that when the family enters therapy, a vast amount of the information in the system will have "collapsed" around the identified problem. Some or all members of the family will be devoting a significant amount of time and energy to solving the dilemma, usually through trying to get another family member to change. Repeated failed attempts to improve the situation increase the strength of the problem attractor. In essence, the more one unsuccessfully attempts to solve a problem, the more captivated one becomes. The pattern around the problem in the attractor becomes increasingly intricate and draws more of the family's attention and energy.

Identified problems often involve the need for a couple or family to make complicated decisions that generate several diverse opinions and options. Seemingly unresolvable disagreements about whether or not to have a child or threats by one partner to pursue a separation are typical problems that pull families into therapy. These periods of indecision have many chaotic features. As Gibney (1987) notes, "By necessity, the system needs to become more complex to move into a more stable condition and yet there are many directions in which it could move" (p. 79). The system is balanced precariously at the edge of chaos through the increase in variety (how to make an important transition, which route to travel, who and what needs to change) that the problem has generated.

The normal fluctuation from problem to solution may be blocked by fear, frustration, and/or lack of experience or information. As many family therapists hypothesize, the problem may also serve an important symbolic function or perceived need in the family. In Chapters 7 and 8, a framework for determining the nature of the impasse or collapse of the system around the problem and methods of intervention specific to these different dynamics will be further explained. Regardless of the dynamics that led to the unresolvable situation, however, the theory indicates that solution patterns in the strange attractor are absent or not functioning as effectively as they have in the past. The ability of the system to make productive use of the information it generates has collapsed. The family engages the therapist to serve as an attractor point focused on solution and positive change. The system seeks something outside itself to provide what it has not been able to generate: a solution.

Chubb (1990) reminds us, "Two structurally coupled organisms can perturb each other but they cannot make each other do anything" (p. 174). That holds true both for interactions between members of the family and interactions between the therapist and family. The concept of "causality" is defined very differently in natural, dynamical systems. Although individuals inevitably describe their experiences in linear terms (e.g., "I yelled at her because she wouldn't listen to me"), the nature of systems is based on complex, nonlinear dynamics in which causality is multidetermined (e.g., "You might have yelled at her because that has become a typical pattern in your relationship, perhaps based on your experience of growing up in a noisy family and your success in being able to intimidate and manipulate others when you raise your voice"). Uncertainty in complex or chaotic systems means we can never establish absolute causality of even simple behavior patterns. As Papp (1983) notes, ". . . no one event or piece of behavior causes another but, . . . each is linked in a circular manner to many other events and pieces of behavior" (p. 8). It may be helpful to remember that relationships between people are processes, not events.

As most experienced therapists know, change cannot be imposed on others. Even the most elegantly designed and carefully thought out interventions do not always perturb the family enough to bring about change. Some type of "perturbation," however, is the necessary component for moving the relationship pattern into a new trajectory. Although in many instances, families entering therapy are already operating at far-from-equilibrium conditions, by entering into a relationship with a therapist, the family incurs greater fluctuations in functioning due to the input of novel information. Several different approaches and methods of adding or containing new information in a manner that is likely to move the family system will be described later in the book.

THE CASE OF THE STRANGE ATTRACTOR

The following case study illustrates the far-from-equilibrium conditions that often exist for couples seeking therapy:

Mark, age 37, and his wife, Ellen, age 41, came in following a frantic call from Mark requesting a therapy session "as soon as possible." Mark was an account executive in a small company; his wife worked as a salesperson in the same office. Mark was extremely anxious and agitated while seated in the waiting room. He appeared much older than his age—balding, paunchy, and stoop shouldered with a rather wrinkled, bland mien. Ellen, an attractive, colorfully dressed woman, arrived late and seemed harried.

Mark called to arrange a session the morning after an argument that had ended with Ellen throwing clothes in a suitcase, grabbing their two young children, and leaving the house yelling threats of divorce as she piled the children into the car at three in the morning. Ellen stated she just drove around until sunrise (the children were asleep in the backseat), and she went home when she thought Mark would be gone to work. Neither had ever been involved in therapy in the past.

THERAPIST: What made you decide to try therapy?

MARK: I tried to hit her, chased her around the house some. That's not me. I've never been violent with anyone before. With my first wife, we never even argued.

THERAPIST: Do you have physical fights? Hit each other?

ELLEN: (very animated) He goes nuts . . . he gets so crazy when we argue. He was chasing me, yelling at the top of his lungs, even opened the front door at 2:00 A.M. to yell so the neighbors could hear. Calling me a slut and screaming I was running around on him. I'm tired of this. Yeah, he hits me and sometimes I hit him back. I don't want to come to therapy . . . this should be private.

MARK: I think she really might try to leave if we don't do something. I know she's not unfaithful, I just get so angry I'll say anything, hit walls, throw things . . .

ELLEN: (interrupting) He can't keep treating me that way. Our house is destroyed—holes in the walls, our bedroom door torn off the hinges. Now he's got my family upset. He called my mother and got her all involved in our stuff. She's really angry with him for hitting me and acting so stupid.

As they described the dynamics and history of their arguments, it became clear that several factors had recently impinged on the pattern and increased the complexity and unpredictability of their fights. Ellen had become much more vocal in her threats to leave and had begun to impulsively act on those threats by packing bags and talking with the children about leaving. Mark had become more threatening and violent. Mark's move to involve Ellen's mother in the dispute served to add to the instability. He had hoped to win her support in keeping Ellen in the marriage by refusing to allow Ellen and the children to stay with her if they left. His plan backfired, however, and her mother was now actively encouraging Ellen to leave. Ellen did not want to consult a therapist, she was embarrassed about being hit during arguments and didn't want "anyone else to know our business."

THERAPIST: It sounds like it's getting harder to keep this private, just between the two of you. Your (Ellen's) mom is involved now and the neighbors must know there's trouble .

ELLEN: That's what I'm maddest about, that Mark just talks to everybody about our stuff. He shouldn't have gotten my mother involved. Now my whole family's upset.

MARK: I just get so upset when she won't agree with me, I just have to win.

THERAPIST: Win what?

MARK: Arguments . . .

ELLEN: (interrupting) He'll do anything to make me stay when I get mad enough to leave . . . he's held my arms, pushed me in the bathroom and held the door shut, threatened me with a knife.

MARK: I know I act crazy, I just can't stop.

Escalations were spiraling out of control and attempts by the couple to manage the conflict within the bounds of their relationship were breaking down. Others were becoming involved, which began to change the pattern of secrecy. Their equilibrium as a couple was being threatened by outside intervention, both from Ellen's mother and from the therapist. All the energy that had been devoted to keeping their conflict a secret was beginning to dissipate and disrupt the balance. In terms of movement into a strange attractor, they were seeking some additional element to stabilize their relationship; something or someone outside themselves to divert them from the dangerous exacerbation in their conflicts.

Couples and families often present as being on the verge of collapse or total chaos. Therapists are consulted in a "last chance" attempt to provide some of the experiences or feelings that have been lost in the system, such as hope, affection, attentiveness, respect, and safety. With the couple described, an early goal in therapy was to advocate for and help the couple direct energy into the areas of the relationship that had atrophied. Establishing patterns that assure safety, creating some distance and autonomy, seeking healthy aspects of their relationship that have remained despite the conflict were tasks that therapy needed to address. The balance of *movement* between points seen in the strange attractor is a reflection of a healthy, vital, evolving system. When too much energy is directed toward only one point (e.g., conflict), the system collapses and becomes dysfunctional and toxic.

Clinicians can begin to understand families by examining where the *information or energy* in the family has collapsed. What issue or problem appears to pull the family like a vortex and limit the *flexibility and movement* of the system? The absence of balancing elements in the patterns of interaction indicate a system that is unable to adjust and evolve sufficiently to manage transitions and challenges. When the pull exerted by a single attractor point is too strong, the degree of spontaneity needed for balance and stability is unavailable to the system.

Therapists serve the function of redirecting the "turbulence" or energy from the attractor point where the family dynamics have collapsed to another source of turbulence. For example, if conflict in the family is avoided and too much energy is being consumed by the attractor of harmony and togetherness, the therapist becomes an advocate for confrontation, appreciation of differences, and increased individuation. The act of entering therapy in itself moves some of the family's energy toward solution and balance by bringing some element of hope to the perceived chaos of the relationship.

PART THREE

CATCHING THE BUTTERFLY— CHAOS IN THERAPY

CHAPTER 5

In the Eye of the Storm

The image of the "butterfly effect" is often applied to systems so
extraordinarily sensitive that a perturbation as small as the
flapping of a butterfly's wings produces a large-scale change of
behavior. Although chaos theory holds that such systems remain
strictly deterministic, they are, nevertheless, so enormously
complex that the exact details of their behavior are, in practice,
unpredictable . . .

—F. David Peat (1995, p. 359)

ANY THERAPIST who has sat in a room with a family and observed how they maneuver through a therapy session has felt the pull of chaos. The behaviors observed in families can come to resemble highly compressed rubber balls that strike something solid on occasion and then veer off in completely unexpected directions. For example, in a therapy session how do we get from the question "Who worries the most in this family?" to a description of an overly intrusive mother delivered in an impassioned monologue by a long-suffering son? Any system whose dynamics may be described as chaotic typically demonstrates a limitless affinity for variety and surprise.

Family therapists and others who delve into the mysteries of human behavior have long sought a suitable metaphor to give some framework to these observations. The behaviorists, who became logical positivism's representatives in psychology, have toiled heroically for decades and been unable to set down a single, immutable law regarding human behavior other than on a very elementary, almost cellular level. Although psychology has attracted some of the greatest thinkers of the past century, when the focus turns to human interaction, no one has been able to predict responses with even a modicum of accuracy. Why?

Perhaps a key to unlocking our epistemological dilemma lies in finding more representative metaphors. Previous metaphors from the "hard" sciences based on hydraulics, machinery, and computers have failed to provide a useful or appropriate model for the social sciences. Cognitive and neurological psychology would be incredibly simplified if we could seamlessly employ the metaphor of the human brain as a giant biological computer. As John Barrow (Appleyard, 1993) explains: "If . . . the action of the human mind involves noncomputable operations, then the quest for artificial intelligence cannot succeed in producing computer hardware able to mimic the complexity of human consciousness" (p. 206).

Thus far, we have not managed to create a computer that develops an unrelenting passion for another computer and pursues a more intimate relationship with the hope of producing some new software. No computer has yet been apprehended for murdering another computer. Computers don't refuse to run programs because they're too depressed (Edelman, 1992). Appropriate metaphors help broaden our understanding of phenomena, inappropriate metaphors restrict awareness. A metaphor that is too confining ensures that important information will be excluded.

Chaos science has produced an abundance of metaphors for those who are interested in exploring a different perspective of human interaction. Many concepts evolving in the realm of chaotic processes have clear implications for human systems dynamics. Among the many metaphors that have been generated in the study of chaotic dynamics, one of the most charmingly titled is also one that has a special significance for human systems. As introduced in Chapter 2 (Theoretical Construct 5), it is a piece of the chaotic puzzle known as "the butterfly effect."

As mentioned earlier, meteorologist Edward Lorenz contributed a seminal piece to the theory of chaos in his concept of the butterfly effect (Gleick, 1987). His goal was a common goal of most meteorologists at that time; to clarify the natural laws at work in creating weather patterns so that the weather would be more predictable. Although the repetition of patterns was never quite exact in his program, there were clearly recognizable structures to the model his computer generated and he was able to see familiar patterns arise over time.

Linear theory would have predicted that a small change in the initial conditions would have had some effect, but that the effect would remain minimal since the change in input was minimal. Fortunately, Lorenz realized that he was on to something more than just a computer error. He recognized that the butterfly effect was no accident. Lorenz also recognized that crisis points where a fluctuation could occur exist everywhere in natural systems. As noted in Chapter 2, other scientists were also finding variations of this phenomenon in many arenas of scientific inquiry. The theory that even minute differences in input can quickly become overwhelming differences in output is also termed "sensitive dependence on initial conditions" and is a cornerstone of chaos theory.

THE BUTTERFLY IN FAMILY THERAPY

In translating the butterfly effect to the psychology of family dynamics, our first task is to understand what constitutes a "butterfly" in human systems. What behaviors or events can sufficiently influence a family by creating just enough turbulence or change in a pattern to allow new patterns to emerge? Critical losses or changes certainly push families to reorganize. A death in the family, a bankruptcy, chronic illnesses, and other events impose a period of transition and adjustment. The therapist is usually called in to change a process, not create an event. For most family therapists, a certain degree of chaos and unpredictability is a necessary prerequisite for change. Paradoxically, although a family may enter treatment seeking to regain a prior pattern of stability, it is often the job of the therapist to introduce some chaos and randomness into the system so that the family can evolve new strategies and patterns of interaction that may be more adaptive. Johnson and McCown (1996) have explored applications of chaos theory in psychotherapy with head injured persons and their families. They emphasize the importance of maintaining some instability during early recovery from head injuries in order to prevent dysfunctional coping mechanisms from becoming chronic, pathological patterns.

Books and journals on family therapy are often replete with examples of therapists introducing increased uncertainty through the use of reframing, paradoxical, or strategic techniques, all of which are designed to intervene in well-established patterns of interaction. Peggy Papp (1983) describes this essential chaos as elements of surprise and confusion that the therapist offers to arouse the family's curiosity and stir up their imagination. Imagination may often be a butterfly that has become dormant under the impact of prolonged conflict between family members. The emotional myopia of prolonged conflict immobilizes behavior, spontaneity, and even hope. Mony Elkaïm (1981) of the Institute for Family and Human Systems Study in Brussels envisioned that the task of the family therapist is to try and push the system away from equilibrium, forcing it to search for a different solution. For Lynn Hoffman (1981, p. 167), the question for the family therapist becomes "How does one disrupt an arrangement that in some ways promotes family stability and instead help the family achieve a transformation that will represent a more complex integration?"

The metaphor of the butterfly effect adds an additional component to the therapist's repertoire. Any small difference that can be magnified by the existing family system can generate new and potentially more adaptive patterns. Providing a tiny push in a different direction, adding some piece of new information, discovering a way to redefine the problem, increasing or decreasing the frequency or timing of a commonly repeated interaction, or introducing just a fragment of some disparate style of communication are all butterflies that can be released in therapy.

The most useful question for creating a butterfly seems to be "What is not stirring in the system?" Then, as a therapist, the task is to make a flutter that will stir the air where it is most stagnant in the family. As noted, crisis points (also termed *developmental bifurcation points* herein) where change can be introduced are ever present in dynamic systems. The simple act of a family or couple entering therapy often begins to change patterns. Now if they have one of their predictable, repetitive fights, the interaction is paraded before another person who can carefully observe pieces of the pattern. As we know from quantum experiments with light, observation has a powerful effect on the observed. This also has been demonstrated in industrial/organizational psychology and social psychology, and titled the Hawthorne effect (Aronson, 1965; Burke, 1982). It has been shown that the mere act of observing people produces changes in their behavior. The sense that someone is looking over their shoulder and may become privy to some secrets can be a significant new element for change. Now some energy is stirring in a sphere of the relationship that may have been becalmed. In a family therapy session, at least one member of the family may openly acknowledge being in need of assistance, and there is the possibility that carefully guarded family secrets will be disclosed to an "outsider."

It is important to recognize that the metaphor of the butterfly influencing weather patterns has other implications for therapists. Although the butterfly creates some air turbulence, it is not a part of the weather system. No meteorologist will report a butterfly's movement on the nightly weather report. Yet, its behavior affects that system. A therapist is not a part of the family, but must move within the bounds of that system to have some impact. A butterfly encased in a jar can flutter furiously but has no impact on the weather. Some activity must be stirred within the context of the family functioning but from a position outside the bounds of the system. Once the turbulence begins a movement in the family, the family members determine how amplified the change will become. In Chapters 7 and 8, we will elaborate on the issues of stabilizing and destabilizing familial dynamics.

Families also find unique ways to bifurcate outside therapy. If they didn't, there would be stagnation and an inability to adapt to changing conditions both within and outside the family. Events such as a death, birth, marriage, divorce, health crisis, or move inevitably challenge family members to find new strategies for survival and growth. An implication of the butterfly effect is that even small glitches in the expected interplay of family members can have profound outcomes. Examples of family-generated butterflies will be given in Chapters 7, 8, and 9. An important aspect of therapy includes obtaining an interactional history that incorporates examples of spontaneous or unexpected transformations that have occurred in the family. This careful examination of change patterns that have previously been activated in the family can help the therapist to identify patterns of transformation. Which member is most likely to bring in new information? What elements outside the family have been influential in the past? How have they adapted before to loss, new additions, and other movement in the structure? This is described in greater detail in Chapter 9, where we also connote the importance and impact of what we term the symbolic client.

FLAPPING THE BUTTERFLY'S WINGS

One implication of the butterfly effect is the importance of the creation or amplification of some areas of turbulence or movement. Transferring some energy from the current storm center to stagnant areas is one goal of the therapist. Therapists utilizing this metaphor must be alert for behaviors and interactions that members of the family believe are lacking or not receiving enough energy. Playfulness, humor, privacy, affection, diversity, conflict, forgiveness, respect, and myriad other types of human experiences may be perceived by some member(s) as unavailable through the family. The stagnation of previously rich, gratifying exchanges or a sense of frustration that stimulating new experiences will not ever occur are often the basis for complaints in couples and families. In addition to understanding where the system is too energized or intense (e.g., disrespectfulness, distance, conflict), it is equally important to determine what isn't happening (e.g., gentleness, affection, support). In our initial discussion of the movement boundary, we described attending to the movement in a system. Therapeutic observation of families is guided by the careful consideration of where energy is directed within the system.

An alternative challenge for the therapist is calming turbulence at the more volatile sites. If certain issues or interactions are assured of creating chaotic energy, helping to establish some eye of calm in the storm becomes the focus of therapeutic interventions. Techniques that help diffuse conflict or that intervene in escalating patterns of disruption can decrease the amount of energy being diverted from other experiences. Consequently, different behaviors and interactions can emerge through the process of destabilization.

Pragmatically, it is useful for the therapist to look for places in the emotional life of the family where the air has been stagnant. If the air is usually moving in patterns of anger or circulates around depression, important turbulence will most likely be introduced from another direction. Interventions that increase the activity or focus on the volatile issues may be less effective because they simply add more energy to a pattern that is already overactive or too chaotic. For example, if a couple already spends an inordinate amount of time being argumentative, teaching the pair "fair fighting" techniques may not be the most useful or efficient way for the therapist to flap her wings. Perhaps humor or playfulness may stir the system more effectively. Assignments that encourage expressions of affection or appreciation can begin to redirect energy from the attractors of anger or depression.

Interventions that involve tasks designed around nonverbal interactions can decrease the amount of energy spent in verbal attack and defend patterns. A homework assignment given to an especially sophisticated, highly verbal, very conflicted couple was to spend 5 minutes a piece in bed at night trading foot massages. This had to be done in complete silence after they had flipped a coin to decide who went first. Although 10 minutes of silence felt excruciating, after a couple of nights they remembered why it is important for couples to shut up at times. As they could become more physically affectionate and close, they became gentler with each other verbally over the following months. A small dose of tenderness with the toes helped to introduce a greater mindfulness of not stepping on each other's emotional toes with quite so much force. Once some energy has been redirected from the conflict, techniques such as fair fighting can be more effectively introduced. Now, there is a greater balance between the attractors of love and fear.

BE THE BUTTERFLY, NOT THE STORM

Like the butterfly, the life span of a therapist's effectiveness in stirring the system may be short-lived. The longer therapists spend settled in a family's storm center, the more likely they are to find their wings becoming tired as the weight of atmospheric pressure increases. Once caught in the winds of the family storm, effective flapping becomes much more difficult. Family therapists have been amply warned by many authorities in the field against becoming captured by the system's patterns and boundaries (Bergman, 1985; Haley, 1973; Hoffman, 1981). This is why in the tradition of family therapy emphasis is placed on supervision in order to avoid being "sucked in" by the family. Techniques such as live supervision and the use of therapy teams were developed to counter this common tendency to join with the family to an extent that the therapist becomes ineffective. The Milan Group's method of employing treatment teams helps to maintain the boundaries between therapeutic members and family members. Having the team of therapists behind the mirror who confer periodically with another team in the room with the family acts to maintain the therapy team's separateness from the family. This keeps the butterfly from being consumed by the storm. Although this arrangement may be impractical in many settings and is typically employed with recalcitrant families, it exemplifies the importance of boundaries in maintaining effectiveness.

Creativity, play, confusion, and the opportunity for unique experience are the identifying marks of the butterfly in therapy. The therapist's ability to flit away from strategies, beliefs, or philosophies that pollute the atmosphere of the therapeutic relationship is a critical skill. Once the therapist joins the family in settling into a pattern that maintains stagnation and avoids change, the wings are gone. Carl Whitaker, a master of confusion and chaos describes, "My tactic has become a kind of tongue-in-cheek put-on, an induced chaos . . . ." (Hoffman, 1981, p. 229).

The metaphor of the butterfly and its importance to chaos theory translates in a very useful way to clinicians who are fluttering about trying to effect some new movement in stagnant patterns of family interactions. Helping families to create and employ new interactional patterns is the goal of most family therapy. Remaining mindful of the areas that are stagnant in family relationships and directing energy to these areas is a focus for interventions based on this paradigm. Saying what's not being said, doing what's not being done, feeling what's not being felt is all territory that a therapist can examine and play back to the family. The art of flapping one's therapeutic wings lies in creating just enough of a stir to draw the family into the creation of new interactions that will establish a more productive, pleasurable, balanced, and understanding atmosphere for all.

To be an effective butterfly, the therapist must:

1. Discover what is not moving in the family by monitoring what we have called movement and/or information boundaries.
2. Be able to redirect energy based on the information gained regarding these boundaries. Specific interventions are determined by this information. These interventions may move the family to stabilization or destabilization.
3. Move within the boundaries of the family without becoming caught in their nets of definitions and despair.
4. Recalling the third paradigm in systemic family therapy, initiate a perturbation that influences the movement of energy in a colorful, charming manner that can capture the attention of the family, and that respects and enhances their ability to self-organize.

CHAPTER 6

Fractals and Forks in the Road

If you knew the algorithm and fed it back say ten thousand
times, each time there'd be a dot somewhere on the screen. You'd
never know where to expect the next dot. But gradually you'd
start to see this shape—the unpredictable and the predetermined
unfold together to make everything the way it is. It's how nature
creates itself, on every scale, the snowflake and the snowstorm.
—Tom Stoppard (1993, p. 47)

DURING THE past 20 years, researchers have looked for fractals and
found them to be widespread in nature, from the branching of ar-
teries to the sculpturing of mountain ranges. Fractals are related
to chaotic phenomena in many ways and can tell us a great deal about the
amount of chaos that is in a system. Fractals are strange dynamic shapes,
created by taking the same mathematical formula and feeding its output
back into an equation as input, again and again. The resulting set of points
is a fractal. Unlike the smooth shapes that we might recall from geometry—circles, squares, tetrahedrons, and the like—fractals are devoid of
transitional symmetry. This means that they are infinitely jagged. Fractals
also possess the strange property of "self-similarity." When such objects
are magnified, their parts are seen to be replicas of the whole.

This chapter will briefly examine the phenomenon of fractals. We will
then apply concepts derived from fractal theory to a specific type of family, the chronically undifferentiated system with few or no boundaries
between family members. We believe that fractal theory may provide a
specific type of treatment for such families. Case studies will highlight
some promising new methods of treatment.

THE STRANGE WORLD OF FRACTALS

A fractal is a rough or fragmented geometric shape that can be subdivided in parts, each part greatly resembling the whole. Fractals are generated from special types of equations. They are easy, if somewhat slow, to generate. Simply take the fractal equation and solve it. Then place your results back into the equation as starting points for the next equation. If we could continue this activity indefinitely, and graph the outcome, the result would be called a fractal. These are often highly colorful and distinctly odd shapes that decorate almost every technical book that has been written about chaos theory.[1] One "popular" example is the Koch snowflake, (Figure 6.1) made by a simple algorithm that successively subdivides a simple triangle.[2]

Fractals exhibit an odd property called self-similarity. This means that if a small section of a fractal is magnified, it will eventually resemble the whole shape. This is why fractals have another curious property, called invariance of scale. Magnify a fractal 1,000 or more times and it looks about the same as if unmagnified. Depending on the algorithm (formula) used to calculate a fractal, randomness may also be introduced. This adds a bit of variety as well.

Despite being bounded shapes, meaning that they have a definite size, fractals can be infinitely complex. A fractal generally contains an infinite number of points whose organization is so complicated that it is not possible to describe the set by specifying directly where each point in it lies. Instead, it may be best described by "the relationship between the pieces" (Barnsley, 1993). Many mathematical structures are fractals (e.g., Koch snowflake and the Mandelbrot set). Fractal geometry is a comparatively new branch of mathematics named and described by Benoit Mandelbrot (1977). It is closely related to the study of chaos. Perhaps the most famous fractal is the Mandelbrot set, pictured in Figure 6.2.

But fractals are not relegated exclusively to the realm of mathematics. Physicists have found them useful to model a variety of processes in nature, including earthquakes and electrical conductivity. If the definition is broadened to include a bit of randomness thrown into our generating equation, fractals or fractal-like objects can be found virtually everywhere in the natural world. The shapes of clouds and mountains, the irregularity of coastlines and the growth of some crystals are all fractal

---

[1] Casti (1992) offers a rather complete description of the mathematics involved in producing fractals.
[2] Fractals were generated from a program by Dr. Ross Keiser.

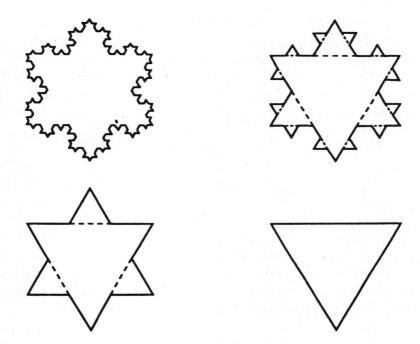

Figure 6.1   The Koch Snowflake, a Simple Fractal.

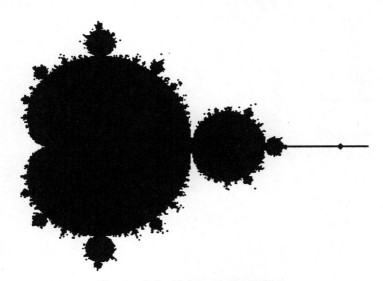

Figure 6.2   A Mandelbrot Set.

(Gleick, 1987). Each of these shapes displays the property of self-similarity across different size or time scales. Figures 6.3 and 6.4 illustrates how fractals may be used to study the irregularity of a coast line. Figure 6.3 shows the Mississippi River, winding towards the gulf, between Mississippi and Louisiana. Figure 6.4 shows a portion of the river magnified 500 and then 5,000 times. Note the similarities across the different scales.

In human physiology, fractal structure is evident almost everywhere; in the patterns of the lungs, blood vessels, capillaries, the intestines, and the brain itself, to name but a few organs (Garfinkel, 1983; Glass & Mackey, 1988; Goldberger, Rigney & West, 1990; Hao, 1984; Skarda & Freeman, 1987). An evolutionary advantage associated with fractals is that they can fold and meander to amplify the surface area of a specific organ without requiring much additional space. Furthermore, due to their repetitiveness and unevenness, fractal structures are vigorous and resistant to damage in the body. Finally, fractal structures may also be much easier to genetically encode, since genes have to pass only formulas, rather than specify an entire placement of complex points in space.

Every fractal may be described mathematically by a number known as its fractal dimension. As mentioned in Chapter 11, there are several different ways to calculate fractals. The higher the fractional number, the more complex the shape. This indicates that a greater degree of chaos or disorderliness has been introduced into the formula. A lower fractal dimension indicates more order and determinism. The fractal dimension is

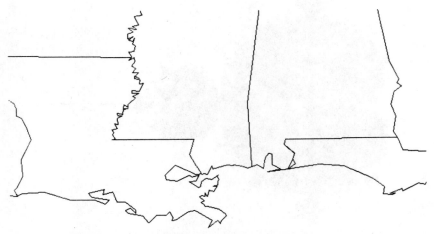

Figure 6.3   The Mississippi River, a Gigantic Fractal.

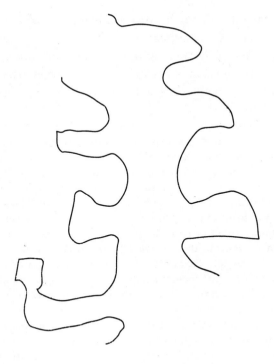

Figure 6.4   An Outline of a Portion of the Mississippi River Magnified 5.00 (Left) and 5,000 Times (Right).

one way we can numerically quantify the degree of chaos in a system. Very high fractal dimensions usually indicate the existence of pure random behavior.

In nature, fractals are particularly likely to occur at boundary points of complex behaviors (Moon, 1992). When dynamical systems bifurcate or begin to become unstable, physicists often describe the route they take with fractals. Fractals may also be useful in compressing information, as we have stated in regard to genetic information. Already, programs that manufacture fractal sets have been used to create stunning and aesthetically pleasing pictures and music, with very little additional human input.

UNDIFFERENTIATED FAMILIES

Fractals may serve as a model for the curious behavior of one of the most difficult challenges that the family therapist faces; the undifferentiated family with boundary problems. Such families are often crisis prone and treatment resistant. They may have multiple members with psychiatric or psychological problems and appear to tolerate stress very poorly. Stresses from one person may seem "contagious" to another family member. Such families are in constant states of turmoil. Their prognosis has traditionally been considered very poor. The following case study is an example of such a family:[3]

> The Green family came into a local mental health clinic in crisis. The presenting problem was that the mother's boyfriend, George, 45, had walked out on the family and moved to another state. The mother, Helen, 49, was devastated by this because "I had no idea he was that type." She stated that she had ideas of suicide, but "could hold myself together" based on her religious commitments and faith. The emergency session was terminated with the therapist being able to extract a "no suicide" contract from Helen.
>
> Two days later, the family returned to the same clinic. Cyndi, 14, had threatened to kill herself. However, when the therapist talked with her, she was happy-go-lucky and cheerful. Again, after two more days, another member from the same family came to the clinic, Donna, 16, with talk about killing herself.
>
> The therapist, who did not fully understand systems theory, knew enough to know he was over his head with this case. He asked the advice of a systems-oriented therapist, who immediately suggested that he schedule a session with the entire family.
>
> Five children, a grandmother, and a sister accompanied Helen. Three of the children had different fathers, the other two were not even Helen's children. All lived together in almost interchangeable roles. None seemed to have a separate personality; each seemed to giggle in an age-inappropriate fashion, but to frequently cry whenever their mother did.
>
> After consulting with the systems-oriented colleague, the therapist attempted to inquire about role differentiation within the family. There was very little. One day a family member might be in school; the next day she might be required to take care of a sick "sibling" and miss several weeks of school. It was not clear who would be cooking on any night, or who would be cleaning up the kitchen. Other household chores were done on an ad hoc basis, and often by an inappropriate member. A seven-year-old might scrub a floor, for example.
>
> Apparently, from her relational history, Helen had fairly little role differentiation regarding the men in her life. Most of her relationships were characterized by dependence and a lack of any ability to differentiate one partner for another. She was not particularly discerning or discriminating. "I've dated all kinds of men. Black men, white men, whatever. . . . My sisters say my standards aren't high enough, but I say, heck, a man is a man."

---

[3] Names and other identifying information have been changed, and these cases have been reviewed by peers to assure that the identities of these individuals remains confidential.

Two of the girls living with Helen had been stepchildren of former lovers or husbands who "just stayed with me because they liked me better than their kin."

At least three of the women living in the house, including the sister Susan, 33, Cyndi, and Donna had been sexually abused by one of Helen's boyfriends. Helen was not particularly bothered by this, stating startlingly matter-of-factly, "Well, my mom had some boyfriends that taught me a lot about sex when I was young. I don't like it, in fact I've kicked plenty of men out for trying to mess with one of my girls, but you know, that's the way men are. It's in their nature to run around. Men ain't got morals the way women do. So you can't blame the man any more than you can blame a hungry dog." The therapist determined that none of the girls were in danger of present sexual abuse, breathing a sigh of relief.

Apart from the mother's bizarre attitude toward sexual abuse, the most amazing thing about the Greens was how stress seemed contagious in the family system. One child might have a bad report card and another would feel guilty. One would get sick and another would have psychosomatic symptoms. One would have trouble with a boyfriend and two or three would rally in anger.

Lest therapists believe that a lack of differentiation is a function only of lower socioeconomic families, consider the Glenn family:

Alan Glenn, age 50, was a computer engineer. His wife, Vicki, 51, was a "psychotherapist," although her training was limited to a few college courses. In a typical pattern first noticed by psychoanalytic thinkers many years ago, this marriage represented a bizarre but common union of opposites. Alan was introverted, morose, pedantic, and completely lacking in spontaneity and charisma. On the other hand, he was careful, conscientious (if plodding), aggressively suspicious, and "a good provider." While Vicki was flamboyant, colorful, carefree, and captivating, she was also impractical, impulsive, overly generous, and a bit profligate. Neighbors described Alan as the "practical, boring guy" and Vicki as "the one who adds the spice." Most people wondered how they could stay together, though they seemed to make it through life superficially well.

The family came into treatment when one of their children, Kendra, age 19, who had been receiving psychodynamically oriented treatment for depression, commented to her therapist that her suicidal ideation was nowhere as bad as her brother Todd's, age 17. This, quite naturally, raised the concern of the therapist, who discussed the situation with a family-oriented colleague who agreed to see and evaluate the entire family, including a third child, Mark, age 15.

On the surface, the therapist noted that this was the "nice" family. She also remembered that they were remarkably superficial, almost like a Hollywood family, or even a caricature of a normal family for a situation comedy.

"Everything about this family was so *pleasant*. The parents were excessively polite and the three kids had a bland sameness about them, almost like they had been hatched from pods in one of those old science fiction movies. It was clear that negative emotions weren't permitted. Nor was there much enthusiasm. They were just bland."

When the therapist tried to speak to one of the family members during a family session, it was not uncommon for another member to answer. An example from the first session is typical:

THERAPIST: So Todd, how have you been feeling?
TODD: Okay, I guess. Maybe a little down . . . I don't know.
MARK: He's been down for a long time.
KENDRA: He's *very* depressed.
THERAPIST: Is there anything particular that's bothering you?
TODD: I guess not. No.
MARK: I think he's upset that Jill (his girlfriend) split up with him.
MOTHER: No, I think he's down because he didn't get into Brown (University).
KENDRA: Yeah, I guess he'll have to go to State.
FATHER: Or stay home. That might be good . . .

The therapist found that every time she questioned a family member about something, other family members would join in to answer. This pattern was repeated throughout the system, with each family member. No one seemed to mind. In fact, the flow of conversation was normal and not indicative of any type of strife or anger over boundaries being violated. Even when asked very personal questions, other family members would leap into the conversation, furnishing apparently accurate information. This is shown in the following remarkable interchange, where the absence of boundaries about both the children's and the parent's sexual behaviors is almost outlandish:

THERAPIST: So Todd, why did you break up with Jill.
TODD: (giggling) I don't know . . .
MOTHER: They fought all the time about sex. That might have had something to do with it (laughing). My son, fighting about sex! Who ever would have imagined . . .
KENDRA: Yeah! Jill didn't want to give him any! (giggles)
MARK: I wouldn't go out with a girl who wouldn't put out. That's stupid.
TODD: Me either.
FATHER: (completely staid): I guess sex is a lot more important in relationships these days than it used to be. If I liked a girl, I'd still go with her. I've always felt that.
KENDRA: It's not important in Mom's and Dad's lives. They don't do it! (giggles)
MOTHER: (giggling) It's true, we don't have a lot of sex. Maybe once or twice a year (giggling). Is that normal? Oh, *I'm* a therapist, I know what normal is.

FATHER: (again, completely staid) Yes, I guess that's true. I just don't have the drive I used to. But, you can still have a good relationship without a lot of sex. We do. There's a lot of love in our family.

TODD: Yeah, not a lot of passion, but a lot of love. They've been like that for as long as I can remember. It's kind of hard to imagine how we all were conceived. That's the family joke.

MARK: Did we tell you they sleep in separate beds?

KENDRA: Seriously! (giggling very loudly) They say it's because Dad kicks, but I just think Mom finds him gross in the sack. That's all I can think of. That's awful, isn't it? Being married to someone who you don't want to sleep with. Probably Dad's real boring.

MARK: Yeah, Dad's real boring in the sack. Just ask him, he'll tell you. Or ask Mom.

KENDRA: Yeah, Mom. She tells me all about it.

FATHER: Now, kids, let's be nice.

Further history and conversations such as the preceding one revealed that the family was exceedingly emotionally enmeshed. Everything was felt as a family and in unison. If one person was sick, everyone would feel bad. If one person did well in school, other family members would feel as elated as if it had been their own behavior that earned the accolades. Some days were "good mood days" when everyone felt happy. Other days were "bad hair days" when the family norm was to moan and complain, commiserating with other family members about how rotten things were. When Kendra announced that she felt premenstrual tension, the family would fight openly for a day or two. When the mother went through menopause, the family carefully monitored her moods and physical changes and appeared to mirror them.

Individual activity outside the family was tightly monitored and discouraged if it interfered with the overwhelming sense of family collectivity. Major decisions were not made individually, but instead were made by the entire system, even when this was grossly inappropriate. For example, when the father needed to hire an associate, he asked his children to choose between two closely matched applicants. He realized that the children had no hiring experience or exposure to computer engineering, but stated that he always had the family help him make any major decisions that he faced.

These families are extremely difficult to treat. They are slow to change and often have no insight into their problems. They are highly crisis prone and also apt to terminate treatment abruptly, especially if their family unity is threatened. Very often, the therapist is seen as a dangerous outsider. Family secrets such as incest or physical abuse may play an important role in encouraging concealment. An understanding of fractals may help provide some additional treatment opportunities for these time-consuming and recalcitrant systems.

FAMILY DYNAMICS AND DIFFERENTIATION

As in previous chapters, before we can highlight the potential contributions of chaos to establishing new therapeutic conceptualizations and techniques, it may be valuable to summarize some of the vast literature regarding family differentiation. Although there are many theories regarding lack of differentiation, two are especially relevant in describing such systems with fractal theory.

MURRAY BOWEN'S THEORY OF FAMILY DYSFUNCTION

Murray Bowen and his associates began their quest for understanding families through research into the family dynamics and etiology of schizophrenic processes (see Bowen, 1978, for a comprehensive review). Bowen is notable for the almost mythological accounts of how he would hospitalize entire family systems. Bowen's theory regarding schizophrenia and other psychopathologies is complex and cannot be easily distilled without oversimplification. Bowen believed that individual psychopathology is due to a "lack of differentiation of the self," a concept related to the degree to which an individual's emotions are distinguished from intellectual processes.

To Bowen, individuals who are low in differentiation view themselves and their families as a common process or an "undifferentiated ego mass." Several generations of intermarriage by persons low in differentiation is hypothesized to produce profound psychiatric disorders. Bowen labels this pattern as the "multigenerational transmission process." He believed that it may primarily predispose a person to schizophrenia but also may make an individual vulnerable to a variety of major psychiatric disorders, including substance abuse, characterological disorders, and sociopathy.

Of special importance in Bowen's theory is the role ascribed to family stressors. In families with low differentiation, external stressors are often "contagious." The stress of one family member effectively vibrates throughout the system, disrupting the entire family. More differentiated families, Bowen notes, are usually able to draw strength from each other in times of stress. However, less differentiated families simply amplify each other's dysfunctioning. In other words, a lack of family differentiation causes excessive stress sensitivity. In its extreme form, Bowen believes, such sensitivity can cause schizophrenic or other severe psychiatric symptoms.

For Bowenians, the theory of stress vulnerability has important clinical implications that therapists of other orientations sometimes miss. The task of the family therapist, Bowen would argue, is to reduce family stressors. Individuals or systems with a lack of differentiation will function extremely poorly during periods of crises and life transitions. At times, the therapist must act like an auxiliary ego, making decisions directly for the dysfunctional family, until the stress is reduced. Ego lending, a process we will discuss in later chapters, becomes a common treatment strategy. The therapist frequently needs to serve as a stress buffer for the family, helping them negotiate the world. Above all, induction of family crises, a popular technique in some schools of family therapy to provide for the possibility of change, must almost always be avoided because it would be too destructive. While we have briefly touched on this earlier, this issue will be described at length in Chapters 7, 8, and 9.

THE CIRCUMPLEX MODEL

The Circumplex Model of family functioning (Olson, Russell, & Sprenkle, 1983) has proven very popular, especially among researchers. It has an outstanding research history and continues to generate important empirical findings. The Circumplex Model consists of three independent (orthogonal) axes that are used to describe independent dimensions of family functioning: *cohesion, adaptability,* and *communication and facilitation* (see Figure 6.5).

The Circumplex Model's concept of cohesion refers to the connectedness of family members. Though a continuous representation is intended,

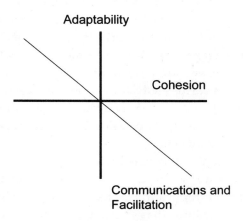

Figure 6.5   The Dimensions of the Circumplex Model.

four levels are usually delineated: Disengaged, separated, connected, and enmeshed. For this dimension, optimal adjustment is curvilinear. The endpoints of disengaged and enmeshed signify pathological levels of cohesion and the midpoints of separated and connected represent healthy levels of cohesion.

Optimal adaptability is also curvilinear, with *both ends of the dimension* signifying dysfunction. Although this variable is assumed to be continuous, researchers have found it useful to delineate levels along this dimension as well. Important categories are the rigid, on one extreme, the flexible and structured in the middle, and the "chaotic" on the other extreme. This word is not used in the way that we use it in this book, although to our knowledge it has been conceptualized this way by at least one researcher (Robinson, 1994). The Circumplex Model is not connected with any advances in nonlinear dynamics or complexity and uses this word in its traditional sense. Families described as rigid are lacking in flexibility, whereas chaotic families are unstable because they are too open to change. Both the structured and flexible family types are found within the arc and refer to less extreme positions on the continuum.

Combining the dimensions of adaptability and cohesion results in 16 types of families. These 16 types are then grouped into three general types, represented by concentric rings of the graphical model. The center circle indicates the highest levels of functioning and is composed of flexibly separated, flexibly connected, structurally separated, and structurally connected families. These families are designated as balanced types. The middle ring represents midrange families and is composed of flexibly and structurally disengaged, flexibly and structurally enmeshed, chaotically and rigidly separated and chaotically and rigidly connected types of families. The four corners consist of the extreme ends of both dimensions and include chaotically disengaged, chaotically enmeshed, rigidly disengaged, and rigidly enmeshed types. These extreme types represent the lower levels of family system functioning. Within each general type, the various subtypes allow for a clearer description of family functioning. The Glenn family, would be an example of a rigidly enmeshed family, whereas the Green family would probably come closer to being "chaotically" enmeshed.

Communication, the third axis, is considered a facilitative variable for both of the two dimensions. This concept is a useful addition to the model and has strong clinical implications. Theoretically, enhancing communication skills within a family has the potential to improve functioning along the dimension of adaptability as well as cohesion.

A criticism of topological theory such as this is that it is merely descriptive. This may result in circular reasoning. For example, we say that the family behaves in a rigidly enmeshed fashion because they are a rigidly enmeshed type. To ascribe cause to a trait or a type lacks explanatory power, unless, of course the trait has an overwhelmingly strong genetic or other fairly immutable basis. This is an important distinction. We can correctly say that a person is outgoing and vivacious *because* she is extroverted. This is an appropriate explanation, since extroversion is a strongly genetically related construct that usually will change very little in life (Eysenck & Eysenck, 1985). Some personality variables such as extroversion have explanatory power because they are temperamental variables, assumed to be related to more basic neuropsychological and neurophysiological processes. Traits remain descriptive and predictive, but not typically explanatory.

Nevertheless, the Circumplex Model is useful because it delineates between behaviors that are associated with enmeshment. It also specifies subtypes of enmeshment, depending on the structure that the family possesses. Finally, the model may have important clinical ramifications and can be used for evaluation or prescriptive purposes (Johnson & McCown, 1996).

FRACTALS, CHAOS, AND DIFFERENTIATION

Using the model of fractals may help us derive new treatment strategies for undifferentiated families. First, however, we need to consider communications patterns in less pathological families and contrast them with families who lack differentiation. For most of us, our conversations are moderately chaotic. In fact, the fractal dimensionality of conversations has been calculated experimentally using a number of different encoding systems of analysis. One involved using the Lyapunov exponent; briefly touched on in the final chapter of this book, it is a measure of the rate at which nearby trajectories in phase space diverge. Chaotic orbits have at least one positive Lyapunov exponent and in general, there are as many exponents as there are dynamical equations driving the system (Moon, 1992). Similarly, additional data was analyzed for its capacity dimension D, or the Hausdorf dimension (Sprott & Rowlands, 1992). In most people's conversations, a high D is found (greater than 3.0). Such a calculation demonstrated that conversations have a great deal of chaos in them, but again, there is little agreement in the literature under what circumstances D represents true randomness.

Perhaps the reader can undertake a better experiment regarding the amount of chaos in conversations. Simply listen to two people having a casual interchange over dinner and try to predict where it will lead in 5 and 10 minutes. Unless conversants have a specific goal in mind, such as negotiating a business deal, such predictions cannot be made. This illustrates how chaotic conversations are. This is natural and good. Conversants are usually acutely sensitive to the presentation of other conversants. Those that aren't are social boors.

However, communications from enmeshed families, whether rigidly or "chaotically" enmeshed (an unfortunate term, given our context) are less chaotic. While empirical research is just beginning to demonstrate this, clinicians can show this very easily. Simply watch a "normal" family, that is a family not receiving clinical treatment and not in a crisis. Ask them to begin interacting about a specific topic. Within minutes, the conversation will have branched and permutated to a different area. Perhaps subsystems have arisen and are communicating with each other. The flow of conversation is chaotic, but not quite random. Very soon, almost anything could be the topic. Levels of participation of each family member change often, indicative of complex nonlinear patterns.

Repeat the same experiment with an enmeshed family. The family chosen can be either a rigidly enmeshed type or a chaotically enmeshed type. In a few minutes, it will be clear that the conversation is meandering less. It may become repetitive, or even strikingly self-similar. Eventually a set single theme will probably become evident, often a theme about a much discussed family topic. The family will perseverate on this topic with little or no flow or progress. There is much less chaos in these conversations.

Observe also how the participation level of family members soon becomes stable and self-similar across time spans. One portion of the conversation is like a fractal of another. The fractal dimensionality of these conversations is low, meaning that very little chaos is in the system. Leave the conversation and come back a few minutes later. It hardly seems as if you have left. This contrasts with less enmeshed families, where there is a dynamic vibrancy and movement to the uncertain course of topics.

What is happening in these two experiments? In the first instance, each family member acts as a part of a fractal equation that produces a chaotic attractor. People respond to each other in unpredictable, though lawful ways, making the conversation highly complex and not particularly self-similar. There is less self-similarity in verbal exchanges, and little similarity in scale. The conversation, although not random, can lead anywhere.

Like the weather, we can only make very short-range predictions regarding the immediate future.

In the second type of family, an enmeshed family, each family member also acts as part of a fractal equation, but one that produces what Barsley (1993) has called a "photocopy fractal." This is a fractal that is excessively self-similar. In other words, there is almost no variety. In extremely undifferentiated families, the topics of spontaneous conversation are almost always self-similar with previous conversations. Similarity in scale is evident in that short interchanges mirror the pattern in longer periods. To outsiders, the conversation is frightfully boring.

Using the analogy of fractals, we are able to see that the lack of boundaries and role differentiations associated with enmeshed families is simply a product of self-similarity. Roles are similar because people are similar. Personality and individual differences are stifled by overwhelming systemic concerns. People lose or are cognizant of their individualities and begin to identify their behaviors collectively. As one patient whom we treated in individual psychotherapy, a woman from a family without boundaries, noted, "It really wasn't until I finished college and started therapy that I realized I had a personality apart from my family's. I don't know how you can go through life and not realize something like this . . ."

Bowen (1978) observed a similar phenomenon in his therapeutic work. Bowen believed that it was often necessary for individuals who came from such systems to make an "emotional cutoff" from these systems. At times this means completely ending contact with enmeshed family members. As family therapists, we recognize the occasional necessity of individual therapy. Yet we remain committed to the concept of family treatment for lack of differentiation, and look to chaos theory to increase our therapeutic options.

Our commitment to family treatment might suggest that a treatment for enmeshed families involves creating a systemic impetus for a reorganizing crisis. Bowen's observations about enmeshed families having poor stress tolerance is very true, however, as determined by our clinical experience and at least one study (McCown & Johnson, 1993). Perhaps the reason, from the perspective of nonlinear dynamics, is that apparently one term in the equation of the family behavior is highly sensitive to stress. It may be, for example, a power function, while the remaining terms are grossly insensitive to any feedback or external changes. Consequently, unless the system experiences stress, the fractal generated by such families will be a monotonous sameness, with each point very near the previous point. As stated throughout the text, only during stress will a pattern of bifurcation arise, which *may produce very unpredictable behaviors.*

Our fractal theory of enmeshment is merely a sketch. But we can speculate on another key component: Why are the behavioral fractals of enmeshed families usually so self-similar? One hypothesis is that this might have something to do with trauma. Although the Glenn case, earlier in this chapter, was an apparent exception, most families without boundaries involve members who have experienced the trauma of poverty, racism, physical or sexual abuse, exposure to traumatic stress, or other lasting damage. Perhaps, for systems that are exposed to these uncontrollable and unpredictable stressors a lack of differentiation of members is functional or evolutionarily advantageous. We have labeled this as the "undifferentiation response." Either prior exposure to extreme stresses or excessive stress sensitivity triggers this undifferentiation response in families that are chronically enmeshed. When this occurs, behavior becomes very self-similar, with practically interchangeable family roles. Such behavior also becomes very singularly focused, perhaps once an evolutionary advantage in dealing with an overriding stress.

Thousands of years ago, it may have been an evolutionary advantage for the family and tribe to become undifferentiated in roles and feelings when faced with an external threat. A wild animal, natural disaster, or human enemy can be dealt with more effectively if everyone has a singularity of purpose and is flexible regarding tasks. Whatever divisions of labor existed in primitive society may have been cast aside almost automatically to fight some of these threats. Such highly undifferentiated systems may also prove to be very difficult to influence from outside sources. Thus, in therapy it may be very difficult to encourage differentiation because in the history of the system it has not been adaptive. It is of little evolutionary advantage for a group or a tribe to be vulnerable, to be loving, when they perceive that a rival tribe is about to attack.

Remnants of such a response can be seen today, although they are rarely functional. As an example, we were able to systematically observe families preparing for a major stressor, a poorly forecasted hurricane. Evacuation time was merely a number of hours before the storm was to make a direct hit on a major city. Family systems that had been remarkable for role rigidity and boundaries appeared to break down in the face of this threat. For example, in one very authoritarian and rigidly hierarchical family, a father was observed hauling clothes from the washer, while his daughter went out to change the windshield washer blades. Later, the father noted that he would have "never usually done women's work like that . . . but I was in the laundry room, so I did it."

The daughter who changed the windshield wipers had never performed this task before. "I just did it because someone had to, so we could get off the island and not get killed." When queried why she did not wait to find her father, who usually performs such tasks on family vehicles, she noted, "It just never occurred to me to look for him with the storm coming. . . . All I could think of was that we needed to get out of there." (Interestingly, the crisis seems to have provided for a higher level of self-organization. The daughter bought a tool kit and is learning some basic home repairs. The father has started cooking, a task he once relegated to his wife.)

Finally, the training of military and paramilitary forces that face unpredictable stress constantly must emphasize role differentiation. As anyone who has been in combat or in a disaster/rescue situation knows, a singularity of purpose dominates the experience. Individual survival is subsumed under the undifferentiated goal of group task completion. Communications become singularly focused, with little variety. Injuries and deaths of comrades are acutely traumatic, yet do not disturb the singularity of purpose. Only training and practice can keep the natural tendency of lack of role differentiation from arising in such a situation. Poorly trained armies at war behave very similarly to undifferentiated families facing stress.

TREATMENT OPTIONS

STRESS AND COPING

Bowen's treatment of undifferentiated families may include a mixture of individual and family therapies. Treatment is usually long term, and only anecdotal accounts exist to indicate treatment effectiveness. Yet in today's managed mental healthcare climate, we are often unable to pursue long-term treatment despite the best interests of the families we treat. Bowenian family therapy is increasingly becoming a privilege of those who can pay out of pocket, which may not be those who are at maximal risk from facing problems due to lack of differentiation. Like psychoanalysis, it seems such treatment requires more than just motivation, and necessitates having a deep pocket as well.

However, Bowen's contributions remain invaluable as a starting point for therapy of the undifferentiated family. He is certainly correct about the devastating impact that crises or family stress has on these systems. Therefore a useful beginning for treatment for such systems is a behavioral or cognitive behavioral intervention designed to reduce general stress sensitivity. This may include any of the popular techniques such as desensitization, cognitive coping, behavioral rehearsal, or group relaxation. Such techniques are usually noninvasive and not apt to raise the resistance of closed and enmeshed family systems. They are fun and have fairly immediate impact. Usually there is little iatrogenic harm associated with these "toughening up" techniques. Finally, the results that they usually display in even one session may help "hook" the family into staying in treatment, resisting the almost natural impetus of enmeshed families to terminate treatment early.

L'Abate and Cox (1992) have a number of therapeutic writing assignments that can be completed outside the therapeutic session to decrease anxiety and stress sensitivity. The problems of completion of the assignments of such tasks is often less than with other types of families. Frequently, family members may complete each other's homework assignments as well as their own!

MACRO SYSTEM INVOLVEMENT

Therapists who receive exposure to organizations with dynamic, aggressive "missions" often note how many undifferentiated families are attracted to such groups. These can include religious or fraternal organizations, self-help groups, or even political groups. Such programs generally have an ideology and a moral or ethical stance. They also provide differentiation of roles for family members, while maintaining a similarity of purpose. If used judiciously, they may be very effective therapeutically, as seen from the Cruise family:

> Jon Cruise and his two sons, Bill, 17 and Ted 18, lived together following the death of Jon's wife. "The boys" as they called themselves, dedicated themselves to carousing and merrymaking. Jon saw his role as "one of the guys . . . out to have the fun that I should have had before I got married. . . ." His sons became his eager accomplices in beer bashes, fast driving, and "getting girls."
>
> Not surprisingly, given the lack of goals in their lives, as well as the high rate of alcohol consumption, the family became increasingly dysfunctional. Bill dropped out of school to work on his Mustang, a vintage car that he believed "impresses the ladies. . . ." Ted continued at community college because "it's the best place to meet girls I've ever seen." Jon quit work during his wife's long and rocky illness. With life insurance in the coffers, he was under no financial pressure to return.
>
> This dysfunction took a strange twist, resulting in an increasing lack of differentiation of family members. Roles around the house were completely interchangeable. Money was shared along with responsibilities. No one kept regular hours. The father and brothers even shared dates at various

times, not being at all ethical or moral in this or any other realm. Sometimes when drunk, the family might share toothbrushes or underwear.

The bacchanalian revelry would have continued except that a neighbor complained to the police that Jon was encouraging underage drinking. Jon's attorney told him that this was a particularly serious offense and that the family might want to visit a therapist so that "the judge will be happy."

When the therapist talked with the family, she noted that they acted more like immature fraternity brothers. They repeated the lines of a popular comedy album in unison, occasionally swapping parts to deliver a punch line. When one person was asked to make a comment, another family member would jump right in and talk. When discussing an emotionally charged topic, such as how they felt about the neighbor that complained to the police about them, one family member might start a sentence, while another would complete it. Attempts to have the family complete psychological testing were thwarted when they jokingly copied off of each other's answer sheets.

Several sessions were conducted with this family system. The therapist realized that they were extraordinarily enmeshed but that they were happy this way. Although their juvenile behavior was dysfunctional, she had little leverage over the system. She sensed that the family's behavior was on some level a response to the mother's painful death from cancer. However, she did not know how to use this information to intervene with the family.

Almost in desperation, the therapist suggested that a fitting tribute to the mother might be to raise money for cancer research. The family agreed, perhaps thinking that they could participate in the zany antics associated with popular charity activities. However, a representative from a local cancer fund-raising institute introduced the family to myriad options. Before long, they were involved in a number of more broadly prosocial activities. At first, it seemed like the family's involvement was primarily because they thought cancer fund-raisers were a good place to "meet girls." But the many activities that the three encountered in the multilayered process of cancer fund-raising exposed each family member to diverse people and different roles. Individual identities began to emerge again. Family members began doing things separately, and not together all the time.

After several months, there was an increased order in the home. The father, who had an outstanding background in business capitalization, spent much of his energy in full-time volunteer work. Cancer funding and education became his passion. Bill went back to finish his last semester of high school, a humbling experience, but one that he thought necessary. He later joined the armed services. Ted actually began fighting with his father, something the therapist considers a positive sign. Ted eventually moved out to share an apartment with friends he met through a network of young people who had lost a parent or spouse to cancer.

Groups such as religious organizations or self-help groups can function similarly, and usually even more successfully. For example, highly structured religious communities, and the numerous self-help groups all seem to be attractive to families with low differentiation and may offer the possibility of development of family members. These groups seem to work by allowing the undifferentiated family an overall umbrella of unity and singularity of purpose while subtly and inadvertently encouraging individual achievement and development. For example, in Alcoholics Anonymous, the alcoholic is encouraged to confront his or her problems *alone* and without the dependence on family members (although the help of other alcoholics is strongly encouraged). Al-Anon, a sister organization for family members of alcoholics, encourages members to examine *their own behaviors,* especially for actions that allow them to lose their personal identity. Younger family members can be shunted to separate groups such as Al-Ateen, which is often segmented by ages and genders. This furthers a contact with larger systems that can help encourage age- and gender-appropriate differentiation.

Clinicians are often asked why they believe it is appropriate to refer addicted persons to a self-help modality that seems to foster dependency on meetings as a treatment. But for undifferentiated families, there can be no question that it is better to attend nightly self-help meetings than it is to remain emotionally stifled in an undifferentiated family system. The clinician, however, might attempt to break any potential for reestablishment of undifferentiation by suggesting that persons from the same family attend meetings in different parts of town. This way they will gain exposure to different sets of people, maximizing possibility of the transition toward differentiation.

INCREASING COMPLEXITY WITHIN THE FAMILY SYSTEM

To successfully increase the differentiation of members between one another, the therapist must exercise caution. Any direct attempts to change the undifferentiated family system may be met with anxiety (Bütz, 1992a), which will provoke further lack of differentiation. The increased anxiety witnessed in such families as they differentiate is equivalent to chaos. Therefore, individual therapy of specific family members is almost always seen as very threatening by those who are not involved and should probably be avoided. Still, there are a number of concrete steps that therapists can use to help encourage differentiation.

Undifferentiated families often have an excessive number of family rituals and myths to preserve the sense that there is safety or specialty in family unity. One method a therapist may use is to discreetly challenge these myths, gently attempting to facilitate personal differentiation.[4] Care needs to be taken inasmuch as shattering of such myths may increase family anxiety, which is countertherapeutic. Yet a reality-oriented approach to these binding rituals may help reduce chronic undifferentiation. The following case example illustrates this:

> The Brown family was composed of five sisters, ages 43 to 56. Two brothers in the system had previously died of cancer. Three of these sisters were married, two were divorced. Although one sister had moved to a large city, following her divorce she returned to the small town where the others lived. Elderly parents lived near the sisters and the sisters took turns supervising the parents' daily activities. Although family members had various jobs, they frequently pooled resources so that the aggregate socioeconomic status placed the entire system squarely in the middle class.
>
> The sisters shared most details of their lives and resources with each other. This included each others' cars, credit cards, and checking accounts, which they shared with impunity. Often the divorced sisters would date the same man, though not simultaneously. Four of them attended the same church. They usually shopped together, and in the evening they all watched television at each other's houses together.
>
> The Brown family came to treatment only when one of the husbands told his wife that he had been having an affair with her sister. His excuse had a ring of truth in it: "I don't know what the big deal is. I practically live with all of you anyhow, so why are you upset?" The sister who had participated in the affair wasn't particularly upset at all, and was more concerned that *her* husband would be angry, rather than her sisters.
>
> The family therapist saw all five of the sisters without any other family members being present. She constructed a genogram and obtained a detailed family history. The family had been wretchedly poor when the sisters were growing up, often not having enough to eat. To hold themselves up with their pride intact during those bleak years, the father had written cute little family jingles and slogans that the sisters frequently sang or quoted. The family had also promoted a number of myths, such as that the sisters were the direct descendants of the English royal family or of the Pilgrims. No one checked these stories for veracity. Yet they were steadfastly believed by all of the family. Of special importance were the heroic deeds of the Brown family during the Revolutionary War. In a custom that was popular with many poor families during the middle of this century, the family "found" an "authentic" crest, obtained from a mail-order firm, with the half Latin motto almost comically inscribed, "Semper Brown" (Always Brown).

---

[4] Essentially, Michael White's technique of narrative therapy accomplishes this task (1986), and is fruitfully explored in the text *Story Revisions* by Parry and Doan (1994).

The therapist was struck by how many times the sisters made reference to "We Browns" or "The Brown way of doing things." She reasoned correctly that the family's framework did not allow for differentiation. The Brown girls saw themselves as too special. Slowly, she began to challenge the credibility of some of the family lore. For example, the Brown children believed that they were morally superior to the rest of the townspeople, since they came from John Brown's lineage. The therapist wanted to know what the proof was, and explained to the family that some of the family lore were probably myths designed to help them maintain their dignity through the crushing weight of poverty.

Slowly, the therapist attacked some of these myths and rituals, like the long-standing traditions of having never missed family holidays together. And very slowly, a degree of differentiation began to emerge. Two of the sisters changed churches. They ended the practice of using each other's checkbooks. One of the divorced sisters moved back to her former home and dated a man who did not know the others. Treatment stopped after a year. From the core of five, only two remained as tightly enmeshed. Oddly, these were the two who originally sought treatment after the affair.

Relatively nonthreatening interventions such as therapeutic writing also may be of assistance in helping families differentiate. L'Abate and Cox (1992) have a number of exercises tailored to families who have difficulty with similar areas such as excessive dependency. Writing modalities can be completed either within sessions or as homework. Unlike the situation with exercises designed to reduce sensitivity to stress, for very undifferentiated families it may be advisable to complete these more personal assignments under the direct supervision of a therapist. This discourages the collaboration and sharing of answers, which often maintain the diffusion of boundaries as the topic areas become more personal.

A third modality of treatment is based on the literature of symbolic interactionism (Meade, 1933) and the Action Identification theory of Vallacher and Wegner (1987). It involves gentle in-session confrontation, where the therapist gradually questions assumptions regarding symbiotic family behavior. The rationale from fractal theory is that family behavior is grossly undifferentiated because members have such a shared symbolic frame of references that aggregate behavior produces a low-dimension fractal. When family members exhibit lack of boundaries within sessions, he gently asks them to state what they are doing.

Action Identification theory states that overlearned behaviors are identified on a higher, more abstract level. For example, a person driving a car to church down a bumpy wet road can describe the process in any number of the following ways: holding the steering wheel and watching the road, trying not to get killed, driving over a rough road, going to church, taking the family to church, doing God's will, or any of an infinite number of other abstract or concrete activities. Undifferentiated families tend to identify each activity they perform with family solidarity and myths. By getting families to identify their behaviors on a lower or higher level, it is possible to encourage differentiation by increasing fractal complexity. The following interchange illustrates how this is done:

THERAPIST: So Kathy, why won't you talk with me today?

SABRINA (16):   Kathy's tired because she stayed out all night with Tom.

THERAPIST: Sabrina, I want you to look at what you just said.

SABRINA: I said—

THERAPIST: I know what you said, but what are you doing?

SABRINA: I'm telling you how my sister feels. She's too tired to talk to you.

THERAPIST: What else are you doing?

SABRINA: I don't know.

THERAPIST: If I gave you a dollar for every way you could describe your behavior, I bet you could come up with another way of describing what you just did.

SABRINA: I guess I could say—I was talking for my sister. Now give me a dollar.

THERAPIST: Good, very good and what else?

SABRINA: I could say I was talking.

THERAPIST: Or?

SABRINA: I guess I could say I was making my mouth move. Or I could say I was talking so that you wouldn't embarrass my sister so [sic] she couldn't answer for herself. Or I could say I'm sitting here, getting bored. Can't we go home yet? Why don't you talk to Kathy.

THERAPIST: Or what else?

SABRINA: Hey, where's my dollar (giggles). I could say I'm sitting here in Pennsylvania, in the US, on earth, in our solar system. In the universe. In this stupid office. This is stupid.

THERAPIST: Good. It's good when you can think about—when you can describe the same action from different—in different ways.

SABRINA: Okay. I'm sitting here in this *stupid* office because my *stupid* mother made me come to see *stupid* you because my *stupid* sister's acting like a *stupid* jerk. How's that?

THERAPIST: Not bad. You get the picture.

Through time, activities that occur outside the session can be queried regarding their action identification, with the intent of gently desynchronizing the shared schemas that these families always use. In our experience with this type of treatment, based directly on fractal geometry, treatment may take six months to a year or more but appears to have less family dropout than traditional methods of increasing differentiation.

CHAPTER 7

At the Turning Point

TWO OF the most widely used techniques in family therapy involve contradictory aims. One entails methods to stabilize families during internal crises. The rationale for family stabilization is that many families report to emergency rooms, clinics, or to the therapist's office in a state of urgency and distress. These families appear to require immediate attention to deal with their behavioral and emotional problems, which can often be severe and spiraling. An effective therapist can frequently defuse ongoing problems and provide temporary or, in some cases, permanent improvement in family functioning.

A second set of techniques involves interventions designed for the reverse process, family destabilization. The theoretical rationale for destabilization is usually that the family is assumed to be "stuck" in a cycle, chronically performing dysfunctional behavioral patterns that resist other forms of intervention (L'Abate, 1986). In such cases, the therapist frequently finds it necessary to nudge, prod, or otherwise provoke the processes of change in a recalcitrant family system. Very often this involves inducing a crisis and temporarily increasing the family's distress in order to foster long-term changes in the family (Fisch, Weakland, & Segal, 1983).

Although both crisis intervention and family destabilization are recognized as potentially therapeutic, they have almost opposite short-term results. In the first case, the family leaves relatively placated, and at a lower energy level than when the session began. In the latter, they may be more agitated and may actually function less adaptively than before the session began. Similarly, the techniques used for these opposing goals are incomplete mirror images; hence they deserve separate treatment. In this chapter, we will discuss the theory involved in family stabilization during crises and how chaos theory affords us a better knowledge regarding these interventions. The next chapter will discuss family destabilization, an equally popular, though often more risky class of interventions.

Specifically, in this chapter we will highlight refinements to existing techniques of crisis intervention and management that are suggested by chaos theory. We will review some of the literature regarding crisis intervention, including the categorization of types of crises. We will next draw analogies between systems in crises and those on the verge of chaos, or technically as it is known, bifurcation. We will then introduce a general philosophy toward treatment that seems counterintuitive, yet is suggested from developments in physics, mathematics, and dynamical systems theories. This new philosophy includes a discussion of negative aspects of crisis intervention. Finally, we will speculate on some other, still relatively untested, interventions that may prove beneficial in stabilizing family systems in crisis.

STEADY STATES AND FAMILY STABILITY

As we have seen previously, the homeostatic model of family functioning has been one of the dominant paradigms in family therapy. First popularized by the physiologist Walter Cannon during the 1930s, *homeostasis* refers to the process through which organisms maintain a consistent internal environment in the presence of varying external conditions. Even the most basic of organisms would die in the absence of physiological homeostasis.

Perhaps the most renowned advocates of the homeostatic model of family functioning were the "communications theorists," a group connected with Gregory Bateson at the Palo Alto Veterans' Affairs Hospital during the 1950s. Bateson's interest in families was partially sparked by Norbert Weiner's theory of cybernetics, a theory of systems control that rose to prominence following World War II. As mentioned in Chapter 1, cybernetics is the science of the way machines use information to maintain a desired output. A common example is a thermostat, which uses information to generate appropriate temperature. By World War II, a number of machines (both electrical and mechanical) had been developed to restrict or increase output to a desired level, based on previous feedback, known as feedback loops.

For the present discussion regarding family stabilization, two important types of feedback loops or processes deserve note. *Positive feedback loops* amplify output to a desired level, such as when the smaller current passing through a transistor modifies a larger current to produce a much greater output. *Negative feedback loops* act to dampen or reduce deviations from a set point, such as when thermostatic feedback turns off the radiator to lower temperature. Homeostatic mechanisms in machines or in physiological processes typically function through a series of negative feedback loops (Gray & Rizzo, 1969), although some may employ positive feedback.

Jackson (1957), a well-known associate of Bateson at Palo Alto, applied the concept of cybernetic processes to family regulation. Jackson probably did more than any other early theorist to popularize this concept. Jackson proposed that a series of homeostatic mechanisms within the family serves to regulate the behavior of family members. Dysfunctional behavior on the part of a family member was seen as a "safety valve," actually encouraging long-term family stability. Based on Jackson's theories, family crises are often viewed as examples of this safety valve in action.

This homeostatic interpretation suggests that in some cases it is inappropriate to treat family crises. If such emergencies serve as a safety valve, then intervening in a family crisis might actually add to a cycle of dysfunctional behavior. In the only study available regarding this point, McCown and Johnson (1991) provided evidence that frequent crisis intervention may cause a dependency on the therapist and may actually stifle optimal family adjustment. The more active the therapist was in helping the family solve their crises, the more likely the family was to return in crisis in the future. These findings, while congruent with a homeostatic interpretation of family crises, should cause family therapists to pause and consider why the therapist's activity might be associated with a poor outcome. Another interpretation of these data may be found by changing our focus from the second paradigm in systemic family therapy to the third paradigm and beyond. As the reader will recall, the third paradigm of systemic family therapy focused attention on general systems theory. This paradigm directs us to consider that systems have both steady and transformative states. Interventions of the sort we have described hold the system back from the next transformative state. Moreover, this type of intervention technique also treats families like machines. In either case, the method runs counter to allowing the system to self-organize out of complexity or chaos as an organic system. Therefore, attending to the system's steady state, rather than its homeostasis-mechanistic tendency is more helpful.

WHY TREAT FAMILY CRISES?

The so-called new solution to mental healthcare funding, managed mental healthcare, has often ignored the role of the family in causing and maintaining mental health (Johnson, 1994). Increasingly, especially among "utilization specialists" (persons approving levels of services) in managed mental healthcare insurance coverage, there is a sentiment that family crises are *irrelevant* to mental health, and at best an epiphenomenon (McCown & Johnson, 1991). Yet despite the sentiment of third-party payers, there remains a strong consensus among clinicians that family crises are important for several reasons.

Foremost is that an inordinate amount of human misery is associated with family crises. Clinical experience amply suggests that family crises often threaten the very existence of the family. Crises are almost always associated with extreme levels of anxiety, depression, anger, and other negative feelings. A corollary is that dysfunctional behavior by family members during these periods may be extraordinarily dangerous to other family members. Incidences of alcohol abuse, incest, physical violence, and other behaviors with lifelong sequelae are most common during family crises (McCown & Johnson, 1991). For example, as Trepper and Barratt (1986) note, incest behavior may be more common among family systems that are experiencing a crisis. As anyone learns in working with incest, physical abuse survivors, or other posttraumatic stress disorders, prevention is a more humane and cost-efficient alternative than treatment (Hynes, 1994).

Family crises also are important because of their direct costs to society. Johnson (1994) cites data that families in crises are the *third* most costly nonhospital expense for mental health clinics, lagging behind only the treatment of schizophrenics and of borderline personality disorders. One reason families in crises are so expensive is that family members tend to receive multiple psychiatric and social services when these crises are not resolved (McCown & Johnson, 1993). For example, alcohol abuse is disproportionally represented in families with a history of crisis proneness (McCown & Johnson, 1993). Such families also may make greater use of nonpsychiatric medical services, such as general practitioners and emergency rooms (Johnson, 1994). It simply makes poor economic sense to ignore families in crises.

Last, and all but forgotten in today's mental health climate, is that family crises are important because they may also have a positive effect on future family functioning. While the early proponents of homeostatic views of family functioning seemed to implicitly recognize this, later authors have emphasized that family crises provide an opportunity for growth and for experiencing a more satisfying life (Satir, 1967). It is often stated that in various Chinese or Native American languages, the symbols juxtaposed to represent the native language translations of the concept of crisis mean two contradictory states: (a) threat, and (b) opportunity. A sentiment among clinicians is that family crises generate a real potential for permanent growth and change within the family. In their survey of family therapists who perform crisis intervention, McCown and Johnson (1991) reported that 87% of 332 crisis therapists who responded to a survey said that they had witnessed at least some families change in a *positive manner* from the experience of undergoing a crisis. Long-term data regarding families in crises are difficult to find. Many families "change" during a crisis only to quickly return to old and dysfunctional patterns when the impetus for change is removed. A common sentiment among clinicians however, is that under some circumstances families in crisis may make long-term and beneficial adjustments or major restructurings. One contribution from chaos theory will be to elucidate how and why this occurs.

CONTRASTING TENETS OF FAMILY THERAPY AND NONLINEAR DYNAMICS

Before we discuss how chaos theory can foster a better outcome for treating families in crisis, it is helpful to review how close the assumptions of contemporary family systems theory and of chaos theory actually are. As described in earlier chapters, family clinicians and chaoticians virtually stumbled into the same domain, at almost the same time. This is remarkable, given the differences between clinicians and chaoticians. Clinicians, as a rule, are not particularly mathematically minded. They are pragmatists, designated with the task of reducing social misery. Chaoticians, on the other hand, tend to frame theories in mathematical terms. Yet despite these differences, there are striking similarities in thought processes regarding complex systems. The experiences of clinicians and chaoticians, however, are somewhat like the Indian proverb of blind men trying to describe an elephant. They may be describing the same animal, but with different emphasis.

A basic tenet of almost all family therapy theorists is that the "whole of family functioning is larger than the sum of its individual family member parts" (L'Abate, 1986). This belief regarding families is now commonplace and hardly controversial. Today, even the more behaviorally oriented family theorists usually recognize that a family has an identity of its own, which is not reducible to the personality and interactions of its members (Mahoney, 1991). Similarly, chaos theorists have also rejected the notion that the world is composed only of constituent parts. In its departure from traditional science, chaos theory argues that the dynamics of systems—the way that it moves and the manner in which parts interrelate—are more important than their individual parts (Goerner, 1993).

Both systemic family therapy theorists and students of nonlinear dynamics explicitly reject the ability of the so-called linear model to serve as a *comprehensive* representation of reality. This sentiment was explicitly stated by many of the founders of family therapy (e.g., Bateson et al., 1956; Selvini-Palazzoli et al., 1978; Watzlawick et al., 1967), though its implications are often not fully appreciated.

As mentioned in Chapters 1 and 2, when scientists use techniques such as multiple regression or the analysis of variance, they are employing the *linear model* as a useful approximation of reality (Cattell, 1982). Examples in the behavioral sciences are hypotheses that a given experience, personality variable, or family type has a specific and proportional effect on cognition, behavior, or other action. Often, scientists may complicate the equation by predicting interactions between independent variables or even introducing cubic or quadratic equations. They may even introduce curvilinear equations or power functions to explain human behavior or performance. However, such models are still mathematically fairly simple.

In theory, if the assumptions guiding the linear model are correct, we should be able to make virtually perfect predictions from such methods, providing the specific model we have developed is both accurate and appropriate to the phenomenon being studied (Kline, 1984). This assumption, rooted in the thinking of Isaac Newton, has greatly influenced the social and behavioral sciences. Based on models of prediction and control popular during the nineteenth century, the accuracy of our ability to predict behavior is thought to be a function of the adequacy of our theorization and clinical conceptualizations.

Chaoticians realize that most complex systems in nature are better modeled by differential equations than by linear models (Abraham & Shaw, 1992). However, differential equations are computationally cumbersome. Another problem with modeling a system with differential equations is that differential equations are harder to use and understand. Traditionally, a differential equation is "solved" by finding a function that satisfies the differential equation (Tuffilaro, Abbott, & Reilly, 1992). Differential equations may provide multiple solutions, and in some cases are impossible to solve. Furthermore, demonstrated in earlier chapters, differential equations often reveal that the systems we are studying may behave in unpredictable fashions.

As we have shown throughout this book, a major reason many systems are inherently unpredictable is that many complex systems are *highly sensitive to initial conditions*, which cannot be controlled completely or predicted in advance (Moon, 1992). Hence, extraordinarily slight alterations in feedback or in the values of initial states may have extreme and literally unpredictable effects (Devaney, 1992). This occurs in many conditions where past system values are fed back into the system to influence future behavior, such as commonly found in population biology, where last year's levels of prey and temperature affect this year's population. This also occurs in social functioning, where one person's behavior affects what another person will do next, such as in a typical conversation (see Chapter 6).

Yet another similarity between family therapists and chaoticians is the belief that unpredictable behavior can arise in even small systems. Family therapists such as Ackerman (1972) and Framo (1982) have commented about how projections or distortions introduced even into a dyadic relationship allow interchanges to multiply and become more complex. This can cause even a simple system to destabilize. Similarly, an important insight to emerge from the new science of chaos is that chaotic behavior—behavior that is mathematically unpredictable—is not necessarily the result of many interacting variables. Even a simple system, with as few as three variables can, under certain conditions, demonstrate extremely complex, unpredictable patterns, as referred to in Chapter 2.

CONTEMPORARY CRISIS THEORIES

STRESS/BUFFERING MODELS

With these similarities in mind, it is helpful to review what clinicians already know from family therapy theory about the dynamics and treatment of families in crisis. Considerable effort in the family therapy literature has been directed toward advocating methods of stabilizing families in crisis (e.g., Bowen, 1978; Haley, 1976; Landau-Stanton, Griffiths, & Mason, 1982). Successful effort has also been directed toward using the family system to stabilize individuals in crisis (Bergman, 1985; Everstine & Everstine, 1983; L'Abate, 1994). Although confusion remains regarding the optimal role of families during crisis intervention (Worthington, 1987), the philosophical underpinnings of family crisis intervention primarily involve a homeostatic view of family processes (Minuchin, 1974). Family stability is usually seen as the norm, until cumulative stress or crises force instability into the system.

The traditional view of the etiology of family crisis usually involves a stress/buffering model (Johnson & McCown, 1996). In this model, the family is assumed to offer buffering protection from individual and collectively experienced stressors. When stress overcomes a family's steady state, the family is placed into a crisis. Early empirical work regarding the efficacy of family stabilization used a variant of this model. Langsley and Kaplan (1968) along with Pittman (1988), pioneered a novel treatment called Family Crisis Therapy (FCT). Begun at the Family Treatment Unit of the Colorado Psychiatric Hospital (Pittman, 1973), FCT focused on identification and resolution of the stress-induced crisis. In this model, family crises are resolved either by the process of allowing the family to make changes or by fostering an adaptation to the stress. Data shows that FCT reduced the need for psychiatric hospitalization (Langsley, Pittman, Machotka, & Flomenhaft, 1968; Langlsey, Pittman, & Swank, 1969).

Presently, there are many competing models relevant to family coping and crises. In general, the most empirical of these are rooted in Hill's ABC-X model (1949), which was based on studies of families struggling with the stressors of World War II. This early model postulated that a crisis (X) was the result of the interaction of three classes of variables: stressors (A), resources (B), and perceptions (C). Various incorporations of this model allow feedback to augment or reduce the outcome of these variables. Notably, the emphasis on perceptions predated the significance attached to symbolic representation of events that is now popular in cognitively based psychotherapies (Mahoney, 1991; Smolensky, 1988).

Perhaps the most popular reformation of the ABC-X model is the Family Adjustment and Adaptation Response Model (FAAR; McCubbin & Patterson, 1983). McCubbin and Patterson (1983), along with their productive research associates, have revised Hill's formulation by postulating the "double ABC-X model." This major revision was conceived to further explain variability in postcrisis adaptation. In this newer model, the same variables that interact to produce a crisis further interact to produce crisis adaptation. Three types of variables interact in the FAAR model: *demand, capabilities,* and *meanings.* Demands include conditions requiring changes in the family system that produce tension until they are met. It is this accumulation of demands that the model postulates precipitate a crisis.

Capabilities are used to meet demands. Capabilities consist of two types: resources and coping. Resources are capabilities a family *possesses,* while coping is a capability the family *actively performs.* Resources may include those of individual members, such as intelligence, knowledge, or self-esteem. They may also be family resources, such as cohesion, adaptability, or communication skills. Resources can also include community resources, such as social support. Coping is another type of capability of the family and refers to the efforts of the family and its members to meet demands. Coping efforts may include either direct action to reduce the demand or action to increase or maintain resources.

The third class of variables are subsumed under *meaning.* Situational meanings refer to the family's perceptions of demands and capabilities. Global meanings refer to the family's core assumptions, such as their sense of shared purpose. Meanings can serve to mediate the balance between demands and capabilities. They may offset the balance by minimizing or maximizing capabilities or by minimizing or maximizing demands.

As stated earlier, there are two phases in this model: adjustment and adaptation. Adjustment refers to the precrisis phase and adaptation to the postcrisis phase. Adjustment is the attempt to maintain a steady state or balance, between demands and capabilities, and using capabilities to resist crisis. Adaptation is distinguished from adjustment in that it occurs after a crisis and, therefore, requires greater change to regain the balance between demands and resources. New resources, coping mechanisms, or meanings must be developed for adaptation to occur.

CRISES AND PATHOLOGICAL FAMILIES

Much of the empirical research regarding crises has dealt with the adaptation and buffering abilities of family systems regarding stress. An equally common clinical sentiment, however, is that specific patterns of family interaction may themselves cause pathology in family members. During the late 1950s and 1960s, progressive clinicians began to investigate the role of the family processes in not only responding to, but also in facilitating psychiatric crises. Interpersonal crises began to be viewed as but one aspect of a dysfunctional family system. Family therapists noted that rarely did symptoms such as alcoholism and depression occur in a systemic vacuum. Instead, family precipitants could often be identifiable in the histories of most crisis cases. Implicit or explicit family rules often seemed to govern the crisis-oriented behavior of family members, as well as other aspects of the family's lifestyle.

Following Jackson's (1965) theorization, individual psychiatric symptoms were assumed to have a systemic function. In its extreme, thinking along these lines explicitly rejected the notion that the identified patient (or "IP" as the patient came to be known) had any specific pathology that was not due to the family system. The behaviors of such patients, whether they were schizophrenic, manic-depressive, or severely depressed persons, were rather naively seen as a metaphor for the illness or dysfunctionality of the entire system. It was once not uncommon for zealous family therapists to tell families to discontinue lithium, antidepressant, or antipsychotic medication for the IP (Levy & McCown, 1983).

Frequently, the functioning of such patients deteriorated. When this happened, family therapists blamed the patients' families. As a result, a few parent advocate groups during the 1980s became extremely critical of family therapy. This, in turn, sparked a mutual sense of anger on the part of therapists. These ripples are still affecting extramural funding of family therapy research and clinical services. This disagreement was truly unfortunate. Data from interventions such as FCT firmly indicated that family therapy could assist family members of chronically mentally ill and reduce hospitalization rates while it reintegrated the patient into the community. Much of the potential good of these programs was lost in the rancor because therapists and family advocacy groups failed to distinguish between *types* of family crisis.

TYPES OF CRISES: A CRITICAL DISTINCTION

McCown and Johnson (1993) have distinguished between two dimensions of family crises: *instrumental,* on one hand and *perceptual* crises, on the other. These two types get their names from the findings of factor analytic studies, which will be described. In the first type of crisis, the family appears to have an instrumental need, meaning an essential, material, or survival-related demand. In these cases, the family is in jeopardy of being unable to function adequately, including providing for the material or instrumental needs of its members. On the other hand, a perceptual crisis occurs when members perceive or believe that they cannot function as a family unit, or at least, cannot function as they previously did. Instrumental crises are related to loss of resources, while perceptual crises are related to changing perceptions about reality. These dimensions were initially thought to be continuous (linear and unidimensional) but now are recognized to fit a two-dimensional space.

In the former type of crisis, a negative event has occurred to one or more members in the family system. This event may impact on the family's survival or capacity to meet its basic needs. The event typically involves a sudden onset, extreme disruption of personal and familial functioning, usually with little chronicity. Generally, instrumental crises interfere with the well-delineated functions of families, as recognized by classic sociological theory (Parsons & Bales, 1955). An instrumental *stressor* is defined as an event that threatens to produce a crisis, if it intensifies or further depletes resources. Unemployment, accident, illness, sudden financial ruin, or natural disaster are all stressors that can instrumentally interfere with the family's survival. Sudden psychotic decompensation or suicidal behavior may also be an instrumental problem, especially when this person threatens other family members. In instrumental crises, family members can usually point to a specific incident that, if changed, would allow their family to function as before. Crisis interventions directed at instrumental concerns generally involve providing instrumental or material needs and appropriate levels of social services. They may also involve methods of increasing coping skills, ventilation, crisis normalization, and methods of identifying and enhancing social and community supports. This is illustrated in the following case study:

> The Smith family appeared at a local crisis agency following the devastation that occurred to their town during a hurricane. The family initially appeared distraught, but this soon gave way to a shared flatness of affect that is too commonly seen in people who have experienced disasters. Although no one in the family wanted to talk, they eventually furnished the following history: By chance, or perhaps Providence, as they would ascribe their fortune to, the family had been out of the house when the storm hit. They rushed home to seek what they thought would be a safer environment, only to have a large tree crash down on their house, seconds before they were about to enter it. Their house was largely destroyed; family pets had been killed. The rear section of their house had simply blown away without warning. Years of heirlooms and family items, such as ancestral photographs, had been damaged beyond repair in the subsequent heavy rains to which their belongings were exposed.
>
> Like many other families in their area, the Smiths now lived in a temporary shelter in a high school gym. However, their adjustment was poorer than their neighbors. The Smith children had been waking up in the night with terrifying nightmares. During the day, they could not sit still and provoked fights with other children. The children's behaviors had been so disruptive that the shelter manager had ordered the family to receive an evaluation before they could continue to stay another night. The manager hoped that "nerve pills" could quiet the kids down. However, a local physician, the first line of evaluation, had refused to prescribe psychotropic medication for children so young, and had sent the family for further evaluation to a family-oriented therapist.

Mr. Smith, a farmer, was acutely embarrassed that he had been requested to seek mental health evaluation. He stated, "They told me it was part of the package . . . part of staying at the shelter. . . . It's embarrassing enough to be there, but to have to see a counselor, I never would have imagined things would have been that bad. . . ." He blamed himself profusely for the tragedy, stating, "I knew I should have cut down that tree. None of this would have happened if I wasn't so lazy. Maybe this is God's method of punishing me for my laziness."

At this point in the interview, Mrs. Smith sobbed uncontrollably, while Eliza, 13, picked angrily at her hair and on some recent cuts on her arm that she had received from flying glass. A younger child, Tom, age 8, simply looked out into a courtyard where there was another uprooted tree from the storm, as if in a trance or experiencing a flashback. Tim, age 4, rocked back and forth in a chair, almost autistically, occasionally peering out the window as if looking at an unnamed dread.

The therapist sought to normalize the situation, explaining that after *any* family had seen their house blow away, a normal response was to be "devastated beyond all words."

"Look," he added, trying his best to convey genuine sincerity, "you aren't going crazy. You are normal people who were put in a crazy situation. Now, I would worry about you if you didn't have this type of response. Then I'd know you *were* crazy. Let me tell you, people who are 'out of it,' they don't have problems from big disasters. It's the normal, hardworking people that react like this because nothing like this has ever happened to you before."

The family seemed relieved to hear this. Mr. Smith said he felt "less crazy knowing I am kind of normal, though I'm not really sure I believe you."

To boost their coping with the situation, the therapist gave the family a daily task for the following week; together, each night they were to draw pictures about the devastation that the hurricane produced. This was an activity they could perform collectively, in their small corner of the high school gym floor. They were also encouraged to seek appropriate federal and private help. The therapist called the family twice a week to make sure that they were following through with this process, since he realized that the family was probably too proud to seek financial aid.

Within two weeks, the family had recovered to the point where the children's nightmares had ceased. By this time, it was no longer necessary for the therapist to prod Mr. or Mrs. Smith about obtaining needed services. The family soon moved out of the shelter and into the home of a relative. While their house was rebuilt they lived in a mobile home where "we got on each other's nerves, but we really learned to care for each other a lot more."

One year later, the family was symptom free, although some of the children seemed especially fearful whenever they watched a TV documentary about hurricane or tornadoes.

Instrumental family crises such as the preceding case are usually accurately modeled by the Hill/McCubbin tradition of ABC-X or double

ABC-X. Instrumental crises are almost always dealt with by appropriate social services, ventilation, and emotional support. Impact of these crises may be long-standing, even if they are treated. Most of the research regarding family outcomes and crisis intervention involves crises that are largely instrumental in nature. Central to crisis resolution may be establishment of an adequate existential framework for such a crisis. Often, religious faith may provide this framework, as it seems to have in the Smith family.

Other types of family crisis do not fit this model so well, however, and these may be more common today than in the past. Represented by another dimension from factor analytic studies are family crises that are best described as being *perceptual* in nature. Perceptual crises occur when an influential person in the family system suddenly says "I've had enough." These crises represent a *sudden behavioral shift* directed toward an unchanging or slowly elevating condition within the family system. Whereas instrumental crises frequently result in a pervasive inactivity and sense of loss, perceptual crises are usually characterized by the sense of behavioral urgency and hypervigilance.

Unlike an instrumental crisis, which almost always has a clear precipitant, it is difficult to explain the timing of a perceptual crisis. Sometimes, such crises are provoked by a belief that a major family rule has been broken (Jackson, 1965), although the same rule may have been violated for a long time without a sense of behavioral urgency. The model of gradually accelerating strains may or may not fit; often no increased strain is felt until a family member looks back and realizes that such strains have been present for quite some time, but have been largely ignored. Most often, though, there is no *clear* precipitant for a perceptual crisis at all, as the following case study indicates:

> The McKeen family made an "emergency" appointment to see their pediatrician. When the physician asked what the problem was, Mrs. McKeen answered that she was about to force her son, Jason, 16, out of the house "once and for all." The pediatrician realized the seriousness in the mother's voice and agreed to see her and her son immediately. While the pediatrician talked with the son, a therapist, who worked out of the same office, talked with the mother. This is part of their interchange:
>
> MOTHER: I've had enough. That's why I'm here. I caught that little fucker with a joint again. I'm throwing his ass out of the house. I've told him he can't smoke dope in my house and this time I mean it. I *really* mean it this time. He's just disrupting everything.
> THERAPIST: How long have you suspected that he has used marijuana?

MOTHER: *Suspected?* (Angrily) You mean *known*, don't you? What do you think I am, an idiot? I've known he smokes dope for two years now. God, at least that long. And *suspected* it for maybe a year more. Maybe two. Look, I used to mess with that shit myself, so I know what it does. I know all the signs. The red eyes, the bad grades, I went through all that myself and it almost ruined my life, let me tell you. (Very angrily) And you tell that to kids these days, that you've been through what they've done and you don't want them to screw up like you did and they just laugh at you. Just laugh at you like you're a moron. . . .

THERAPIST: I'm wondering why—what about today made you feel you needed to seek treatment now? I mean—it sounds like he's been using for four years.

MOTHER: I don't know—*I just feel like I have had the last straw* (italics added). I know I should have come here earlier and you might tell me it's too late. I don't know. I've just had enough. Enough's enough, isn't it. He's just ruining his life, and he doesn't understand it. Maybe we could send him away to treatment. It just makes me sick, all we've done for him.

THERAPIST: Was there *anything* about today? Anything you can think of that prompted you to seek help?

MOTHER: I don't know. Maybe that I had the day off—no—I've had lots of days off—I don't know. I just guess I got fed up (throws hands up into air). Something today just pushed me over the edge, that's all I can say. What more can I tell you? *Maybe I'm just noticing more these days* (italics added). Look you've got to do something. Send him away or something. Give him something to make him sick when he smokes that crap. Anything. There's got to be something. We can't go on this way.

THERAPIST: I'm still perplexed. This is (sic) been going (on) for some time. Why is there a crisis today? Why not last week, last year? Anymore stress in your life? Anything else happening?

MOTHER: Why are you trying to blame it on me? I don't know what happened. I guess you're going to lay some trip on me about how I should have gotten here earlier. Okay. I admit it, I screwed up. *But it didn't seem like a crisis until today* (italics added).

Whereas the timing of instrumental crises is generally explainable, perceptual crises are relatively unpredictable. Because these two variables represent underlying linear dimensions, the instrumental/perceptual distinction is not binary. Crises may have mixtures of each aspect. An example is the housewife whose husband "suddenly" leaves her, after an affair with a coworker has gone on for several years. Instrumental concerns include loss of economic status, necessity to make a livelihood, and loss of a marriage. Perceptual concerns in such a case include why she was not able to detect this behavior earlier and what she should have done to "prevent this mess."

CHAOS THEORY AND SYSTEMS IN CRISIS

The dynamics in both instrumental and perceptual crises can be captured through chaos dynamics. In instrumental crises, external containment of family parameters, described in the McCubbin/Hill tradition, are generally effective. Perceptual crises demand a greater reliance on the family's internal resources for the family to self-organize at a more evolved level. Stress-buffering models such as those out of the McCubbin/Hill tradition are usually the most helpful for explaining the effects on the family of a death, disaster, the lingering impact of medical illness, or a sudden loss of income. Theory-driven interventions derived from models such as FAAR (McCubbin & Patterson, 1983) include decreasing the stressors, increasing coping and support, increasing resources, and changing the meaning of events. These usually are helpful for practically any therapist attempting to assist a family following an instrumental crisis.

Chaos theory is extraordinarily helpful for advancing our understanding of perceptual crises. To the chaotician, the period where a stable system approaches chaos represents a crisis in the system (Devaney, 1992). Behavior may wildly vacillate between extremes or it may become totally unpredictable (Moon, 1992). The underlying attractor of such a system has become unstable, resulting in wildly fluctuating behaviors. By using the model that perceptual crises are better represented by systemic chaos, we can learn a great deal about potential methods of stabilization of systems in perceptual crisis. To illustrate this, we will begin by discussing ways in which chaos is similar to perceptual crises. We will next highlight some of the limits or caveats to crisis intervention suggested by the science of complexity. This phase of the discussion will highlight how family therapists may be inadvertently harming families in crisis by acting too quickly or competently. Finally, we will highlight potentially new interventions suggested by chaos theory.

LEARNING ABOUT CRISIS FROM CHAOS

Chaos theory can tell us facts about systems that we as clinicians may have already known, but may not have recognized as particularly important. These facts may be directly relevant to the clinician's efforts toward managing crises. They include the following: Abrupt changes in complex systems are ubiquitous in nature and such crises are usually self-limiting. Furthermore, crises are largely unpredictable and sometimes may be of benefit for the system. These characteristics parallel what we already know about family functioning, further illustrating how chaoticians and clinicians are beginning to think similarly.

First, chaos theory tells us that abrupt change is inherent in complex systems. Cellular development, plant growth, infant motor development, brain anatomy: Not only do the dynamics of these systems resemble the chaotic global models of physical properties and mathematical and physical laws, but they all seem to be in a constant state of flux (Rapp, 1987). One of the findings from this new science of chaos is that many complex systems—in fact most complex systems that involve feedback to constituent parts—alternate between periods of predictable stability and chaotic instability. During periods of stability, numerical values associated with measurement of the system are also very stable. Then, suddenly, they fluctuate wildly. Following periods of extreme apparent disorganization, order arises again, as if by magic. This pattern is now recognized as being so common in nature that it appears intrinsic at every level, from the behavior of subatomic particles to the motion of stars (Devaney, 1992).

This ubiquitous flux followed the pattern of order to chaos and back again to order. In other words, crises are usually self-limiting. These findings may have first been noted by the pioneering research of Steven Smale (Gleick, 1987), who theorized that almost all systems in nature are continually changing over time. He concluded that these changes progress from order to chaos, and that the resulting chaotic state had its own rules of structure and order. Similarly, Feigenbaum found that in a surprisingly large number of natural systems, a sequence existed of order, followed by turbulence and chaos, and finally resulted in a new state of predictability (Loye & Eisler, 1987).

Chaoticians also know that periods of chaos are unpredictable over the long run. While we can describe the general *shape* of the behavior graphically, or illustrate its general and probable range, we cannot predict the behavior of many complex systems with accuracy (Abraham & Shaw, 1992). An example is the prediction of hurricanes. We can categorize certain times of the year as "hurricane season" and frequently accurately chart the behaviors of storm systems within 6 to 12 hours. But as one of the authors who recently had to evacuate his home unexpectedly can affirm, we do not have highly accurate models for predicting complex systems, and perhaps chaotic systems, such as storms. Their nature makes long-range forecasting impossible. They are much too sensitive to initial conditions.

Chaos theory also tells us quite seriously that a little chaos once in a while can be a good theory. The reason for this involves the capacity of systems to *self-organize*. Perhaps the most exciting finding today regarding complexity is that chaos may resolve itself with a superior systemic organization and functioning (Kauffman, 1993). Systems that function chaotically or "on the verge of chaos" frequently self-organize after periods of chaos to function better in the future. They violate the classic laws of thermodynamics, as Ilya Prigogine discovered about two decades ago (Prigogine, 1980) in his research regarding chemical reactions. Classic thermodynamics states that systems tend to become more disorganized through time, eventually breaking down into apparent randomness. Yet Prigogine clearly found a class of chemical reactions where a higher degree of organization occurred through the passage of time. These reactions were "self-organizing" because they did not require additional input from any other agent to organize to a higher level of complexity.

During the past 15 years, extensive research has occurred regarding the capacity for self-organization of complex systems that are on the verge of chaos. In many systems, the following predictable pattern occurs: Order begins to transition into a state known as a bifurcation, otherwise described as oscillation or wildly fluctuating behavior. Following this, there is a further transition into a period of apparent randomness or more complete chaos, where everything seems to break down. Eventually the system seems to slow down, as if drained of energy into a period of stability. Often, though not always, there may be a superior organization following this period of chaos. Systems do not have to become completely chaotic to self-organize into more sophisticated functioning, and there is actually greater chance of self-organization if the system stays on the edge of chaos. Stuart Kauffman (1993), the renowned biologist, believes that this capacity of systems on the verge of chaos to self-organize into a higher, more superior level of functioning is what is responsible for both consciousness and the process of evolution. Davies (1992), a well-known professor of mathematical physics, interprets this capacity in a theological light, in but one example of how the new physics and theology may be converging.

The four observations about chaotic systems also apply to families in instrumental crises and to a larger extent to families in perceptual crises. Such crises are frequent, they are self-limiting, they are unpredictable, and finally, they represent a chance for an improvement in functioning (McCown & Johnson, 1993). It is the last point that is the most important to the practicing therapist.

Several proponents of chaos theory suggest that the maximal opportunity for change or self-organization occurs in systems that are near to, but not actually at the point of behaving chaotically. These systems are the most likely to self-organize toward higher functioning (Kauffman, 1993). Data regarding family therapy and crises indirectly supports this belief about complex systems. McCown and Johnson (1993) found that the faster a crisis is dissipated in a family, the more likely the family was to return soon with another crisis. These authors attempted to cast their explanation for these findings in the traditional paradigm of social learning theory. A newer perspective, suggested by chaos theory, is that families whose crises have been externally solved quickly by powerful outside agents such as therapists have not had time to develop a sufficiently complex self-organization. Therefore, they will remain crisis-prone and excessively vulnerable to future problems. The following two examples, with similar case histories, will help clarify this concept.

CASE 1

John Blevins, 42, sought help from his managed mental healthcare provider because he was having difficulty with his son, Jeremy, age 16. Jeremy claimed to have "converted to Satanism," much to the distress of his Evangelical Christian father. Jeremy had recently tattooed the numbers "666" on his forearm and claimed to be praying nightly to the Devil. Oddly, his school grades were unchanged, and he remained a fairly quiet, studious youth, apart from listening to heavy metal music that his father claimed was evidence of his "Satanic possession."

When questioned about why the father brought the son in for treatment at this time, the father noted that the son was "obviously getting worse . . . more possessed every day. . . ." Both father and son showed mild but objective evidence of depression, as measured by formal psychological testing. Yet there was no definable reason why the father had reached his personal breaking point or why he felt it was necessary to start treatment at this particular time.

The practitioner who evaluated Jeremy was an experienced family therapist. He believed that the family was reaching a crisis regarding rebelliousness and adolescent decision making. He noted that John's style was aggressive and authoritarian. The only way family members could gain his attention was to shock him. Under the constraints of the deadlines of the six sessions provided by managed mental healthcare, the therapist attempted to treat the problem at hand through a rapid crisis-reducing set of interventions. He allowed each member of the family to ventilate their concerns and anger in front of one another and then included a paradoxical intervention. The father was to encourage the son's Satanism with the rationale, "I'm glad you're interested in religion."

For the short run, the intervention worked extremely well. The son, having been given permission to be a Satanist, lost interest in this once forbidden area. Having had a chance to complain about his father to a professional, the son felt vindicated, as did his father, who received professional imprimatur for his parental concerns and hatred of heavy metal music.

However, six months later, the family returned to the therapist and sought additional treatment. Both the mother, June, 38, and Jeremy were very depressed. This time, the therapist obtained a more detailed and multifocal history. There had been glaring omissions in his original formulation of the family's problems. John, the father, was a "control freak" according to his wife. "He doesn't believe that anyone in the house should have any say at all. He believes that he's the one that should make the rules for everyone else. It's like the military or something. He just has this view that the man should be the head of the house and that we're his slaves. . . . He claims to get it from the Bible, but I tell you, it's not in my Bible. Every time we argue with him, though, he just tells us we're going to hell if we keep believing *(sic)* against him."

The therapist realized in retrospect that he had defused the crisis of a system that was attempting, quite legitimately, though not too adeptly, to claim more authority for others of its members. By providing his quick interventions, the therapist had inadvertently solidified the workings of a pathological and authoritarian family. Not surprisingly, the family continued to do poorly, with symptoms appearing in a number of other areas than suggested by the initial presenting problem.

CASE 2

The same therapist, some weeks later after the Blevins family returned to treatment, encountered a similar case. The identified patient was a 14-year-old adolescent named Jennifer, who claimed to be using marijuana and had set up an "altar" to Satan in her room.

She was brought into treatment when her step-father, Tom, 45, claimed, "I've had enough of this nonsense. All the kids I raised came out normal except this one. It's not my fault. . . . I just want her put away, that's all. I want her out of the house right now." Tom was a long-distance truck driver, who was rarely at home. "When I am there, I don't have time for this voodoo she's into. It's just disruptive and I'm sick of disruptions in my life."

Jennifer's mother, Laura, 33, had been diagnosed with depression that had been evident for at least five years. She was treated with antidepressant medications, though had not been involved with any psychotherapist, since "I can't afford to pay for a Christian therapist, and I won't go for one who isn't born again. With our insurance, all they do is give us a list of who we can see and none of them are Christians." Other family members refused to participate in treatment, each claiming that they were too busy. This was a signal to the therapist that something serious was amiss in the family system.

The therapist viewed Jennifer's "Satanism" and her mother's depression as responses to paternal authoritarianism. A perceptual family crisis was evoked when the father begin to feel that he was losing control over the system. To employ and maximize his control, he frequently verbally berated his long-suffering and religious wife, who, on theological grounds, believed that it was inappropriate to object to such action on the part of her husband.

The therapist determined not only that the family had a history of being crisis-prone, but also of quickly dropping out of treatment, apparently when the crisis was stabilized. Detailed notes from other treatment providers indicated that virtually no one felt that the family system had obtained any real changes, but that crisis intervention acted only to restore the family's authoritarian hierarchy. The therapist was justifiably worried about this family's outcome.

Rather than allow the family to return to their precrisis pathology, the therapist tried a different technique. In retrospect, he noted, "What I did ran against my training as a strategic therapist and emergency counselor. I always thought the best thing was to defuse a family's tensions as quickly as possible. But this time I tried something different."

Using a psychoeducational model of treatment, he actually kept the family in greater crisis. Sessions were spent teaching family members about role-appropriate requests for autonomy and assertiveness, and teaching the father different methods of problem solving and discipline other than yelling and berating. These efforts acted to increase Jennifer's marijuana smoking, though her Satanic interest seemed to decline. The father dropped out of treatment four times, almost once a week. However, when realizing that his family was changing without him, he agreed to continue on each occasion, perhaps out of fear of losing what control he had.

Tension built in the family over the next few weeks. The mother became more depressed, the daughter used more marijuana, and the father tried harder to be an authoritarian and to maintain control in the only way he knew how. The therapist felt sorry for the family. Their lives together must have been very uncomfortable. Still, they needed to change, and this was the only way he saw such change as possible.

However, nine weeks into treatment, the father received an "insight." He noted, "I was reading my Bible and something came to me. I was reading about Abraham and Isaac and it struck me—well the Lord revealed to me, I guess—that I should be gentler to my family. It wasn't Christian to yell at them. And then I read what St. Paul said about "Husband's love your wives as Christ loves the church." Now it occurred to me, did Christ constantly yell at the Church? No! Did he try to control the Church. No, he let us learn on our own, by trial and error because He loves us. That's what it took. I started to think, maybe the Christlike way is to loosen up."

The therapist worked with the father alone for four more sessions, helping him maintain authority, yet teaching him to do so in a nonauthoritarian style. In response to either the father's changes, or occurring simultaneously with them—it is impossible to say—June developed a less traditionally subservient role and became more insistent that her opinions around the home be heard. She found out that she had special sway over her daughter, who would often listen to her, but not listen to her stepfather. At the two-month follow-up, family tensions were markedly reduced; and there had been no more crisis sessions.

What was the difference between the failure in the first case and the success in the second? On the basis of two cases, we can't conclude much. Yet, on the basis of chaos theory, we believe that in the second case the family demonstrated a higher level of self-organization. While reluctant to criticize "divine intervention" in this case, we suggest that this change occurred because the therapist did not act quickly to solve the family's problems. He permitted them to remain in a constant crisis for several weeks. In the first case, however, the therapist's insistence on acting rapidly had a long-term effect. While the family's problems were temporarily alleviated and they felt better, they did not make the changes necessary to prevent the recurrence of problems.

The major contribution from chaos theory regarding crisis intervention can be stated as follows: *Perceptual crises that are allayed too quickly will not produce optimal change.* This is because optimal change involves self-organization, which can only occur if the system is allowed to remain at a crisis point for however long is necessary to produce this change. *To increase the possibility of self-organization, interventions should be as noninvasive as possible.* The more controlling of the system an intervention is, the less likelihood that the family will self-organize. In other words, *don't just do something—sit there!*

With this in mind, the goal for the therapist is to intervene in such a way that the family will remain in a therapeutic crisis, but will not completely disintegrate. Here we aim to do two things, keep the family near chaos, but not actually in chaos. This is optimal according to certain proponents of chaos theory. Or, on the other hand, keep the family in chaos long enough to promote self-organization. This requires an understanding of the different levels of family crisis and the way to match levels of intervention to the family's needs.

As one might expect, families demonstrate the process of self-organization in different ways. We want to introduce two ideas about how to conceptualize family dynamics. Certain families, such as single-parent or blended families always seem to be in crisis. We would view this as a crisis of adaptation. These families, more so than many others, are required to adapt to environmental changes on an almost constant basis.

While we have at times described these families as crisis-prone, they make up but a small subset of this population. Other, more adaptively oriented families we describe as *rapid cycling* families. These families are rapid cycling in the movement through the process of self-organization (via complexity or chaos). They move through these processes rapidly, adapting to one new environmental demand after another. We might place these families in the chaotic region of the Circumplex Model, whereas those we describe as *slow cyclers* would tend to be correlated with the more rigid region of the Circumplex Model. Together, these descriptions add dimension to the movement and information boundaries described earlier in the text. Our goal here is to provide family therapists with tools to identify the familial dynamics we continue to witness in our work.

LEVELS OF INTERVENTION:
THE VARIABLE OF CONTROL

The more controlling a therapeutic technique is, the less likely that the system will be able to self-organize. Specific interventions can be classified according to their controllability of the family system. These rankings are somewhat arbitrary and theoretically based. There is no absolute way to know how one particular set of interventions will be perceived by a family or what sort of control it will have. We can speak only in probabilities. In some cases, methods aimed at extreme control of particular families may be viewed by target families as hardly invasive at all. For example, we have treated many families where going to jail is seen as less controlling than going to weekly family therapy sessions! Yet despite large individual differences, some generalities are apparent across families.

The most extreme method of the spectrum of controllability and invasiveness involves institutionalizing family members. Using this method, we find we can control any family crisis. All we have to do is hospitalize and drug the members experiencing distress. Similarly, members can be jailed if they are uncooperative. Only slightly less invasive are techniques that physically separate family members. Sometimes these interventions are necessary, but they must be recognized as usually being the most controlling and in the long run are probably countertherapeutic.

On the other extreme of the continuum are completely noninvasive and noncontrolling interventions. Such interventions exist only in theory. Chaos theory indicates that any time we intervene at all into a system, we can never be certain of our impact (Moon, 1992). Interventions that come closest to theoretically being of little controllability involve providing information or tension reduction, such as conjoint relaxation. Even providing information may disrupt a family system, just as hospitalization or institutionalization may paradoxically have a minor effect on family systems. Some families are so rigid that they would rather have two or three members hospitalized than have these same members receive appropriate information about medical or psychological problems that could keep them out of the hospital.

In between these extremes lie an infinite number of other interventions routinely performed by therapists. For heuristic purposes, we may divide these into general classes, including the two extremes of the continuum previously discussed. The first class of interventions are those on the extreme end that restrict the family's ability to choose. Such interventions act to stabilize a system by grossly restricting the options available to it. Hospitalization or confinement is one of these interventions, but also included are techniques such as removing disparate parts of the family system from each other (for example, separating feuding spouses for the night).

Next on the spectrum of controlling behavior are interventions in which the therapist makes a decision for the family, usually over the family's tacit or overt objections. This technique has been labeled as "ego lending" (McCown & Johnson, 1993), a name culled from the psychodynamic literature regarding the treatment of very disturbed individuals. In ego lending, the theory is that the individual or family is so temporarily impaired that the therapist must lend his or her higher cortical functions to the system, to assist the members to make a rational choice. Police engage in forms of ego lending routinely when they redirect the perpetrators of minor inappropriate behavior toward more acceptable courses of action.

Ego lending, like psychiatric hospitalization, is often a necessary evil. When families are in instrumental crisis and cannot adequately make decisions to end conditions that might threaten their safety, well-being, or survival, the therapist often has to do this for them. This is most likely to occur when the family encounters extraordinarily unexpected instrumental stressors, such as a sudden death or a natural disaster. Biopsychological factors may prevent rational thinking and these may be rooted in the neurochemistry of exposure to uncontrollable stressors. Ego lending is much less necessary for perceptual crises and may be countertherapeutic. Sometimes the therapist has no choice but to make major decisions for a client in crisis but most therapists are correctly cautious of such actions.

The next class of interventions, in terms of controllability to the system, involve those designed to manipulate behavior by changing roles. Most therapists are aware of the numerous techniques involved in manipulating systems through changing roles or expectations. These include such common techniques as paradoxical interventions, empowering specific family members, drastically changing family roles, behavioral prescriptions, encouraging overcompetent behavior, and other systemic interventions. One problem with using them for crisis intervention is that they rarely work quickly enough. Another problem is, that like more controlling techniques, their results may be unpredictable. Such techniques usually work better for destabilizing family systems, which will be discussed in Chapter 8.

In the next cluster of intervention are techniques, such as family problem solving, negotiation, and reframing, all of which are moderately invasive and controlling techniques. These are often the treatments of choice for families who are crisis-prone, but have a history of disappearing once real changes are demanded of them. Reframing, however, remains controversial. Some authors feel that it provides insight. From the perspective of a chaotician, reframing works because it allows diverse subsystems to attune their functioning. It is not the cognitive component of reframing that is essential. Instead it is the change in dissipative energy into the family system. Reframing per se may result in a decrease in behavioral frequency of problem behaviors, but this is often only temporary.

Perhaps the most common class of techniques for family stabilization involves such therapeutic procedures as ventilation. Ventilation is a classic psychodynamic term related to a hydraulic model of personality (Cameron & Rychlak, 1985). It is often thought of as a method of allowing an individual or family to "blow off steam." However, the therapeutic use of ventilation involves listening to as many family members as is possible, allowing all of them to be equally heard. Ventilation is often not as benign as it seems, since it may work only when energy is evenly dissipated across the system. We make a mistake when we let the dominant member of the family system speak, to the exclusion of other members, which often happens. Listening to one family member and not others serves to legitimatize or challenge structural aspects of the family system and if this is the goal, it can be accomplished more directly.

Providing information to a system is usually seen as the most benign function of a family therapist. Presenting information to a family in a crisis may have a profoundly calming effect. Sometimes, as we have seen earlier, there can also be a disrupting effect. Yet in general, providing information is the least controlling of any family therapeutic intervention. Information normalizes a situation, legitimizing family feelings and actions while suggesting that the crisis situation is transitory; and it promotes the ability of the system to begin a process of successful self-organization.

A major mistake that therapists in training often make is to present information only once or to only one family member. It is common therapeutic practice to find the most "stable" member of a family system and instruct her or him about whatever information needs to be imparted. Actually, a classic paper in information theory proves that an alternative strategy is better. Kelly (1955/1986), a scientist at the Bell Telephone Laboratories, investigated the accuracy of informational exchange in systems that display varying degrees of noise or uncertainty. His goal was to develop algorithms for determining the maximal faith we should have in such communications and how we should allocate resources under varying degrees of line noise (or entropy in a system) in order to make sure that an accurate message is received. Using the analogy of a wager at a racetrack, Kelly mathematically demonstrated that the gambler—analogous to the person sending information in a noisy system—has more chance of winning (getting the message across) if he or she spreads the bets around, rather than relying on one or two "sure horses" in each race. Kelly established a complex formula for the bankroll of a gambler, where the size of the bet is proportional not only to the odds of winning, but also to other bets made within the same race or system. The surprising conclusion from the "Kelly Criteria," as horseplayers fondly call it, is that it is more effective to spread out your wagering dollars across the system, rather than concentrating your money only on the wagers that you think have the best chance of success.

The exact calculations necessary to determine the optimal combination of odds and financial investment are probably of interest only to mathematically oriented horse handicappers. Yet Kelly's theorem suggests that it is better to present information to diverse family members, than to only to one or two of them, despite the appearance that they will not understand the intervention. In other words, when facing a system which does not conduct information well (such as any system in crisis), the therapist's maximum likelihood of getting the information across is to present it at several times to several members. It is better to make several small bets than one large bet. (Technically oriented readers will realize that Kelly's racing example is a special case of general systems entropy, which is now a popular topic among chaos theorists, and sometimes referred to as Shannon's entropy (Proskauer, 1996).)

In review, we have seen that the more likely a technique is to dissipate a family crisis, the more likely that family is to return in future crisis. Therapists can come to confront this problem by realizing that different levels of intervention have different degrees of control over a family (Proskauer & Bütz, 1996). In general, especially for perceptual crises, the less invasive, the better. The more invasive a therapist is, the more likely it is that the therapist has impeded self-organization.

NOVEL TECHNIQUES OF CONTROLLING CRISES

Chaos theory also allows us to develop new techniques of family intervention. These techniques have the advantage that they are usually minimally controlling of family behaviors. They allow stabilization, yet also allow maximal possibility for self organization.

CRITICAL FEEDBACK STABILIZATION

A. B. Çambel (1992), a well-known chaotician who is concerned with the practical aspects of chaos theory, argues that chaos can be controlled by application of feedback performed only at critical periods. This is based on some very interesting experimental work out of several sources, which is now just entering the physics literature. These findings show that directed feedback occurring only when the system is beginning to bifurcate may help stabilize a system very quickly. This is probably what happens in some forms of crisis intervention, especially when performed by therapists who seem intuitively gifted or talented and able to obtain exceptional therapeutic results with little intervention.

Critical Feedback Stabilization (CFS) is a technique developed to provide this type of feedback. During CFS, the therapist performing family intervention for the purpose of crisis stabilization allows the family to go in any direction that they want. He or she only "brings them back" when they are in danger of precipitating an unmanageable crisis. An example is when it is likely that something a family member does will result in the termination of a session or when a family member is physically threatening to other family members or to people outside the session. Family members may be halted from attacking other family members who are incapable of responding, such as those in tears or who are too anxious to talk.

CFS therapeutic interventions are brief and to the point. Usually, the therapist prefaces the session by having each family member sign a contract regarding rules for the session. One of the rules is that when the therapist thinks that a specific family member's behaviors are "out of bounds," the therapist will say so. Otherwise, the therapist is fairly silent. In transcription of CFS-based therapy tapes, therapists made an average 0.38 interventions per minute ($SD = 1.45$, a somewhat skewed distribution).

CFS sessions typically take anywhere from one-half to two hours. Preliminary analysis of data suggests that CFS is effective as a method of crisis intervention, at least as effective as traditional, more active techniques. Long-term results are unclear, but may indicate a trend toward fewer subsequent crises. More data are required before definitive statements can be made.

One disadvantage of CFS training is that many therapists, including some of the present authors, find it difficult to remain fairly passive while the family "goes at it." Consequently, considerable supervision is required during training; frequent training "booster sessions" may also be necessary. A major caveat is that CFS is often contraindicated with instrumental crises, where much more therapist activity may be necessary. Nor does CFS abrogate the therapist's responsibility to evaluate the crisis potential of family systems, including assessing such traditional variables as suicidal and homicidal ideation and plans. It may be that due to the therapeutic skill required to manage a crisis without saying much, only outstanding therapists are capable of CFS training.

WHITE NOISE THERAPY

From a dynamical systems perspective, crisis intervention involves one of two processes, either draining dynamical energy from the system, or swamping the system with stabilizing energy. The analogy with fluid dynamics is appropriate. A turbulent lake may be stabilized, for example, by draining energy from it through heat transfer or fluid reduction, or by adding vast amounts of water evenly across the lake. Ditto, Rauseo, and Spano (1990) have demonstrated the experimental control of chaos by application of white noise to a system. White noise is defined as the equal spectrum of waves across the band. A common example visually is the blank picture seen on televisions, that is usually called snow . . . white noise.

We have discussed, by analogy, white noise stabilization for family dynamics for some time. We have made initial attempts to use it as a technique, one of which will be described in this section. The technique seems to work, but we aren't certain if it is really analogous to what occurs in the world of physics. Essentially, the family therapist, equally engages and rewards each member in the family system within each therapeutic session. There is no goal to any session, except that each family member be engaged approximately equally. Unlike CFS, the therapist remains very active, speaking in about 40% of the content of the session. Material is not directed toward crisis-provoking material and ventilation is expressly not allowed. Associations are almost loose on the part of the therapist. This technique may seem simple and fun, but it is exhausting and requires training and supervision. The following case study is an example of "white noise therapy":

> The family made an emergency appointment to visit the therapist, who was covering for a more traditional psychodynamically oriented clinician. The identified patient is Tiffany, 16, a very bright young woman with an eating disorder. Following disclosure of the fact that the parents are planning to move to another town, Tiffany has threatened suicide. The mother angrily responds toward the father, blaming him for placing his career above the interests of his children. The father has asked for Tiffany to be hospitalized, while the mother does not want to consider this option. We begin the transcript about 10 minutes into the therapy session, after the therapist has determined that Tiffany has mild suicidal ideation, but with no discernible plan.

THERAPIST: Anyone see who the (New Orleans) Saints signed today?
SEAN: (age 8) They didn't sign no body.
FATHER: I don't see what this has to do with anything. I'd like to get her in the hospital as soon as possible. Really. We've been here—
THERAPIST: And who cares? I mean about the Saints. Not about the hospital. But more importantly, who can tell me who got out of retirement this week.
SEAN AND STEVEN: (age 11) (In unison) Michael Jordan!
THERAPIST: And who cares? His playing days are over!
SEAN: Man, you're nuts. The Bulls are going all the way. Go Bulls!
STEVEN: All the way home! Go Bulls!
THERAPIST: Mom, what do you think?
MOTHER: Well, I don't know much about basketball. I mean I've never been a sports fan.
THERAPIST: Well, what do you like?
MOTHER: Movies, music . . . gardening.
THERAPIST: Okay, here's a bit of trivia for you movie fans: Tommy Lee Jones—the Oscar winner, used to be the roommate of Al Gore. *The* Al Gore, the Vice president.
TIFFANY: You mean that stiff guy? The one that doesn't move much? He's fat. He should lose some weight.

THERAPIST: Tommy Lee Jones isn't a stiff guy . . . anyone like music?

TIFFANY: Yeah.

THERAPIST: What groups?

TIFFANY: (Painfully) Alternative. Green Day, Live, the Cranberries. I hate the radio. I used to like Pearl Jam.

THERAPIST: I know, but their last album wasn't very good. It was better than Nirvana's though.

STEVEN: Hey I gotta joke about Kurt Cobain.

THERAPIST: We don't want to hear it. We're here to discuss the fact that Tiffany wants to kill herself. She thinks she's too fat. I'm too fat. What do you think, Dad? How much weight should I lose? Forty, fifty—

FATHER: I'm not really certain what all of this is about? I mean . . .

THERAPIST: Well, Kurt Cobain was the lead singer from Nirvana who killed himself. Tiffany might need to hear that joke.

TIFFANY: I've heard it before. It's not funny. It's gross.

THERAPIST: Okay Steven, if Tiffany doesn't want to hear it, whisper it in my ear. (He does and the therapist reacts.) That joke is awful. I heard it and *I* want to kill *myself* and I have more mental health than anybody in this room.

TIFFANY: (to the therapist) What kind of music do you like? You look like you would be a Deadhead or something.

THERAPIST: Me? A Deadhead? Your Dad's the Deadhead! (Kids laugh). I just like TV theme songs. From the old, hokey shows—*Mr Ed, Lassie, Gilligan's Island, The Brady Bunch.*

STEVEN: The Bunch sucks. Yuck!

THERAPIST: I beg your pardon. The Bunch *rules.*

SEAN: Can we leave now?

THERAPIST: Not until everyone who hates the Brady bunch morphs themselves into Brady Bunch Fans. Mighty Morphing Brady Bunch.

TIFFANY: (to therapist) God, you're weird.

THERAPIST: (Looking to heaven) Did you hear that, God? Tiffany says you are weird! No wonder she wants to kill herself. She thinks God is weird! Mom, Dad, you heard it, too! Your child is not an atheist. She has started a new religion. The God Is Weird church. Can you imagine? Every Sunday we've been giving our money in the collection plate to this guy whose really weird.

TIFFANY: No, I mean you're weird. You're weird. But I like you better than Dr. Zach. All he wanted to do was ask me about my problems.

THERAPIST: Dr. Zach, did you know that he used to be a figure skater? Really! Now can I leave, you guys are boring me. You are making me stiffer than Tommy Lee Jones. I should be home watching wrestling. Hey, Tiffany, they don't have MTV in the hospital.

TIFFANY: Come on! They must!

MOM: Doctor, it looks like you agree with me. About the fact that she doesn't need hospitalization.

THERAPIST: I agree that Tiffany watches too much MTV.

The session ended about an hour later with Tiffany denying that she felt suicidal; she was able to sign a "no suicide" contract and agreed to call the therapist if she again had ideas about hurting herself. She called once more three days later, but only to say that the kids in the family all concurred that "You're really weird." Tiffany then suggested that the therapist might need some drugs to slow him down.

APPLYING CHAOS TO CHAOTIC SYSTEMS

The preceding intervention and therapeutic style overlap to some extent with that of the renowned Carl Whitaker (1975), who seemed to use therapy to prove to a family that he was crazier than they were. Why would this strategy work? Chaos theory gives us an explanation. Çambell (1992) argues that chaos can also be controlled by applying chaos to chaotic systems. Again, this must occur when systems are in periods of instability, or, in the case of families, are in crisis. This has been demonstrated experimentally by Shinbrot, Ott, Grebogi, and Yorke (1990) who have shown that applications of chaos to chaotic systems at specific points may control systems and cause them to maintain a more stable trajectory.

For families, the implications for this finding may be quite astounding. This may be the reason that "out-crazying" the family system provides stability. It may also explain other findings from more traditional family crisis intervention. Elsewhere it has been noted that one of the more effective techniques for providing for family stability during crises involves the process of assembling disparate members of the family system (McCown & Johnson, 1993). This method may provide stability by applying chaos to chaos. If we seriously consider Çambell's (1992) summary of the literature, then adding "crazy" members to an already crazy family therapy session may act to stabilize the system further, a hypothesis that is counterintuitive. Consider the following case:

> Janet and Roger Hughes, both 48, fought constantly. Although they had no diagnosable disorders per se, there was a constant amount of family friction, resulting in extraordinary symptom changes, varying almost by the hour. The couple fought frequently over any number of petty topics. Often these arguments would accelerate beyond either of their control and someone would have to leave the home for a few hours or more, to allow "things to cool down."
>
> Traditional marital, social learning, and family interventions were not effective in reducing shared or alternating symptoms. The therapist was increasingly alarmed because the couple's arguments had become more pronounced and there was the possibility of serious domestic violence.

Based on Çambell's (1992) observations, the therapist decided to add chaos to the family system by adding another member who was behaving chaotically. Roger's first wife was offering to give him custody of his 14-year-old son, who was proving unmanageable for her and had recently gotten into legal trouble. Traditional family or individual therapists would have attempted to steer the family away from a new inclusion of this obviously stressful additional member, reasoning that it would not do either the son or the couple any good to be further encumbered at this time in their relationship. But the therapist decided to encourage the son's entrance into the home, hoping to provide some stability to chaos by adding chaos.

Results were quite impressive. The couple reached a degree of symptom stabilization within a few weeks of the son's arrival. They were able to work together to help treat the son in a consistent manner and give him necessary guidance and space to transition through a difficult period. Moreover, Roger and Janet stopped their constant bickering and petty fighting. Within a few weeks, they even volunteered that they loved each other. Although no formal psychometric follow-up was attempted with the son, it is notable that he did not engage in illegal or uncontrollable behavior while with the family.

ADDITIONAL TECHNIQUES

A number of other potentially therapeutic techniques derived from chaos theory have been developed and are being tested including methods that directly *increase* family stress during crises, with the goal of providing for rapid self-organization. Some of these methods may be especially helpful for family systems dominated by individuals or couples who are best described by the traditional nomenclature of personality disorders. Family interventions for personality disorders may prove an important area of therapeutic intervention during the next decades, since the treatment of personality disorder by traditional techniques is expensive and personality disorders almost always negatively affect the family system.

Presently, a number of clinical interventions are underway involving the treatment of families of people with traumatic brain injury and dementia with chaos theory (Johnson & McCown, 1996). The focus of these interventions is to allow the individual with neurobehavioral compromise and his or her family to self-organize. Therapeutic techniques involve exposing chaotic and crisis-prone families who have a neurobehavioral compromised member to *structured crises;* since these techniques may involve the process of crisis induction, they will be discussed in the next chapter.

CONCLUSION

As scientists learn more about controlling chaos, a number of other techniques will naturally suggest themselves and may be fruitful areas for designing additional interventions. To develop and test these interventions, family therapy will require the training of empirically oriented practitioners who are open to experience and creative enough to be able to translate, at first by analogy, results from other sciences into the arena of therapeutic relationships. Given the incredible creativity of family therapists during the previous decades, we are optimistic that today's experimental interventions may be tomorrow's orthodox treatments.

CHAPTER 8

Trying to Unscramble the Eggs

T HE CONCEPT of the therapeutic destabilization of a family system is integral to family therapy and common even among the early family therapists. In traditional systemic approaches to family therapy, there are two reasons to disrupt a family's steady state. The first involves the possibility that such action will allow superior stabilization processes to help the system. In other words, by temporarily disrupting the family, a superior level of functioning may emerge rather quickly.

As we have seen from Chapters 1 and 7, Jackson (1957) applied this concept of cybernetic processes to family regulation and probably did more than any other early theorist to popularize it. Jackson proposed that a series of homeostatic mechanisms within the family serve to regulate the behavior of family members. Dysfunctional behavior on the part of a family member was seen as a "safety valve," actually encouraging long-term family stability. For the family, there is less danger of destruction if they tolerate or even encourage this dysfunctional safety valve behavior. By temporarily upsetting the homeostatic mechanisms within a family, Jackson believed that it was possible to allow other homeostatic processes to dominate, thus, in essence, allowing the system to heal itself. Again, application of this mechanistic model to the family is inappropriate in the current paradigm as families are organisms.

A second reason often mentioned in the family therapy literature regarding the induction of crises is to replace dysfunctional or stifling aspects of a family's steady state that might be restricting a family. This thinking is largely based on the pioneering work of Virginia Satir (1967), a promoter of humanistic influences in family therapy. From our current perspective, Satir's major contribution was her recognition of the potentially negative aspects of homeostasis. Whereas authors such as Minuchin (1974) and Haley (1980) generally advocate the beneficial role of homeostatic processes, Satir saw the same tendencies as too often potentially stifling of a family's growth. Satir viewed homeostatic processes as possessing the ability to restrict a family's new experiences. Frequently, these promoted rigidity and resistance to change in the face of life situations that demand flexibility.

For Jackson and advocates of his techniques, disruption of homeostasis is a temporary or brief process. For Satir, the process may be a more intense and humanistic journey, necessitating longer term family therapy. Neither theorist is "correct"; some approaches work better for some families or specific problems, whereas others are best tailored for a different set of family problems. In this chapter, we will discuss the contributions that chaos theory can make to help us better understand the process, potentialities, and risks of family destabilization.

SUCCESSFUL FAMILY DESTABILIZATION

Most of the major approaches in family therapy involve components designed to unsettle previous patterns of family processes (Framo, 1982). For maximal efficacy, states the traditional wisdom, a therapist often needs to be influential, in control, and occasionally disruptive of the family process (Gurman & Kniskern, 1978). Paradoxes and reframings, techniques that are usually considered "innocuous and commonplace" by family therapists, can startlingly and fundamentally alter a family's epistemology (L'Abate, 1986). Even the act of assembling the various members of a quarrelsome family system can have profound impact on family functioning and may in itself precipitate a crisis. Few family therapists, with the exception of Murray Bowen and his associates, discussed in Chapter 7, routinely practice without using methods of family destabilization or family crisis induction. Bowen's work exemplifies earlier comments on the impact of having an observer in the room. Family therapists would be well advised to remember this fact. As the Milan group (Selvini-Palazzoli et al., 1980) has pointed out, collecting enough information in the presence of the family may be intervention enough to move the family toward more adaptive behavior. It is important to remember, our mere presence in the room and the collection of information are "interventions"—in and of themselves, this may be enough.

Methods of destabilizing a family system or a family's hierarchy are so common that they will not be reviewed here in detail. Excellent accounts exist elsewhere. Some techniques include joining with underrepresented family members, giving families tasks that they will fail in completing, empowering members, prescribing specific behaviors to upset family balance, forbidding specific behaviors, isolating scapegoats or identified patients (IPs), joining family subsystems against major obstacles, and many other common techniques.

Despite its popularity, however, family destabilization is not as routinely performed as it was a decade ago (Johnson & McCown, 1996). One reason seems to be a greater respect on the part of family therapists for dangers inherent in destabilization. Another reason involves the limited number of sessions that family therapists are increasingly operating under, due to the constraints of managed mental healthcare. The following case study is an example of a destabilization of a pathological family system, and is an example of the power such interventions can have in causing long-term and beneficial changes:

Imal, age 13 was an African American male who lived part-time with his mother, J'wan, 33, and part-time his grandmother, Shonda, 52. Imal was recommended for treatment because of poor grades and a "bad attitude" at school. Anecdotal accounts from teachers suggested a history of extensive substance abuse, although this could not be corroborated by family members. Imal was seen by a local community counselor, who realized that this young man's problems had more to do with his family than any other reason, and who subsequently recommended him for family therapy at a local agency. There was a long waiting list for such services, and by the time Imal saw a family therapist, his behaviors were well entrenched in the family system.

Upon obtaining a detailed family history, the therapist recognized Imal's behavior as a classic pattern that single-parent youths are at high risk to follow. Because of a family configuration that was first widely recognized following the work of Minuchin (1974), Imal was able to negotiate between his mother and grandmother until he had practically no supervision or rules. J'wan, who worked full time as a nurse, and Shonda, who took care of a number of neighborhood children, competed for this young man's attention and affection. Continually, Imal successfully played off one of these adults against another, until he had cleverly worked himself into a situation where he was almost totally without any adult restraints. He slept at either house, depending on his mood and whims and who was willing, at any particular time, to offer the least restrictive environment. Usually, this was the grandmother, who often gave Imal spending money as an inducement to stay at her house and assist with chores.

Imal would soon grow tired of his grandmother's somewhat domineering ways, and then would return to his mother, who lived a few blocks away. When the mother would try to regulate his behavior, he would return to his grandmother, who would initially indulge him and then gradually enforce rules. Once rules were enforced, Imal, like most teenagers who might be in this situation, would return to his mother who was willing to allow him a honeymoon period in order to court his affections. A very stable but pathological family system had evolved in just a manner of months.

Had this been the only problem in this family, behavioral interventions or even psychoeduction might have solved the predicament. But the dynamics of this family were deeper. Anytime J'wan began to be interested in having a life outside the house or her work, Imal would hurtfully complain to his grandmother, who would always side with him. This would empower Imal to disobey his mother and also would act to rein in his mother from contact outside the family.

Two processes were operating in this system to create this pathological condition. First was Imal's manipulations. Second, and probably harder to treat, was the fact that the both Imal and the grandmother responded to J'wan's desires for outside affiliation by attempting to restrict these behaviors. Both apparently felt threatened by J'wan's church activities and any men that she might meet. At this point, J'wan had figured out more of the family dynamics than many therapists might have. She was angry with her son and mother, and threatened to "just tell that boy he has to stay with her and can't come back," although both she and the therapist knew that she would probably never make this decision.

To upset this family stability, the therapist proposed a somewhat paradoxical intervention. Identical sets of rules were advanced and accepted for both the mother's and the grandmother's households. However, rules were only to be enforced during the first 48 hours of Imal's stay at either house. Following that, he could do as he pleased, and stay out as long as he wanted. Furthermore, for two days, neither member could undercut each other's authority. With a great deal of coaching, the family was able to maintain the "48-hour" adherence to mutual rules. This strategy reduced the ability of Shonda to control J'wan's church and dating activities, since she couldn't "out-nice" J'wan to gain control over Imal.

Very quickly, a crisis developed. Shonda called the therapist with what seemed like almost paranoid ideation. She was angry and almost incoherent. She accused J'wan of being on drugs and also being a lesbian, which from Shonda's cultural background, was an egregious behavior. Ironically, she also vituperously attacked her daughter's heterosexual morals, accusing her of having multiple sexual partners. She was afraid that J'wan was HIV-positive, although there was no evidence to support this fear. She also accused J'wan of being financially irresponsible and "giving all her money to that church because she's in love with that Bishop there" (who presided over the church).

The family therapist scheduled an emergency session between the mother and daughter. By this time the tension had decreased and Shonda was denying that she felt any hostility about or fear from her daughter's behaviors. The therapist then reminded her of her previous diatribe. This provoked an angry interchange between the two women. After over a half hour of arguing, Shonda stated that her real fears were that J'wan would enter another abusive relationship. Apparently, several of her boyfriends had severely beaten her, a behavior somewhat normalized by the relationship that J'wan had with her abusive father.

When the therapist pointed out to Shonda that her own husband had been the first person to physically abuse J'wan, the mother began to cry uncontrollably. She stated that she realized that she had "messed up" J'wan's life by allowing her to be beaten by her late husband. "I know I ruined her for men and I don't want to hurt her again." Following this, Shonda revealed to her daughter that she also had been physically abused in childhood and that this is why she had allowed her late husband to be so violent with their own children. At that point both mother and daughter began to sob uncontrollably at this new insight.

The therapist suggested that J'wan obtain counseling from a local women's network, since she might be at high risk for other abusive relationships. He also suggested that Shonda seek similar therapy. Finally, a few more sessions were scheduled to help maintain consistent behavior toward Imal.

One year after these interventions, Imal's behavior continued to improve. Both his mother and grandmother benefited from support groups and psychoeducational interventions designed to alert them of dysfunctional patterns in their relationships, due to histories of early physical abuse. J'wan realized that in some cases her mother's fears, while exaggerated, had a spark of truth. J'wan, like her mother, tended to become involved with men who were abusive. Although she is not dating now, J'wan remains active in her church, without generating any inappropriate concern from her mother.

It is not hard to destabilize families that are exhibiting dysfunctional behaviors. In fact, supervisors are constantly reminded of the difficulty that they face in reining in student trainees who seem overpowered with the ability to disrupt family processes. However, what is difficult to teach the recently empowered trainee is that there are often vast differences in outcomes following family destabilizations. Some work, others do not. Still others produce unpredictable "side effects," which sometimes can be worse than the original symptoms that prompted the family to seek treatment. The following case studies illustrate how destabilization can occur. One case had a relatively positive outcome, the other a more negative one.

CASE 1

Robert and Anita Fineman, both 47, were rapidly rising professionals. Robert was a corporate attorney who traveled frequently throughout the world and was home less than one week a month. Anita was a dermatologist, with a large, demanding, practice. The couple had one child, Nathan, age nine, who had been in psychoanalytically oriented treatment for three years following the death of his older sister, who had died of cancer.

At age eight, Nathan, who spent many hours with his grandparents when his parents were working, tried to kill himself. Although his attempted method—jumping off a one-story roof—had a low chance of lethality, the family was justifiably concerned and took him to an emergency room for treatment of cuts and for evaluation. Following this, he was psychiatrically hospitalized for a month and symptoms remitted somewhat. Still, the child appeared chronically depressed, morose, and extraordinarily serious. One of his physicians somewhat cruelly nicknamed him "Little Father Time," after the strikingly melancholy young lad who killed himself in a Thomas Hardy novel.

Nathan's case was so severe that he was started on antidepressants, which was rare at this time for children. These drugs had little apparent effect and after he was discharged from the hospital, his depression increased. A few months later, his suicidal thoughts also increased. The attending physician even considered electroshock therapy, but rejected it on a child so young. At the advice of the analyst who was somewhat desperate, the parents entered family-oriented treatment. Nathan was also briefly rehospitalized.

After obtaining a history and talking with the couple, it became clear to the therapist that they didn't really know each other and that their marriage was more perfunctory than real. The therapist, a strategically oriented social worker, interpreted Nathan's depression as his own clumsy way of keeping the couple together. This was a destabilizing move. The couple were then told that they would have to make a decision if they expected Nathan to get better. Either they would have to work very hard to become a "real" family, or they would have to choose to divorce. They were given a week to think about their decision. During this week, Nathan was also discharged from the hospital, largely because his insurance had run out.

To the therapist's surprise and dismay, the couple stated the following week that they had decided to get a divorce. The therapist was worried; she hadn't planned on this response. She strongly believed that the couple had a salvageable relationship and that a divorce would be devastating to Nathan. She realized that this would represent a major, and much worse, destabilization of the family system than she had initially anticipated. Regardless, the therapist helped the couple find a divorce mediation specialist and also made plans to tell Nathan, who by now had figured out the couple's decision and was threatening suicide again.

Although Nathan's response was to become very upset, it was not necessary to hospitalize him. For the next few months, both parents spent more time with him. Within several months, the child's depression remitted, and he resumed a normal childhood. One year later, Nathan is still a serious, introverted child. Yet he jokes about his depression and states that he wants to be a child psychiatrist "to help children like me out who get sick." His grades have become very good and he now can name children in his class whom he considers to be his friends. Although the parental divorce was a major side effect from the crisis induction, this case must be considered a success.

CASE 2

Jerry and Cleo Jenkens, ages 67 and 62, were a working-class couple who had recently retired. Jerry had been a welder, while Cleo had a variety of jobs. For seven years, they had lived with their son Oscar, 37, who had sustained severe head injuries in a street crime during the mid-1980s.

Oscar was disagreeable, cantankerous, and obese. From the time Jerry and Cleo awoke each morning, all they ever saw him do was sleep and eat, vaguely watching television. Oscar hated other people and would not go outside. He refused to leave the house and became frenetic when forced to ride in a car. During the last time he had to ride somewhere, he resisted so strongly that he injured his face trying to get away. When company came over, Oscar hid in the house, once hiding behind the stove. A visiting niece did not see him once during the three days she was present.

Although Oscar's brain injuries were severe, they were not, according to his neurologists and neuropsychologist, severe enough to produce the gross behavioral deficits that he displayed. For example, he had recently developed the habit of refusing to get his own food, but instead liked to sit across the room and mutter loudly that he was hungry until someone in the household brought him what he wanted to eat. Sometimes he would urinate on the walls or floor, claiming that the toilet was too dirty to use. Individual psychotherapy and medications had been of no help, and in fact, made him worse.

The family had also been unable to follow an operant reinforcement program of behavioral management to reduce certain targeted behaviors. This failure was considered critical by Oscar's care providers, since his behavior was apparently deteriorating and his parents were intimately involved in the cycle. The behavioral psychologist who treated the family had noted that the couple appeared to be sabotaging each other's efforts. If Jerry fulfilled the rigid requirements of record keeping and operant reinforcement during one day, Cleo would ruin the treatment, "accidentally." The reverse might be true the following day, with Cleo's efforts being exemplary and Jerry the one to blame. Regardless, Oscar kept getting fatter and lazier; for the first time, a physician had suggested that Adult Protective Services might need to step into the family and mandate Oscar to an alternative living arrangement. As a last step, the couple saw a family therapist following their failure to implement this behavioral program.

The family therapist, an extremely competent provider, took a careful and detailed history. He determined that Oscar held too much power in the family system. The long-suffering parents had gradually ceded almost all control to Oscar, even though the man was brain damaged. Yet the parents were unable to realize this, at least on an emotional level, and couldn't stand the idea of "being strict." Both parents felt guilt over Oscar's injuries and the fact that they hadn't done more to rehabilitate him. Another child had died of heart disease, largely due to obesity and hypertension and the parents felt Oscar had little time left. Therefore, "we might as well indulge him" as the father noted to the incredulous therapist.

The therapist knew that he needed to destabilize this dysfunctional relationship. He was able to get the parents to allow Oscar to be hospitalized for extensive medical testing and for psychiatric treatment. Although Oscar's physicians had pressed for this course of action for several months, the parents had steadfastly refused. But in the meantime, one of the physicians managed to get Oscar involuntarily committed for psychiatric evaluation. What had been the family's choice was no longer optional. The family was very angry and in a crisis.

With the help of four policemen, Oscar was taken from the home by ambulance and was combative the entire way. The therapist had kept the treating physicians closely appraised of this difficult family. The physician wrote an order forbidding that the patient talk or visit with his parents, to the consternation of the therapist.

By now the couple were in an utter state of crisis and returned to the family therapist for advice. The therapist thought he might act to intensify the crisis, thereby inducing behavioral changes. He suggested that they use this time—estimated to be two weeks—to take a vacation "someplace fun." The family chose sunny Florida, a bright, festive contrast to the winter bleakness and rundown feel in the couple's own fading working-class neighborhood. Although they felt very guilty leaving Oscar, the therapist made it clear that they would not be able to visit him.

Somewhat pitifully, they acquiesced and made vacation plans. The therapist thought that the family would return after only a day or two. He would use this behavior to demonstrate how dependent the family had become on Oscar's injuries for any sense of satisfaction or well-being they derived out of life. The therapist agreed to give them weekly updates, instead of the daily information about their son that they sought. This added to the family's sense of crisis and frenzy.

To everyone's surprise, Cleo and Jerry loved Florida. Every day they would look out into the ocean lazily and reminisce about their lives. Yet even more importantly, they enjoyed being away from Oscar. They felt a burden had been lifted, exactly as the therapist had hoped. Yet things changed too fast. Within a few days, they did not miss him at all, and by the end of the first week they dreaded seeing him. They seethed with anger at themselves at how he had dominated their lives and how they had allowed themselves to be involved in his behavioral escalations.

The family's behavioral pattern probably would have been unremarkable had it not been for a chance occurrence. While in line for dinner at a popular nightspot, the couple met another couple from a neighboring town back North. They actually had met each other before, back when Oscar was in the hospital, but during the next few hours they became friends. Over drinks, they exchanged stories involving disabled children. This neighborly couple had a similar problem with a daughter who had developmental disabilities. They had successfully sued the state to force the government to find appropriate housing, other than with the couple. Not surprisingly, they were now zealous advocates of "the rights of the mentally handicapped to live alone." The couple suggested to Cleo and Jerry that since Oscar had been judicially committed to treatment, the couple could refuse to accept him back. The state would have an obligation to house him, as long as the parents did not intervene.

"After all," said their new friend, "we thought it might be cruel, but what's going to happen in a few years when one of us gets sick and dies? It's better that we start the process now . . ."

Cleo and Jerry had a sleepless night mulling over everything that their new friends had told them. Both were heavy smokers; they knew they probably had a limited life expectancy. It would be much better to make sure Oscar was ensconced in a residential facility that could take care of them after they died. And what would happen if one of them got sick and Oscar was still at home? Certainly, he would go out of his way to be even crazier, trying to get their attention. This was what the family therapist told them, so they knew it to be true.

By morning, the vacillation and anguish had ceased. The decision was clear and they were relieved. They called the family therapist and not at all sheepishly told him of their decision regarding Oscar. They were moving to Florida. Since it had been countertherapeutic to let Oscar talk with them while he was in the hospital, they couldn't see how it would be helpful for him to see them now.

The therapist was incredulous, but unable to make the couple change their minds. He realized that something had gone terribly wrong with this destabilization. Within a few days, the couple showed exactly how serious they were; they sold their house to a relative at a loss. They took the money and bought a small one-bedroom condominium in Florida next to the beach. The decision for a one-bedroom unit was deliberate. They did not want to be able to impulsively change their mind about taking Oscar back.

The parents agreed to fly North and break the news to Oscar themselves. Armed with an unshakable confidence from a recent involvement with a parents' support group, they were unflappable. Although they later both broke down in private, in public Jerry and Cleo were expressionless. Later, they would bring their own lawyer to meet with a hospital social worker and her supervisor, both of whom were in a state of panic. It was simply unthinkable that such down-to-earth people would abandon their child. Yet for each argument the social worker put forth, the carefully prepared parents had a counterargument. The parents left the meeting convinced that they were doing the right thing for everyone.

Because there was no place for Oscar to go, he stayed in a psychiatric hospital for a number of weeks. The parents maintained their silence, writing him at decreasing intervals. Oscar was then placed in several residential facilities, but failed to make an adequate adjustment to any of them. Finally, he was placed in a nursing home, to live out the rest of his life. His adjustment there was poor as well. He hoarded other patients' food and urinated in public to express his anger.

His parents used to visit him frequently, but do so only once or twice a year now. Jerry notes that seeing Oscar "seems to make everyone unhappy." Cleo bakes cookies for Oscar every week, but since Oscar is a diabetic, he is not allowed to eat them. Cleo knows this, but continues to bake them regardless.

Both Cleo and Jerry have called the therapist and told him privately that they feel extraordinary guilt, living 1,700 miles away from their head-injured son. Yet they now state that they are "too old to let him back in our lives" and despite second thoughts about their decision, still refuse to budge.

The therapist now uses this case as a training aid for his own students regarding the dangers of family destabilization. He has spent hours talking with the family, trying to ascertain their reasoning at each critical juncture in their decision-making process. However, in reviewing this case, which the therapist often does, the therapist has difficulty in determining what he would do differently.

DANGERS OF DESTABILIZATION: THE ETHICS OF CHAOS

The case of Cleo and Jerry is remarkable in that families rarely behave this poorly toward their members. Occasionally, however, it does happen, and the family therapist is advised to consider the warning. Chaos theory suggests that it is impossible to specify the effects on a system in crisis of an intervention. As the system becomes more oscillating, or chaotic, predictions become even less exact. Consequently, the potential for inadvertent, therapy-induced harm to a family system is greatest in systems that are in crisis. Oddly enough, many clinicians continue to believe that families in acute crisis should routinely be placed in further crisis, despite the observation that systems in crisis may need assuaging rather than exacerbation (L'Abate & Cox, 1992).

The dangers involved with inducing a crisis in families that do not stay in treatment is outlined more clearly in the following case study of a spectacular treatment failure:

John and Mary Kurtz were a middle-class couple in their early 40s. The couple had a history of three brief attempts at marital therapy, all occurring within the past 4 years of their 16-year marriage. Each time after "attempting" therapy, the couple terminated because the therapist was "not to our liking." The terminations all came within the first three sessions and were all unexpected by the therapists involved.

The couple began a new round of family therapy with Dr. Smith, a well-known family therapist. This new attempt occurred at the advice of their child's pediatrician. Their only child, John Jr., seven, had recently developed a school refusal syndrome that had proven retractable to behavioral interventions prescribed by the pediatrician. Previously, John Jr. had been a well-functioning, outgoing child with no noticeable behavioral deficits. An extensive physical workup also failed to find an organic basis for his disagreeableness, temper tantrums, and constant anxiety about being left alone or going to school.

During the first family session, a working hypothesis of the family's major problem became obvious to the therapist. John Sr., a rising corporate executive, was usually home less than three nights a week. Mary, a successful freelance business consultant, worked almost as many hours. Consequently, the parents were not home much, especially in the evenings. Child care was usually left to a live-in surrogate who spoke poor English and was more interested in watching television than in child rearing. When John Jr. departed for school each morning, he usually did not know when he would see his parents again. Hence, he behaved quite logically for a seven-year-old; he refused to leave for school at all.

Attempts to get him to go to school showed the couple just how much out of control a seven-year-old could be if he put his mind to such a task. John Jr. would lie on the floor screaming, only to run upstairs and hide. Once he pulled down all the dishes from the cabinets. Another time, he angrily threw the contents of the refrigerator at his parents. He had even grabbed a kitchen knife and threatened to kill his parents if they made him go to school.

Despite John Jr.'s desire to stay at home, the family's life together was an unhappy one. While at home, the parents rarely talked civilly or calmly. They were simply too tired. Occasionally they argued, mostly about child care. The subject of John Jr.'s school phobia provided one of the few occasions the parents had deeply conversed in several months.

The therapist closed the first session with a strategic intervention designed to increase family tension, though one that appeared simply to facilitate time together. He anticipated that the family would be unwilling to carry out his suggestion of spending an hour together each morning and this failure would be used therapeutically in subsequent sessions. Dr. Smith's behavioral prediction was accurate. The family effectively sabotaged any increased interaction.

During the middle of the second session, Dr. Smith made a logical (and not particularly dramatic) reframing intervention. He asked them if they thought marital affairs would have an effect on their child. Both agreed such behavior would be terrible for John Jr., and in fact, might invoke a school phobia similar to the one that he was presently displaying. The therapist then quizzed each parent regarding their extramarital affairs. Both laughed in a somewhat annoyed manner, stating they were too tired to do anything but work. The therapist then gently contradicted them, stating that their careers had become their other lovers. The parents were dumbfounded but amazed and both began crying at this seeming insight.

Dr. Smith then planned an intervention designed to boost marital intimacy and to allow both parents to spend more time with their son. Initially, the parents were highly enthused about the reframing and seemed to accept the accompanying intervention. During the third session, a more detailed plan was painstakingly drawn up to allow them to spend more time with John. However, the plan was never to be implemented. The family failed to show for the following week's session. A call to the family indicated that John Sr. "had to work late—unexpectedly" and "we were just too busy to make it tonight." The family promised to reschedule, but was vague about when they would call again.

The family was a "no show" for the next session as well. They were eventually terminated from treatment by the therapist after missing six subsequently scheduled sessions. John Jr.'s behavior continued to deteriorate, and he eventually developed an apparent agoraphobia. This was remarkable considering his young age and the fact that agoraphobia primarily affects adolescents and adults. The child was later psychiatrically hospitalized.

In the ensuing weeks, John Sr. and Mary became increasingly bitter toward one another. While John Jr. was in the hospital, the couple were coerced into another try of family therapy. During this forum, they blamed their open and mutual hostility on the "realizations we obtained with Dr. Smith." Mary stated, "I guess John made his choice, choosing his work over me and his son. That's one thing I've learned from all those therapies. . . . It's his work or me. . . . This made me understand that I just can't stay married to him." The couple later divorced, intensifying John Jr.'s problems.

Given the potential disruptiveness of many of the popular techniques in family interventions, the possibility for therapist-induced deterioration in client families is not a trivial concern (Ackerman, 1967; Haley, 1980). Clinical observations suggest that some families benefit greatly from family therapy, but that a small number eventually function worse. Therapists who perform potentially destabilizing interventions must do so with trepidation, since they have little basis to assess the riskiness of their interventions in advance (Coleman, 1985).

Yet if a given intervention fails, a family is at minimal risk provided it remains in treatment. Any adverse consequences from interventions can usually be corrected by a competent therapist. Additional interventions can be proposed and developed, with the goal of eventually targeting the family toward a desired course of action. *But this is true only if the family stays in treatment and the therapist is able to adjust treatment to emerging or unexpected problems.*

From these case histories, it becomes clear that it is ethically questionable to administer destabilizing interventions to families with a high probability of terminating treatment. The potential risks are often excessively large and it is impossible to specify with any accuracy what the effects of these interventions will be, as chaos theory has shown us.

An analogy with medical interventions may be useful. It is simply incomprehensible that a physician would perform invasive procedures or risky therapy on a patient that he or she knew would refuse follow-up and proper medical management. It should be equally incomprehensible that family therapists disrupt dysfunctional systems by invasive interventions when there is a high likelihood that the family will not submit to ongoing treatment in the management of their ensuing disequilibrium. Chaos theory tells us quite plainly that we cannot predict the effects of these interventions on such systems. If there is a reasonable probability that the family will cease treatment, then destabilization is unethical.

PREDICTING WHEN DESTABILIZATION IS COUNTERTHERAPEUTIC

Destabilization may be countertherapeutic when a family is at high risk to drop out of treatment. Yet too few empirical attempts have been made to identify families at high risk for termination or deterioration in family therapy. One exception has been the work of McCown and Johnson (1993), who have investigated the conditions that are necessary and sufficient for family therapy-induced deterioration of functioning. Using traditional linear model statistics, these researchers were able to identify a subset of families who terminated treatment early, based on the not-too-surprising variable of past history. Between 10% and 30% of the variance in early termination could be explained, depending on specific clinics that were sampled (smaller variance was accounted for in a cross-validation). This low number is not surprising. Termination itself is somewhat chaotic. Too many variables probably interact to produce this outcome, with variables shifting in importance depending on what phase of therapy is ongoing.

McCown and Johnson (1993) have developed a specific technique of crisis intervention and family systems consultation designed for family systems in crisis that may be likely to terminate early. Labeled ADEPT, this method is based on several strategies:

1. Lowering, rather than increasing the family tensions that may prompt early termination.
2. Prepping the family for more extensive therapy by enabling them through enactment of minor changes.
3. Pursuing aggressive problem solving or "first order changes" until the family has demonstrated a commitment to therapy.
4. Encouraging the family to accept responsibility for treatment termination.

Families are also invited to make use of potentially stabilizing resources such as other functional family members, church, self-help groups, and other persons or groups that can decrease the family's frequent crisis-proneness. The therapist using such a system avoids performing interventions that could result in a decrease in family functioning if the family abruptly terminates at any time.

Other authors have recommended potentially innocuous but powerful interventions for resistant family systems that can be applied to families in crisis with a high probability of early termination. L'Abate (1986; L'Abate & Cox, 1992) advocates the use of structured paratherapeutic writing for many family systems. L'Abate illustrates how these techniques can be applied to specific problems likely to be encountered in families that may terminate early such as lack of family intimacy, families with lack of communication, impulsiveness of IPs, and substance abuse problems. Structured writing assignments rarely provoke family crisis and disharmony. Their risk is quite low, while their potential is large. This class of interventions may be a treatment of choice for families unlikely to return past the first session or two. It contains the energy of the family system, where adding more energy would precipitate early termination. We view that energy in these families places them at an evolved state of complexity—teetering on the edge of chaos. As Kauffman (1993, 1995) notes, maintaining complexity that evolves into self-organization is less risky developmentally than going through chaos and self-organization. Therefore, we conceptualize early terminations of this sort as pushing the family into chaos without containment toward functional adaptation. Attending to the boundaries we suggest earlier will aid therapists in detecting when this might be the case.

As shown in previous chapters, it is often necessary to spark a recalcitrant system into a deep change. We believe, however, that such change should be evoked most cautiously and only after considering possible consequences, which according to chaos theory, may be impossible to predict. Reframings, strategic interventions, structural rearrangement, and other potentially antagonizing techniques are probably more likely to *work with a family that has adequate rapport, trust, and experience with a therapist.* In other words, this is a family that has consented to ongoing treatment. *Perhaps one of the most unethical services we perform for our client families is fitting extraordinarily difficult systems into brief models that state change will be quick and relatively painless.* This simply is not so!

CHAOTIC SYSTEMS AND DESTABILIZATION: BEYOND LINEAR PREDICTIONS

Using traditional linear statistical techniques, we are able to accurately predict early termination about one tenth of the time. If premature termination was a low base-rate phenomenon, like homicide, such a forecasting inability would be satisfactory. However, early termination is quite common; in some cases, more than half the families that are seen by therapists in particular settings quit treatment against the therapist's advice (McCown & Johnson, 1993). As clinicians, we face an ethical dilemma.

Destabilization is a very powerful technique and sometimes necessary intervention, but it also may have tremendous side effects. The side effects cannot be predicted in advance but may frequently be corrected providing families stay in treatment. Yet we are not able to predict whether families will stay in treatment. *Therefore, is it ever therapeutically indicated to destabilize a family system?*

One of the contributions of chaos theory is to suggest that we can do better than the preceding predictions based on the linear model regarding early termination. Chaos theory can give us a theoretical rationale for when it is and isn't appropriate to destabilize a family system that will reduce the amount of iatrogenic (healer induced) difficulties (Morgan, 1983). Chaos theory can help us approximate when our interventions may have unpredictable results.

This enhanced prediction that chaos theory allows us may seem ironic. Abraham and Shaw (1992) note one of the paradoxes of chaos theory that is relevant to the prediction of the therapeutic effects of destabilization: An understanding of chaos both enhances and limits our knowledge of complex systems. Our knowledge may be enhanced because we are aware there are often hidden patterns amid apparent randomness. Unexplainable occurrences, formerly believed due largely to chance and error variance, are looked at as potentially ordered phenomena (Moon, 1992). In this manner, we heighten our knowledge and understanding of the *general behavior* of complex systems, *although our capacity to make specific predictions may be limited.* More directly, as Abraham and Shaw note, qualitative descriptions may be made more accurately, even with the realization that direct quantitative descriptions are meaningless.

The clue to using chaos theory in understanding the appropriateness of destabilization is the by now well-known concept of sensitivity to initial conditions. Research has shown that this unpredictability and sensitivity to initial conditions in complex systems are especially likely to occur when systems are undergoing a *transitional phase of instability* (Abraham, Abraham, & Shaw, 1990). Although we may speak probablistically about the behavior of complex systems, chaos theory demonstrates—as the mathematician Poincaré demonstrated almost 100 years ago—that it is not mathematically feasible to make long-term, accurate predictions of many complex nonlinear systems (Waldrop, 1992). *The more unstable the system is, the less accurate our numerical predictions regarding the system's future behavior are likely to be* (Casti, 1992). Furthermore, instability is most apt to increase the effects of unpredictability when the system is at a critical point of transition. While we can describe the general *shape* of the behavior graphically, or illustrate its general and probable range, we cannot predict any complex system's behavior with accuracy (Abraham & Shaw, 1992). Such systems, as Poincaré showed, always have the capacity for generating the unpredictable behavior we now call chaos (Moon, 1992).

A principal application in applying chaos theory to family therapy is that *family transitional points* are where there is the most sensitivity to initial conditions. In other words, at specific and identifiable critical periods in a family history, families may be extraordinarily influenced by very small events, which may have extreme and unpredictable implications for future family functioning. *It is at these critical points where destabilization is to be avoided.*

CRITICAL DEVELOPMENTAL BIFURCATIONS: A RISK ASSESSMENT

How do we determine *critical developmental bifurcations?* One way might be to examine the family therapy literature. There are numerous developmental models regarding family functioning, all of which have heuristic value. Yet families are complex systems and are too diverse for us to postulate that each goes through identical and necessary developmental sequences. The traditional models assume that families are particularly vulnerable at certain times such as at childbirth, entering of school of the children, adolescence, when children are leaving home, at the transition to retirement and at the death of a member. This usually is the case, but sometimes it is not. Models are heuristic, meant to guide and educate, but not to limit our constructions of reality. Whether a particular model is applicable to a specific family is a complex question. Often a model may be applicable at a specific time, but not at another time in the family's developmental history. A model may also produce iatrogenic harm if the therapist follows it so rigidly that he or she observes or creates pathology that others would not find.

For the chaos theorist, a better way of determining whether a family is at a point where members are likely to be particularly sensitive to initial conditions involves evaluating the emergence of symptoms, in terms of length and severity. *The hypothesis here is that if symptoms appear suddenly and without substantial buildup, they are generated by a family system that is undergoing significant levels of instability.* This concept is not new, and actually was rooted in the work of several family systems theorists, including Jackson (1965) and Haley (1980). We can state now, however, that such families are likely to be exquisitely sensitive to initial conditions and hence since they are at a critical developmental bifurcation there is greater chance that the destabilizing intervention may have untoward effects.

The following family therapy failures illustrate the danger in applying family destabilization when symptoms are newly emergent.

CASE 1

Jim and Eric were a gay couple who lived in a fashionable area in a large city. The couple had been together for approximately seven years, in a relationship that Jim called "totally faithful" and Eric labeled as "monogamous most of the time." Together, the couple had purchased and refurbished an expensive home. They had even talked about adopting a child. In the eyes of their friends, they were a "perfect couple" and no one expected them to have more than an occasional quarrel.

The couple sought treatment when Jim found out that Eric no longer had orgasms during receptive anal intercourse. As Jim noted, "I know it's irrational to be bothered by something so stupid. But one of the things that was so special about our lovemaking was that [the fact that they were able to experience orgasm simultaneously]. I'm just so hurt now, and I know it doesn't make sense . . . I just feel like I am falling out of love and I'm scared." Not surprisingly, Eric became very insecure when he heard this, increasing his sense of guilt and anger at himself for a process that he felt he could not control. Anger and guilt spiraled, resulting in the decision to seek help.

The couple's therapist was well known for his ability to treat resistant families by his reliance on applying pressure until the families experienced severe crises. Then, according to the therapist's account, "I get down in the trenches and help them reorganize." However, he had little experience offering reassurance and information and even less experience working with gay men. The idea that a gay couple could break up over something seemingly as trivial—at least to a heterosexual male—was beyond his belief. Given his orientation and training, it was perfectly rational that the therapist searched for a deeper meaning to the symptoms.

The therapist tried the techniques he knew best: strategic interventions that were rich in metaphors. He conjured that the couple had lost capacity for intimacy because of an emphasis on sexuality. This would serve the function of avoiding a public relationship commitment, something the couple's families were adamantly against. The therapist attempted to induce crises through a number of actions, including having both partners tell their parents that their sexual orientations were "permanent," something neither was prepared to do. Both sets of parents harbored the common illusion that their children's gay experiences were simply phases of development that they would outgrow. Homosexual commitment was very threatening to the parents, since it implied that the sexual orientations were not going to change.

The couple had a family meeting where they affirmed their commitment to each other in the presence of their parents. Yet they felt more embarrassment and pain than ever. The intervention did not help. Tension increased as did hopelessness. For a time, they stopped speaking to one another and had a few casual sexual relationships. Therapy obviously was not working. The couple's lives became miserable, with bouts of constant distrust punctuated by periods of bickering and self criticisms.

While discussing the case with a colleague, a gay psychiatrist, the psychiatrist suggested that the couple should be evaluated by a physician who specializes in diseases of gay men. The therapist suggested this to the couple, and a physical exam revealed that Eric had a slight prostate infection. With rest and medication, he was cured. Moreover, the physician was able to educate the couple about the decreased likelihood of orgasm from passive anal intercourse with increasing age. This allayed both of their fears, since both had been concerned about pleasing the other partner, but lacked the necessary information that they needed regarding physiological functioning.

In retrospect, the therapist learned an important lesson beyond the obvious failure fostered by cultural insensitivities: Don't look for deep metaphors or induce crises when symptoms have a sudden onset.

This case involves a physical problem, but the general principle it illustrates is true regardless of the type of presenting problem. Crisis inducement is counterindicated when a symptom has appeared suddenly. How long is "suddenly"? We still do not know, but operate on a rule of thumb of six months for adults and three months for adolescents (American Psychiatric Association, 1994). A shorter periods for adolescents is based on the fact that they often have transitory dysfunctional behavior. It is almost routine for identities and strong feelings to be shifted frequently. Perseveration of a particular symptom for a extended period is usually more significant in this age group.

The second case, involving an adolescent, illustrates the preceding point. Like the case of Eric and Jim, it is remarkable because of the therapist's cultural insensitivity. Yet beyond this, it is another example of how the sudden onset of symptoms indicates that a family is sensitive to initial conditions and that family crises should not be induced:

CASE 2

David was a 15-year-old Orthodox Jewish adolescent who lived with his mother and father in an orthodox neighborhood, a very homogenous *shtetlach* where remnants of Yiddish are often spoken in addition to Hebrew and English. Like all the males his age, he attended *yeshiva*, an orthodox day school, and walked to Saturday services at *shul*, where he constantly heard *musser*, or pleas for greater religious devotions. Sometimes he slept through these lengthy and often pedantic services, but generally he paid attention, as most boys his age were expected to do.

One day David decided he had simply had enough of his family's orthodoxy. Like many decisions of adolescents, this one appeared "out of the blue," shocking his devout family. There was no apparent precipitant. While David agreed that he would follow the *Halakah*, he told his parents that according to his interpretation of the Talmud, he alone was responsible for his spiritual observances. From this point forward, he would no longer keep *kosher* and would play sports on *Shabbes*, or the Sabbath. Worse, he stated that he would shed the ritualistic garb that the family wore, stating that it had "nothing to do with true religion . . ."

In most families it is realized that adolescents frequently make decisions that offend their parents. Yet this decision struck at the heart of the family system, which was defined by its religiousness and adherence to Orthodox rules. It sparked several days of arguments in the family's house, culminating in David's refusal to attend *shul* (school). But David's parents were worried for more than one reason. His older brother, Alan, a brilliant graduate student in mathematics, had recently experienced a schizophrenic break. Alan's first symptoms were a general oppositionality to everything in his culture that was Jewish. This progressed to a full-blown thought disorder that required his hospitalization. Alan's prognosis was still unclear and he had to quit graduate school, at least for a semester. The parents feared that David might be next.

At the advice of David's physician, the family took him to a mental health professional, a family therapist with little experience treating or even understanding the experience of Orthodox Jews in America. The family was reluctant to talk with this provider, but their health maintenance organization, which insured the family, gave them little choice among providers. Although the therapist herself was Jewish, her involvement with religion was admittedly nominal. She probably had less in common with David's family than she would have with a middle-class Episcopalian clan.

By the time the family entered treatment, David and his father had been verbally exchanging insults for 18 long days. The father's cajoling just made David more recalcitrant, while David's oppositionality simply made the father more antagonistic and worried. There was constant tension in the home that seemed to spill over to behavioral disturbances in David's younger sister, age 10.

The therapist's conceptualization of the family's dynamics was that David was appropriately rebelling against cultural constraints placed on him by his Orthodox parents, much as her own grandparents had done. The therapist wanted to interrupt this cycle by inducing a crisis. She had quite a bit of therapeutic success in using similar tactics with families of bulimics and anorexics. Using Breunlin's (1989) theory of family transitions, she sought to paradoxically encourage the father's *absolute* insistence that the son follow cultural and religious rules. Her goal was to broaden the conflict beyond the religious domain, with the hope of encouraging a family breakdown. During this intended crisis, the therapist planned that the family would be able to renegotiate their roles, perhaps with the help of strategic therapy interventions, such as meeting together with a rabbi.

The father, who was basically a reasonable and easygoing man, felt awkward in the role of a religious authoritarian. He believed in dialogue and hoped the family would be able to resolve "David's problems" through a slower process. Nevertheless, the therapist convinced the father that this new course of action was absolutely necessary. The father, very trusting of the therapist, agreed to be a "hard liner."

At the same time that they planned this intervention, however, David felt considerable guilt and rumination about his behavior toward his father. Parental disrespect was not part of his value system and once he realized how he was acting toward his father, he quickly began to recant. As rapidly as his "symptoms" started, they stopped. He again became a typical conforming, Orthodox youth. Yet his father was unable to "turn off" his own overbearingness (which had been prompted, in large part by the family therapist), attributing his son's change of attitude to a sudden strictness and reinforced seriousness toward religion. The father began to assume this attitude to other family members as well, believing that what had saved his son was his own stern piousness.

Having lost a major battle with his father, David quietly acquiesced. During the next few months, he became deeply depressed, perhaps because of the lack of parental kindness that he was used to, and the fact that his father was increasingly inaccessible and stern. David's mother told the therapist that since they had first sought treatment, she felt increasingly alienated from her husband, whose newly found and rigid interpretations of their Orthodox faith she could not understand. Finally, tension increased between David's sister and her father, resulting in the onset of a number of apparently psychosomatic symptoms.

While Cases 1 and 2 share hegemonic therapeutic practices (Bütz, 1995b), their suddenly emerging symptoms were also treated unsuccessfully by crisis induction techniques. From a conceptualization furnished by chaos theory, we can surmise the following:

1. A problem in the system emerged suddenly (perturbation or bifurcation).
2. This problem was poorly dealt with by the system (period-doubling route to chaos).
3. Adding strain to such a system overwhelmed the system's capacity for self-organization (chaos).
4. It was impossible to predict whether such an intervention would have a negative impact, because the system was especially sensitive to initial conditions, which could not be predicted or fully known.

This may seem like a contradiction to our attempts to add chaos to chaotic systems discussed in Chapter 7. While the case with Jim and Eric was clearly a misattributed instrumental crisis, that with proper treatment would have ameliorated, we have, on the other hand, the case of David. This was clearly a perceptual crisis that called for a "hands off" approach to allow a relatively healthy family to self-organize. The critical distinction here is "don't fix what ain't broken!"

GUIDELINES FROM CHAOS THEORY
CONCERNING CRISIS INDUCTION

Probably the best guideline from any adherent of chaos theory is that all guidelines are flexible (Freeman, 1995). Family therapists should know this quite well. All families are different. Circumstances are infinitely different and complex. Hence we are reticent to prescribe guidelines, for fear that they will be taken as "divine writ." Consider the following as "highly useful suggestions" for therapeutic practice.

A first suggestion, discussed at length in this chapter, is that it is dangerous to destabilize systems that will drop out of treatment. As chaos theory shows us, it is impossible to accurately predict who will and won't drop out of treatment. Certainly nonlinear factors are at work in determining which families quit treatment. However, even though we share a general distrust of many things linear, it is foolish to disregard what we already know. Families with a history of terminating treatment early should not be treated with crisis-inducing methods. While naive therapists may make the attribution that "destabilization is an established technique and should be used," therapists of this sort will likely invoke unpredictability also to justify not understanding appropriate use of therapeutic interventions. As we will discuss in Chapter 10, however, family therapists would do well to consider the credo of "do no harm."

A second suggestion is that destabilizing a system that is already in crisis is risky, especially for perceptual crises. Few practitioners, unless they are working with persons in the hospital, are willing to do so and for good reason. Chaos theory suggests that it is impossible to specify the effects of a therapeutic intervention on a rapidly cycling family system. As the system becomes more oscillating, or chaotic, predictions become even less exact. Consequently, the potential for inadvertent, therapy-induced harm to a family system is greatest for systems in crisis. Oddly enough, many clinicians continue to believe that families in acute crisis should be placed in further crisis, despite the observation that systems in crisis need assuaging rather than exacerbation (L'Abate, 1992).

A final suggestion, directly attributable to chaos theory, is that destabilization is most likely to be adverse to a system that is entering a transition from one state to another (Garfinkel, 1987). This is what we have called a critical developmental bifurcation. In other words, sensitivity to initial conditions is maximized during transitional states, including mental states or periods of adjustment (Langs, 1992). Behavioral patterns of families that have been rather stable and show no signs of changing are not as likely to be disrupted as patterns that are new, experimental, or have not been in the family's behavioral repertoire for a long period. Families who are at transitional points are apt to be disrupted by more minor changes and may, like other complex systems, begin to behave wildly erratically and inconsistently. We speak of these families or any other system functioning in this matter as being on the verge of chaos.

For many years, clinicians have recognized that certain families may be at strategic change points, or ready to modify their behaviors on their own. Chaos theory now gives us an explanation for why this is so. Behavior of complex systems is not linear, but ever changing. At certain periods, especially those marked by transition, systems will be especially sensitive to outside agents or internal sentiments that otherwise were ignored. These systems may use this energy to self-organize on their own (Kauffman, 1993), a concept that has been known at least since Satir's work (1967), but is now only being discussed in the world of hard sciences.

As clinicians, our job is to foster this change. Yet our dilemma is that we cannot always predict the results of our interventions. Chaos theory suggests as a general guide that induction of crises is counterindicated for symptoms recently emerged.

CHAPTER 9

The Critical Moment

IN PREVIOUS chapters, we have described how ideas from chaos and complexity theory may be applied to the dynamics of family therapy. These concepts have included sensitive dependence on initial conditions (Lorenz, 1963), the edge of chaos (Kauffman, 1995), strange attractors (Ruelle & Takens, 1971), and self-organization (Jantsch, 1980; Prigogine & Stengers, 1984). Here, the focus will be on two case studies that describe the ability of families to transcend chaos, and even suicide. Each case study will depict a period of a family's development from a self-organizing perspective: In one case, we will follow the family from a bifurcation point through self-organization; whereas in the other, we will describe a family in chaos, and its subsequent self-organization. One case is actually a collage of three families that have been in therapy over the past four years in one of our practices, and the other family comes to us out of another coauthor's practice. As stated earlier many times, in each case names, ages, and circumstances have been altered to maintain the confidentiality of these clients. While each therapist worked from a somewhat different theoretical orientation, the process is similar in terms of global dynamics, but not the point in time or with reference to intrafamilial dynamics.

BIFURCATIONS: AN INDICATOR
OF A FAMILY'S HISTORY

At each bifurcation point in our system's past, a flux occurred in which many futures existed . . . one future was chosen and the other possibilities vanished forever. Thus our bifurcation points constitute a map of the irreversibility of time. (Briggs & Peat, 1989, pp. 144–145)

Bifurcation points are the history of a system's life, and like the branch of a tree, may describe the degree of stress the system was under. However, they serve only as historical markers, and as such they do not indicate a future. Approximation of what the system will do next is "the best one can do."

> Bifurcation points are the milestones in the system's evolution; they crystallize the system's history. . . . in bifurcations the past is continually recycled, held timeless in a sense—for by stabilizing through feedback the bifurcation path it takes, a system embodies the exact conditions of the environment at the moment the bifurcation occurred. (Briggs & Peat, 1989, pp. 144–145)

Bifurcations are "forks in the road" that on examination reveal the irreversible path cut by the system over time. Where are family therapists able to look for bifurcations in family systems? In the history, of course. As described in Chapter 3, understanding the role of stability and its transitory nature is important in working with change processes. As we have discussed, of equal importance is recognizing that each system has its own unique stability that may be radically different from the stability of other systems:

> You could add noise to this system, jiggle it, stir it up, interfere with its motion, and then when everything settled down, the transients dying away like echoes in a canyon, the system would return to the same peculiar pattern of irregularity as before. (Gleick, 1987, p. 48)

Reviewing a family's history will indicate if its communication and behavior have been stable as well as at what times in its history the system has bifurcated as is grossly demonstrated in genograms (McGoldrick & Gerson, 1988). The key here is information, the flow of information that constitutes the boundary of the system:

> In fact, matter and energy literally flow through it and form it, like the river water through a vortex. On the other hand, this very openness somehow makes the structure resistant to change. (Briggs & Peat, 1984, p. 169)

This description comes from Briggs and Peat's elaboration of Prigogine's idea of the dissipative structure, which lives "out" at far-from-equilibrium. While cryptic, this is a pretty good description of a self-organizing system that has a boundary, though like phrase space, informational boundaries, and movement boundaries, it is difficult to perceive unless we have a context. Briggs and Peat introduce dissipative structures, which we believe are similar to families, in this manner:

> The name comes from the fact that to keep their shape these structures must constantly dissipate entropy so it won't build up inside the entity and "kill" it with equilibrium. To dissipate entropy requires a constant input of energy and new materials, which is why dissipative structures must form in energy-filled, far-from-equilibrium situations (a vortex wouldn't form in a still pond). (1984, p. 169)

So, for families not to be "killed" by maximum entropy, *information must flow through it*. Thus, the criticality of the difference between describing systems as open versus closed. Indeed, a fully closed system, like our horse in Theoretical Construct 2 (see Chapter 2), would die very quickly without new information and/or sources of energy (hay for the horse). But, how do we explain family systems that appear to be closed? Remembering the Circumplex Model, there is definitely a region where rigid or enmeshed families are cut off from sources of information. Therefore, their information boundary will be attenuated, whereas open systems have freely flowing amounts of information available.

When a system self-organizes, this new level of organization may be seen as emerging from the system's ability to move beyond its previous parameters of existence. There, it gains new information enabling it to adapt to the destabilizing element it had "run up against" during this change period in its evolution. The key element here is *new information* found through chaotic behavior that allows the system to become more complex and more adaptive in the face of novel situations or stimuli: "Prigogine says, 'This mixture of necessity and chance constitutes the history of the system.' It also constitutes the system's creativity. The ability of a system to amplify a small change is a creative lever" (Briggs & Peat, 1989, p. 145).

Seeking solutions beyond previous bounds is a creative process that Prigogine describes in biological systems. Surely creativity must also be expected in family systems. We contend that families develop through a similar process. Enlarging our context for a moment, we believe that families evolve in cooperation with other social entities around them, nations, communities, and even therapists. There, solutions are found together as systems coevolve (Gibney, 1987). Coevolution says that changes which take place on the microscale instantaneously effect changes on the macroscale and the reverse. Neither really "causes" the other in the usual sense (Briggs & Peat, 1984, p. 194).

Using these premises as a framework, perhaps we will be able to better understand the experience of our families in this chapter.

CASE 1: THE "COLLAGE" FAMILY

This collage family is an Euro-American lower-middle-class single-parent family. The family's nucleus is made up of four members who share the household, a mother, two boys and one girl, depicted in the genogram shown in Figure 9.1. The family is involved with a number of social service agencies, school officials, and mental health professionals. Both the mother, Sue, and the children, Chris, Joe, and Peggy respectively, have extensive psychiatric histories.

Our involvement begins with the family when they request a psychiatric evaluation for Joe, the middle child. The mother is concerned about Joe's preoccupation with *hurting himself*. He presents with some vegetative signs of depression, and an amorphous plan for self-harm. While intensive outpatient therapy and partial hospitalization were given as therapeutic options, Sue chose partial hospitalization. As part of the treatment process, family therapy is broached, only to find that while each member has been in individual therapy and more restrictive environments, family therapy has never been initiated. After consultation with previous therapists and agencies, no reason can be found for family therapy's absence as a treatment modality. The respective individual therapists involved opt for conducting this therapy at the psychiatric hospital in conjunction with the partial hospitalization program. In a treatment team meeting conducted before Joe begins the partial hospitalization program, one team member remembers the family from a year before and comments, "They were doing so well last year."

The members of the adolescent treatment team began reviewing the history (which included the psychiatric evaluation and treatment summaries obtained from different agencies and therapists) provided as the case was

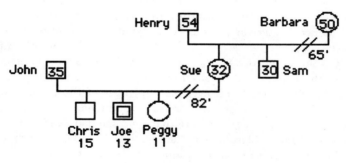

Figure 9.1   The Collage Family.

presented. The presentation revealed that John, the father of all three children, had been unavailable to the family since the divorce 10 years earlier. He now lives several states away, and the only contact he has with the children is a phone call about once a year that Sue tolerates "for the sake of the kids." Sue has not been romantically involved with anyone in the past several years and appears to be avoiding intimate social contact with others in her peer group. She works as a home care nurse where she is often isolated. She is most closely aligned with her mother, Barbara, who, like Sue, divorced her husband shortly after the birth of her last child. Both Henry and Sam, Sue's father and brother respectively, do not have strong family ties. Both live several states away, and have not had contact with either generation for several years now. Sue and Barbara live in the same town, and Sue spends a great deal of time at her mother's house, especially under stressful situations. While on these visits she brings her daughter, Peggy, and has since she was very young. The boys are left at home.

In the evaluation, Joe, the identified client, complained that his mother either "isn't around" or "she looks at all my stuff." While Chris, the oldest boy, echoed these complaints, he appeared detached and unavailable to the immediate situation. Meanwhile, Peggy remained close to her mother, mirroring the majority of her mother's actions. Joe stated that he is angry with his mother for shuffling through his room, and intermittently not being home "when I do need her."

Sue listened in the evaluation with nearly flat affect, and responded in "fits and starts" to Joe's statements and Chris's lack of involvement, stating "pay attention." The subsequent retorts from the boys inspired a volume audible several rooms away. Now Sue's affect was animated. Neither Sue, nor the boys, seemed to register a word the other was saying. Meanwhile, the volume went up to a level that was uncomfortable for the therapist. Apparently, the family was used to communicating at this volume. At one quiet moment, Chris simply walked out of the evaluation room and other family members appeared to "shut down" in his absence. The volume of the session decreased, Sue and Peggy began to talk between themselves as the therapist attempted to continue the evaluation addressing Joe and then Sue. When Chris returned 15 minutes later, the high volume of their communication quickly resumed over discrepancies in the history. With each question in the evaluation, there was this "fit and start" quality, where periods of dead silence or side conversations contrasted with exceptionally high volume exchanges. Forty-five minutes into the evaluation, Sue lamented quietly and again with little affect, "We were okay until a few months ago."

So the therapist asked if anything significant had transpired a few months ago. Blank faces fell over each member of the family except for Peggy. Like her mother, she responded without much affect, "Grandma moved near us." Apparently, before that time she had lived some 30 miles away on the "other side of town," even a bit, 20 miles, outside of town. Given the poor condition of Sue's automobile, they had only attempted a visit once a week or during stressful situations. Now, Sue and Peggy saw her almost daily for hours at a time.

It should be mentioned that some general evaluation questions revealed that Sue, Chris, and Joe showed minimal signs of substance abuse, gave no history of sexual abuse, but some mention was made of loud and physical fights that had occurred while Sue and John were married. A similar history was noted between Sue's parents. No current thought disorders were described, although both Sue and Joe have had inpatient hospitalizations with diagnoses featuring some auditory hallucinations and some delusional content that abated with time.

So what did this family look like when it was relatively stable? As mentioned earlier, a member of the treatment team and Sue recalled they were "doing so well" a year prior. We might venture a guess that this state continued until several months ago when Barbara moved closer to the family. It turns out that, while somewhat disengaged, the boys had more contact with their mother. So we may begin to look at different aspects of the history to find out how well the boys were functioning.

As mentioned, the family was well connected with a number of social service agencies. These agencies functioned as containing elements that kept the family stable following Joe's past hospitalization (Bütz, 1993b). We see this type of "containing" approach also used with chaotic systems (Ditto & Pecora, 1993; Neff & Carroll, 1993; Strogatz & Stewart, 1994) where either coupling or slowly limiting the parameters of a chaotic system's behavior assists it organizing, as discussed in Chapter 3.

As a result of Joe's previous hospitalization, Sue had gained some new parenting skills through a psychoeducational class. In addition, Joe had resolved a number of issues around his father's absence. While there were obviously other factors, these two additions to the family's coping abilities in conjunction with the social service agencies' coupling and containment served to move the family into a new stability at that time.

Once Barbara moved within close proximity of the family, this stability was challenged. Barbara acted as a new element in the family's environment with which they had to cope or adapt. However, based on earlier family dynamics (Sue's enmeshment with Barbara), the family as a whole adapted poorly. The new dynamics led to the boys' alienation, and Sue's withdrawal from some of the helpful interventions from social service agencies. While interventions continued at school for the boys, Sue's preoccupation with her mother limited her attention to supporting continued therapeutic activities. The key element in the family system had withdrawn—Sue. Subsequently, the boys were left to their own devices, and Chris, an already somewhat distant member, moved further away from the

family toward his peers leaving Joe alone. Sue vacillated between neglect-
ing Joe or being intrusive with him, and Chris began to constellate as the
gradually disappearing father figure in the family's life.

We can speculate on how and why certain dynamics started to acceler-
ate ultimately landing Joe in a structured therapeutic program. Since we
have a general idea of the dynamics that were driving Joe to become the
identified patient, or as we sometimes refer to such patients, the "symbolic client" (Bütz, 1993a, 1995b, 1997), it seems sufficient to state that the
family was deeply affected by Barbara's move. The family stability was
interrupted resulting in a bifurcation, and eventually a state of chaos
where one family member, Joe, held an overwhelming amount of anxiety
for the entire family. Remember, that following a steady state, if a new
perturbation disturbs the stability of the system sufficiently, it will bifurcate. Pushed even further, it will move toward a chaotic state, after going
through a period-doubling route to chaos. The treatment team was only
able to witness the family during periods of stability or chaos. Maintaining complexity just seemed to surpass the family's collective abilities. We
could only hypothesize that Barbara's move and Sue's subsequent involvement with her are the elements that destabilized the family system.
Speculating on how or why this ultimately resulted in familial chaos
(where we have one person overwhelmed while attempting to contain the
entire family's anxiety) would require more time. Therapeutically, Joe appeared to be the hinge to the entire family. With him was the hope of
keeping the father figure Chris close to the family, and the hope of open-
ing up the closed relationship between Sue, Barbara, and ancillarily
Peggy.

The hypothesized precipitator is Barbara's move within reach of Sue
and the reenmeshment that constellated. The family as a unit was caught
unable to adapt to this dynamic, which, at this phase of the family's development was powerful generationally. What is not so apparent is the
task of therapy. We hypothesized that this phase of the family's development was a critical window for redirection that might integrate the two
sexes into one family. Joe's behavior had made all this possible, and attempting to understand it symbolically during therapy would provide the
necessary insights to turn the crisis into an opportunity for integration.

As a team, we felt that therapy would need to include Barbara, since without her presence the pull toward her as an attractor for an old system dynamic would severely hamper the prognosis. Another key issue was who
would act as the therapist. Because of the family's pull to disintegrate along

gender lines, treatment would be led by a female and a male cotherapy team to model this integration. Joe's symptomatology became the focus of the therapy as he continued to symbolically draw attention to the basic issues the family was struggling with. His behavior was interpreted in a symbolic fashion over the course of therapy, where each symbolic act revealed one of the family issues.

As one of the elemental issues in therapy, Chris's slowly growing distance from the family was connoted as a growing absence experienced as a loss of the father figure. For example, Chris was out late with friends one night, and that evening Joe sneaked out of the house to find him. Unable to do so he came home very late to find his mother waiting for him. This was addressed that week in therapy. When he was asked about this, Joe stated, "I wanted to be with him." The therapist asked him why, and he stated, "because with him I feel safe." This was interpreted as a need to be near a father figure, whom Chris had come to represent.

Therapy continued, but as many therapists are aware progress was not small incremental steps toward more adaptive organization. In was in fact, a nonlinear process with peaks and valleys. One lurch forward came when unexpectedly Peggy began to describe the loss she had felt from her brothers' absence in her life. This came out of Peggy's perceived betrayal of the female triad, when she said she missed the boys. Barbara was notably upset, and turned away from Peggy. This was a turning point in therapy, since the focus had now shifted from Joe to Peggy. Peggy was describing her own anxiety, and we found that she wanted her whole family together. She also changed her position in the room, moving from between Sue and Barbara to between Sue and Joe.

With this symbolic bridge between Joe, Peggy, and Sue, which may be seen as an initial organizing event, an integration began to spread. In self-organizing theory, a similar event is seen as the seeds for a new form of adaptive order. Typically, this order spontaneously spreads throughout the system either gradually or seemingly all at once. We also see this with our collage family. A key piece of information assisted the family's self-organization. Barbara had experienced Joe and Chris as threats to her intimacy with Sue. Subsequently, a new organization spread from Peggy and Joe's reconnectedness to include Sue with Chris and ultimately Joe and Chris with Barbara. Spontaneous self-organization has a snowball effect of pulling together a number of previously disparate elements that assist the individual or family to adapt. For example, once this process was set into motion, the family reconnected with agencies and reinitiated their individual therapies after weeks of resistance.

CASE DISCUSSION

This therapy lasted 10 sessions (an average of the three families that make up the collage), and what may be seen is that Joe was the initial symbol of the family's difficulties. However, as the therapy progressed, the issue was addressed by another member, Peggy, and eventually Barbara took the baton. Joe's stay in the day-hospital program was only six weeks, since his symptomatic behavior decreased as his actions were better understood. Peggy and Barbara's roles in change then took over for the remaining four weeks. Barbara's issues may be seen as the strong generational undercurrent or "rules of the game" (Watzlawick et al., 1967). When these rules were not followed, she began to act out in instances such as the one described earlier, with more overt gestures occurring outside therapy. Once the triad of issues were addressed, the family moved from a chaotic state toward self-organization where a number of significant changes were witnessed. The family reconnected with social service agencies, reinitiated their individual therapies, and Barbara began to visit Sue's home spending time with both the "boys" and the "girls."

Numerous issues still remained unresolved. What about reintegrating the other male figures in the family? How long would this stability last? How much change is enough? The behavior of the family members will indicate when they are ready for more change. Another crisis will emerge. Whether or not it will require therapeutic intervention is another issue. As we have described, some families are rapid cycling families. Their timetable is to do a lot of change in a short amount of time. As soon as one crisis is over, another arises. At this time, it seemed this family had done as much work as it wanted to do.

SUICIDAL BEHAVIOR: A LOOK AT CHAOS IN THE FAMILY

Observing how suicidal behavior becomes part of a pattern of family interaction may offer a framework for clinicians to observe the dynamics of chaos. Many theorists and clinicians have examined the phenomenon of suicide from a family systems perspective (Farber, 1977; Hutchinson & Draguns, 1987; Pfeffer, 1981; Richman, 1979, 1986; Sands & Dixon, 1986). Most, however, have pursued the goals of delineating the precursors of a suicide attempt (with the goal of identifying predictive factors) or of defining a "family type" that produces suicidal members. Most family theorists studying suicidal behavior view the suicide attempt as a disastrous endpoint of a series of interactions. For example, Richman (1979) hypothesizes that there is a "suicidogenic family pattern" based on "intense symbiotic ties combined with inordinate fears of separation and change" (p. 132). Chaos theory offers an alternative framework. The theory offers the view that a suicide attempt is not an outcome, but rather is an event, embedded in a more complete and complex pattern of inter-action in some families. A suicide attempt is a part of the pattern, but does not encompass or define the entirety of the pattern.

While there are some commonalties in families with a history of sui-cidal behavior (e.g., previous deaths in the family from suicide, problems in the marital relationship), the circumstances of an attempt of suicide remain unpredictable. Like all other behavior, suicide is constrained by time, place, and certain other elements such as substance abuse, the avail-ability of the preferred method for making an attempt or the presence or absence of rescuers. It is important for clinicians working with suicidal behavior to be familiar with the factors that increase the likelihood of an attempt, and to know how to take appropriate actions to protect a suicidal person. The ability to assess lethality is critical when working with peo-ple who are potentially suicidal (Monahan, 1977, 1984, 1992). Farberow (1981), Wekstein (1979), and others (Applebaum & Gutheil, 1991; Bendar, Bendar, Lamber & Waite, 1991; Bongar, 1991; Monahan & Stedman, 1994; Swanson, Holzer, Ganju, & Jono, 1990) offer useful guidelines for assess-ing suicide potential. These guidelines, however, are largely focused on the individual who is a candidate for attempting suicide. The addition of the model proposed by chaos theory can help expand our understanding of suicidal behavior in families.

Unlike other theoretical models of suicidal behavior, chaos theory sug-gests a descriptive, not a predictive model. It provides the framework for an alternative perspective from which to observe, understand, and inter-vene with families in which there is a threat of suicide. Although a death from suicide is certainly a "difference that makes a difference" in creat-ing structural changes in a family, suicide threats and nonlethal attempts may have several different effects.

Bergman (1985) defines suicide threats as just another symptom that serves to maintain equilibrium in the family. Suicidal behavior may serve as a means of preventing change (chaos) and maintaining stability (order). For example, a child's suicide attempt may unite parents who are conflicted or apathetic. Periods of chaotic transition or disruption may activate a stabilizing negative feedback loop in the family that slows or prohibits significant change such as a member leaving the family. Those are typically what we refer to as slow cycling families. Although a death from suicide would certainly exemplify a positive feedback loop by changing the basic structure of the family, threats and incomplete at-tempts may serve as corrective strategies to restabilize the family by blocking further change.

Conversely, a suicide threat may also serve to destabilize a family that is not adequately responding to change and is somehow "stuck" in more of the same when a difference is needed. A spouse may become depressed and suicidal after failed efforts to change a pattern of substance abuse in his partner. The appearance of suicide may be a way to increase the chaos in the system to a crisis point that will necessitate the family taking some new action to reestablish the prior steady state, such as making contact with a psychotherapist.

The challenge posed to the clinician by chaos theory is how to begin adding new information or behaviors to the existing pattern that will help move the family to a "far-from-equilibrium" state while also reducing the threat of death from a suicide attempt. Complexity theory indicates that for a reorganization to occur in the family, there must be an increase in the instability or disorder. The negative feedback loops that attempt to correct the system without changing its structure must somehow be inactivated, blocked, or removed. At the level of family systems, this may translate to increasing the confusion about the nature of the suicidal threats, changing the pattern of interaction among the members when a threat is issued, or focusing on other issues in the family.

For example, if a suicidal threat in an adolescent has previously been dealt with by hospitalization, using a more family-based intervention such as a "suicide watch" (Bergman, 1985, pp. 151–160) may change the pattern of interaction in the family. The suicide watch, in which family members maintain a 24-hour surveillance of the suicidal member until the crisis lessens, may serve as a positive feedback loop that increases the level of dissonance or intimacy in the family. This alternative may block the stabilizing influence of the suicidal member. It is also important for clinicians to be aware that the repetition of other family members' attempts to save the life of the suicidal person (e.g., through bargaining, hospitalization, seeing the person individually instead of with the family) are likely to interfere with change if the suicidal behavior is serving to maintain stability.

Psychotherapy with suicidal persons has generally focused on issues of prediction and control (Monahan, 1992; Kassen & O'Connor, 1988). Certainly, in a life-or-death situation, most clinicians would opt for intervening in any manner necessary to control and protect a suicidal client; and rightly so. Safety must always be the first priority. Although chaos theory does not offer a means of prediction, it can provide an alternative reference for viewing the patterns in families in which suicidal behavior is likely. In some families, the pattern of fluctuation between periods of

chaos and order can be marked by severe disruption, such as suicidal behavior. In the following case study, we describe the chaotic nature of a
spontaneous "intervention" that reorganized the family. The family illustrates the transition from a chaotic period of suicide attempts and unsuccessful treatment to a rather unusual steady state. The following
examples of change occurring outside the context of therapy offer interesting information about the patterns and responses a family may generate in critical situations. The dynamics in the family will be discussed
using the theoretical constructs of chaos described in Chapter 2.

CASE 2: TILL DEATH DO US PART

This case presents an example of the process of change in a family in
which suicidal behavior emerged during a time of transition and increasing disequilibrium (see Figure 9.2). Because the events described occurred
prior to entering therapy, the historical perspective allows a clearer look at
a significant shift in the family that was maintained over time.

> During an initial family therapy session, the therapist was first told of the
> following incident that had occurred almost five years earlier. Therapy was
> being conducted with the father, Joe (age 47), the mother, Martha (age 48),
> and the youngest daughter, Susan (age 22) who was staying with her par-
> ents. An older sister, Lucy, had been out of the family for several years and
> was living with her husband in another state. Joe and Martha had initially
> contacted the therapist requesting help in dealing with Susan's most recent
> "psychotic break." Susan had been hospitalized against her will when her
> parents became concerned about her sleeplessness, irrationality, delusions,
> and apparent hallucinations. The three came in for the initial session a
> few days after Susan was released from the psychiatric unit, which she
> described as a "jail." Susan presented no symptoms of depression and
> strongly denied any suicidal intent. Instead, Susan was openly angry and
> belligerent that they had involuntarily hospitalized her. Both parents ap-
> peared sad and concerned about her welfare and stated they were primarily

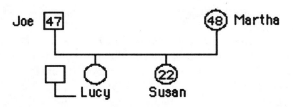

Figure 9.2   "Till Death Do Us Part."

seeking therapy to help Susan with her problems. In obtaining some history from the family, they related the following incident. It provides a curious example of how chaos, unpredictability, spontaneous change, and self-organization can occur in a family.

Susan's first "break" occurred when she was 16 years old, shortly after her older sister, Lucy, left for college. During this time, her parents were experiencing a dispute in their marriage over whether to live near Martha's family in the Midwest or move to California where Joe thought he could expand some of his interests and build a new life for the family. Lucy (who was 18 years old) had moved to another state several months prior to the father's decision to move the family to California. Although she left to attend college, both parents felt her leaving was a clear statement that Lucy wanted to "get away from the family." Martha and Susan had decided to stay where they were while Joe went to find a home in California. At that time, Joe and Martha were uncertain if they would stay together. The stress of disputing the options for moving and Lucy's leaving the family combined to push both parents to consider divorce. It appeared that Lucy's role of peacemaker and stabilizer left the family feeling jumbled and precariously unbalanced once she left.

Martha finally decided to follow Joe to California. Approximately two months after Martha and Susan joined Joe in California, Susan made her first suicide attempt by swallowing lye. Neither parent could remember any single precipitant for the attempt and they did not have any overt warning from Susan. Joe described feeling very ashamed and helpless at his daughter's attempt. It reminded him of his own mother who was chronically depressed and "crazy." He began to "tune out" and retreat and let Martha and a psychologist take over the care of their daughter. Joe and Martha also began to see therapists individually. They continued to feel unsettled in California with Martha resentful of the move and of being such a long distance from other family "back home." Susan became increasingly withdrawn and continued to behave in an unpredictable manner. She had periods of deep depression marked by withdrawal as well as times when she was openly hostile and delusional. She made a second suicide attempt by overdosing on the only drug her parents kept in the house—pennywort. Because there was no ill effect, she later went to her mother and told her what she had done. Martha and Joe continued to rely on the therapist involved with Susan to provide the critical factor in controlling her suicidal behavior. They became increasingly alienated both from each other and from Susan. The shared sense of frustration, helplessness, and instability continued to magnify.

Within a month, the third suicide attempt took place. Martha had gone to Wisconsin to stay for a few weeks with her mother. Joe came home from work one afternoon to find Susan's wrists bandaged. She showed her father the wounds and described "trying to find the best way to cut her wrists." Joe believed that if Martha had been there, "I would have withdrawn as much as possible" and things would have gone differently. They would have at least talked over what to do before taking any action. Without his wife available to intervene with their daughter, Joe began to feel provoked and desperate to do something to "make her want to live." He hit on the thought that if Susan were threatened with immediate death, she might be forced to fight for her life. In essence, he spontaneously created a reframe of the situation from "I have to keep her from committing suicide" to "I have to make her want to live." Joe then went in to his daughter's room, gripped her tightly around the throat in a strangle hold and told her, "You've got to want to fight to live." After a moment of shock, she pushed his hands away and he left the room to make arrangements for her to go to residential treatment and called Martha to ask her to come back to California. Susan was again placed in a hospital prior to her mother's return.

The common pattern of interaction around Susan's suicide attempts now had a very different "punctuation." Instead of Susan trying to take her own life, her father was now "trying to kill her" and she was given a chance to struggle against the threat of death. Although Susan's behavior continued to be unsettled, both Martha and Joe describe that things were better after Susan came home from that hospital stay. At 18, she moved out on her own with her boyfriend. So far as they knew, during the following four years their daughter had never become suicidal again. Susan had continued in therapy and was being treated for symptoms of bipolar disorder when she came to live with her parents after the relationship with her boyfriend ended. At the time they consulted with the therapist, their primary concern was with the tension between Joe and Susan based on Susan's fear that her father might try to kill her even though there had never been any further threats or aggression on his part. In fact, Joe presented as an extraordinarily docile, quiet, nonviolent man.

How can we begin to understand this family's experience from the perspective offered by chaos theory? A brief review of some of the theoretical constructs in Chapter 2 and the application of this paradigm to the case described may help to capture chaos in action.

CASE DISCUSSION

Innumerable alternative explanations exist relative to the dynamics of the family described in Case 2. Where there is no absolute objectivity (Theoretical Construct 1), there is no ultimate "right" explanation. As noted in the description of the case, traditional interventions had repeatedly been attempted. The daughter had been hospitalized, family members were involved individually in therapy, and patterns had been established regarding how the members interacted when the daughter attempted suicide. The events described by this family were a bizarre guide for how to avert suicide through threat of death. Everyone (except Susan) had defined their role in the pattern of interactions as being responsible for keeping Susan from dying. Only when her father accidentally took a significant turn and decided instead to make her want to live did the pattern begin to shift. This was the bifurcation that provided an opportunity for the development of a new pattern that would shift the family to a new steady state.

The case offers an elegant example of how some of the characteristics of chaos theory interplay in family systems. Although we have yet to recommend to any families that they threaten to kill a suicidal member, an awareness of how fluctuations can occur during periods of intense chaos does help to provide a guide for observation. Fluctuations that offer new information and novel pathways to a different level of order are embedded in all patterns of family interaction. In viewing the case from the perspective of chaos theory, it is important to focus on difference rather than cause and effect. Her father's behavior did not cause Susan to struggle for her life, but it certainly provided some new information for her!

Fluctuations in the patterns of interaction among the three family members began when a crucial member, Martha, was absent during one of the periods of Susan's suicidal behavior. As outlined in Chapter 2, the various constructs suggested by chaos theory can help us describe and understand the dynamics at play in this family. The fluctuation in the sequence created when the mother was not there during a confrontation changed the structure, creating a "butterfly effect" (Theoretical Construct 5) that provided an opportunity for the family to reorganize the entire pattern. In her absence, the ensuing level of chaos made it more likely that father and daughter would find some way to act outside the previous boundaries, as described in earlier chapters.

The situation became more "far-from-equilibrium" and chaotic. A "critical moment" (Theoretical Construct 6) occurred in which the father's behavior became increasingly unpredictable (Theoretical Construct 9) and he did something so different that it made a difference. This increase in the level of chaos offered a greater opportunity for the family to undergo a substantive change in their pattern of behaviors. It may help to remember that nothing new can be taught to someone who already believes he has all the information he needs. Confusion (cognitive chaos) is necessary for change to occur. Finally, a self-organization could take place in the family (Theoretical Construct 7).

In retrospect, this was not a gradual change from a pattern including a suicidal child to one including a homicidal father. Instead, the transition in the family was sudden, unexpected, and spontaneous, as the model of "punctuated equilibria" would suggest (Theoretical Construct 8). It appears that once the typical pattern of interaction around Susan's suicidal behavior was interrupted, the old and new pattern could not coexist. There was no going back. Something "irreversible" (Theoretical Construct 2) had apparently taken place in the family such that the members did not return to the previous pattern of behavior in which the threat of suicide was embedded. New patterns had to be established that provided a different structure and order for the family.

It is impossible to predict exactly how family therapists will respond to the challenges posed by chaos theory. The concept of a science based on unpredictability and complexity presents an alternative to the pursuit of reductionistic, empirical thought. But, in true "Kuhnian" (Kuhn, 1962/1970) fashion, they are not likely to blend together given the significant differences of the two paradigms. The effects of such a dramatic shift from empiricism not only would be difficult for the social research scientist but would have a profound impact on the clinical practitioner as well.

Clinicians and theorists have been working through the past three decades to translate ideas about uncertainty and, more recently chaos, into psychological theory and clinical technique. Perhaps one of the most significant contributions of chaos theory is that it may "offer our culture one of the greatest opportunities it has had to heal this fundamental split between the dark and the light, chaos and order" (Bütz, 1995a). As Keeney and Ross (1985) have noted, it is the pattern of the constant interplay of stability and change that the clinician must address.

This line of thinking argues against the idea of a "suicidogenic" family type. Applying the theoretical constructs of chaos theory, family systems should be no more amenable to accurate prediction than weather systems. Although we can safely hypothesize that it will generally be warmer in Mexico than in Canada, within the boundaries of those separate countries, it becomes increasingly difficult to predict the movement of rain clouds or the timing of blizzards or hurricanes. As one moves from the general to the specific, the patterns become much more complex, intricate, and unpredictable. As family therapists, we can use information about factors that place people at a higher risk for suicidal behavior. However, this does not make the family suicidogenic, and it certainly does not limit high-risk families from engaging in a vast number of other behaviors. We can also predict that families that have several professional people may encourage higher education and promote their children to engage in professions. Yet, we don't label these families as "professionogenic."

The label of suicidogenic implies that suicidal behavior is a property of the family and that only a certain type of family produces suicidal members. Richman (1986) proposes that suicidogenic families are characterized by an inability to accept change, interpersonal conflicts, a disturbed family structure, unbalanced intrafamilial relationships, affective difficulties, transactional difficulties, and intolerance for crisis (p. 58). However, many families will display all these factors without ever precipitating suicidal behavior. If a suicide attempt occurs in families that do not meet the criteria of the "suicidogenic family," how are we to explain the event? Suicidal behavior is a process and a part of a pattern that occurs in families, not a trait of the family. It is not the nature of any family system to be suicidal; it is only our observations that label it as such.

Chaos offers the premise that there is an underlying order in all interactive systems. As previously noted, suicidal behavior can emerge as either a form of positive (an attempt to induce change) or negative (an attempt to inhibit change) feedback. In understanding the development and appearance of suicidal behavior in a family, we can discern several parts of a pattern. These are neither exclusive to suicidal families, nor are they predictive or all-inclusive. The pattern's appearance may serve, however, to alert clinicians to observe the family more closely for signs that suicidal behavior or threats may surface.

Suicidal behavior is always embedded in a pattern of interaction in the family set in motion by some threat to the system. The threat may be either to force change (e.g., a member leaving) or to force stability (e.g., a member being prevented from leaving). The behavioral sequence that includes suicidal behavior will also have some meaning for the family (e.g., it is dangerous for people to leave home). Understanding the symbolic act characterized by suicidal behavior is an important part of the assessment and treatment planning. Deducing the meaning of the threat will help guide the therapist in deciding whether to help increase or decrease the level of chaos in the family. This is where attending to movement and information boundaries again is so important, as well as monitoring the energy in the phrase space of the system.

CONCLUSION

So, what does understanding chaos theory and self-organization theory do to help us with families in therapy?

1. As mentioned in Theoretical Construct 4, it provides a new way to look at development from an organic perspective, where systems do

not fall apart in chaos and we do not treat organisms such as families like machines.

2. It does not mean we need to reinvent therapeutic approaches; evaluate therapeutic techniques against the developmental framework we have described.
3. We learn to emphasize the history in therapy because it indicates what stability once was and what was the perturbing event. Lorenz's attention to the history of his computer-simulated weather system indicated that a radically new order was emerging from minute changes in variables.
4. If we are aware chaos is a necessary step in development, then we know it is there to:
   a. Assist the system adaptation.
   b. Drive the system to look for new solutions.
   c. Integrate new solutions with old ones.
5. Change is an ongoing process, it can be rapid or slow cycling.
6. Organisms have a tendency toward a creative life and a "desire" toward wholeness.

In the framework of chaos theory, symptoms and problems must be conceptualized and treated as part of a more encompassing systemic pattern of organization. Those behaviors that appear the most chaotic are also the foundation for stability and order. Therapeutic communication in other orientations has focused almost exclusively on attempting to induce change. The new "art of therapy requires successfully handling requests for both change and stability" (Keeney & Ross, 1985, p. 54). In attempting to be helpful, therapists will "organize the problem either as part of a process of self-correction or runaway and oscillation (Keeney, 1983, p. 162)." Clinicians, if they are to find chaos theory useful, need to redefine their role. Rather than simply pursuing the goal of helping people change, we need to consider the stabilizing nature of some patterns of behavior and how changes may create disorganization.

As the ideas inherent in chaos theory become more prevalent in other areas of science, they are certain to have an increasing impact on clinical theory and practice. Can a new, more unified system in the social sciences be the outcome, or will we splinter into increasingly separate factions? The quest for scientific validity that has been such a strong motivating force for the past 500 years is not likely to change without a period of significant disruption. It will be fascinating at the end of the next decade to look back and see if in fact we are now at that "critical moment."

PART FOUR

NO PREDICTABLE PERIOD

CHAPTER 10

From Chaos to Order,
or . . . From Order to Chaos

INTO THE CHAOS

O VER THE course of this text we have addressed the cornucopia of
ideas found in theories on chaos, complexity, and the new
physics. Noting how the more quantifiable aspects of these theories are still in need of greater definition in Chapter 11, we have provided
qualitative analogical models that bring these new notions in science to
family therapy. There, we have provided our reader with a host of pas-
sages through which interested therapists may come to understand and
talk about nonlinear change in family therapy.

The touchstones we have outlined come from the developments in systemic family therapy to date. We have witnessed how the seeds for what
has become truly systemic therapy grew out of attending to patterns in
communication. For over a decade (Hoffman, 1981), systemic family therapy has been poised to transform those early dynamics in communication
into more fluid descriptions thereby moving from a metaphor of machine
to that of a biological life form. Linearity has been replaced with a more
recursive frame of reference, where the unpredictability of the human
condition dominates, and reversible time finds a home only in our minds
(Bütz, 1997). It is as though, we, like Thomasina in Stoppard's *Arcadia*,
have just figured out that "Newton's equations go forwards and back-
wards, they do not care which way. But the heat equation cares very
much, it goes only one way" (1993, p. 87). Transformation in these models

connotes a one-way self-organizing process at both the edge of chaos and the other side of chaos as these systems move toward greater adaptations. The process of transformation also informs us that there are more steady, perhaps coherent, states of existence sandwiched between the complexities, bifurcations, and chaos of development. These new kinds of order do not simply reflect an incremental growth process, but punctuate their birth with a new form of coherence that announces the system's increase in sophistication and adaptation. Ideas such as these are characteristic of what we have described as the fifth paradigm in systemic family therapy. These touchstones also reflect the translation of chaos and complexity theory through what we have identified as theoretical constructs.

Objectivity has melded into the relief of the family therapy session as we come to appreciate system's sensitivity to initial conditions. There too, we have found that there are critical moments, where systems bifurcate, and therefore, choose a path where one set of possibilities fades away forever as a new one unfolds. Notions such as these inform us about the vivid portrait which this holistic epistemology conveys to each branch of knowledge that embraces it.

For family therapists, our hope is that attending to boundaries will take on new meaning. While boundaries have always been a central concern, the mindful therapist may now begin to watch the quality of information and the patterns of movement within the family determining where in the process of self-organization this system finds itself. As awareness of communication is at the systemic approach's center, we encourage others to attend to phrase space to understand these dynamics. Core to this set of ideas is the underlying assumption of energy—where it is and where it is not. Questions we may ask are; Is there too much energy here and not enough there; Does the system have enough energy to survive chaos or would a complex self-organization at the edge of chaos better serve them? These, and an array of other ideas we have attempted to share in this book are directed toward how to care for families as well as ourselves.

Sometimes we have found it is better for a butterfly to generate energy in a system where its small contribution may join with others to have a disproportionately positive effect. Other times, we must learn to move about quickly and discreetly, so as not to get sucked into the storm in which the family has so long found itself entangled. In still other situations, inventively, we must learn how to contain the chaos. These dynamics must be contemplated with great regard as we consider how to intervene. There are ethics here that demand our caution, as we will describe in this chapter.

Chaos is nothing to trifle with, as "those dynamics" and "that energy" bring many families to our door despite the immense capacity these systems have for adaptation. As Ford (1989) states, "What is chaos, that we should be mindful of it?" Well, mythologically, it is no less than the "unorganized state of primordial matter before the creation of distinct forms" (Webster, 1989, p. 226). We're talking real wrath of God stuff here. . . . And, in science it has come to mean many things as we demonstrated in Chapter 2, but they too experienced it in the mythological sense first (Yorke, 1975) before the field was able to take wing.

So, our journey to this point has indicated where we feel family therapy has been and what allegories may be shared between chaos, complexity, and the new physics in science and our discipline. The entire text is filled with these suggestions, but what of the future of family therapy? As we have stated numerous times, we cannot predict it, and discontinuous change is, as they say, "part of the ballgame." Still, we can tell you our thoughts about the future and extend those notions into a consideration of ethics that in our estimation hold not only for systemic therapists, but the entire field of family therapy.

CHAOS, COMPLEXITY AND THE FUTURE OF FAMILY THERAPY

Vandervert (in press) suggests that proponents of chaos theory and nonlinear dynamical models ask themselves how their respective disciplines will be different if the new paradigm that they advocate becomes more widely adopted. For family therapy, this is a difficult and perhaps unanswerable question. This is because the field of family therapy is itself a complex and nonlinear system, characterized by positive and negative feedback loops that interact in elaborate and often unpredictable patterns (Boscolo & Bertrando, 1992). In other words, the social systems that incorporate family therapy as a treatment modality may themselves demonstrate chaos at various times from a dimensional standpoint (Bütz, 1991). This includes the medical service delivery system, which in the United States has been recently thrust into a period of crisis, ostensibly for the purpose of cost reduction.

Therefore, it is impossible to specify with any degree of certainty what changes may occur if our conceptualization of the family therapeutic process transpires. Chaos theory tells us one thing is certain: The future of complex systems is impossible to predict (Loye, 1995). Nevertheless, some fundamental modifications in the assumptions of family therapy, clinical practice, and training may be likely if the paradigm of chaos theory gains the level of acceptance that it has found in physics, mathematics, and life sciences. The following are just a few of the possibilities; we encourage readers to add their own revisions and ideas to the following discussion.

Foremost, we hope that this anticipated paradigm shift toward a nonlinear conceptualization of human behavior will encourage a rebirth of theoretical and therapeutic creativity. Family therapy arose when the restricting mantles of earlier paradigms were overturned by therapists who had the creativity to view behavior from new perspectives. Perhaps the greatest genius of these founding therapists was their mental flexibility and their refusal to be limited by previous notions. The paradigm shift that we advocate can help revitalize this creativity. By reflecting on alternatives generated by nonlinear systems theory, the reader becomes a participant in this new paradigm and has already begun a fruitful and creative transformation process.

THEORIES THAT CHANGE OUR IDEAS ABOUT FAMILIES

Throughout this book, we have been critical of theories of family functioning that rely solely on the concept of homeostasis because homeostatic models of systemic functioning are usually heuristic simplifications. Almost every system of interest in nature is nonhomeostatic or, as they are technically known, dissipative or open (Prigogine & Stengers, 1984). Rather than maintain a steady state, such systems take in energy and transform it, an entirely different dynamic than systems that strive for balance. Ironically, the theory of cybernetics, where the concept of family homeostasis was derived, was initially a theory of machines (Wiener, 1961), not of human or life systems functioning. Machines, not human systems, are usually closed, as outlined in Chapter 2.

By viewing families as open systems, rather than closed ones, a number of possibilities emerge. First, we will no longer be wedded to a unidimensional view of what families are or how to "properly" define them. We will recognize that the concept of family is itself open, dynamic, and "fuzzy" (in the sense that this word is used in systems and set theory; Terano, Asai, & Sugeno, 1994). Given the changing nature of familial constitutions, about the best definition we can provide is that families are "networks of systemic relationships, characterized by a high degree of emotional involvement." Other definitions may exclude important classes.

Yet even this definition may exclude legal situations where people are biologically related but have made emotional cutoffs (e.g., Bowen, 1978) from other family members. The word *family* is so open and dynamic that we err the least by defining it as "anything that anyone labels with this term." In other words, if we want to find out what a family "truly" is and what its definition should include, we should simply allow the varieties of present-day families to flourish or extinguish on their own, as Gould might suggest (1980).

That we should deliberately define families ambiguously has some important political considerations. Increasingly, especially in the United States, we hear claims that the institution of the family is in crisis. This rhetoric comes from both the political right and the left. The right uses these arguments to bolster the moral regulatory policies that it favors, while the left uses the same claims to press for greater government intervention in solving social problems. Undoubtedly, there is some truth to these concerns, regardless of their sources. Crime is perennially up and divorce rates remain high, while many children live in poverty. Spouse abuse and child abuse are too common, as is adolescent and preteen substance abuse. Numerous exhaustive demands are placed on the family that only two generations ago were met by the community or the church. Pressures from declining wages and parental overcommitment to work have increased throughout the years and show no sign of slowing their rate of acceleration.

It is tempting to try a quick legislative fix for these social problems. Yet chaos theory suggests that we be very careful before we design social policy for the family. Political action usually tries to artificially stabilize a particular definition of what a family is and what a family should be. Chaos theory helps us understand why such interventions usually do not work. They restrict diversity, which almost always has disastrous consequences. Kauffman (1995) cites growing evidence that maximal adaptation in complex social systems occurs where there is maximal diversity. In fact, maximal adaptation seems to occur when systems are diverse and near the edge of chaos. If we truly want to strengthen the institution of the family, then we must allow for maximal diversity in family types and patterns.

As well-meaning as proponents of both the left and the right are, we must criticize them for their naive science, which may have untoward social consequences. In one obvious example, the American liberal agenda of the 1960s defined what was an "acceptable" family by its regulations regarding entitlement benefits. The rich familial social networks of economically disenfranchised families were often stripped as a prerequisite for receiving government support. That social policy was a drastic failure, as most everyone will admit today. The conservative agenda that many now advance wants to define "family" and family values by certain Judeo-Christian (mostly Evangelical or Fundamentalist Christian) traditions. These beliefs will by definition largely exclude extended families, unmarried couples, many blended families, single parents, same-sex unions and probably a host of other "untraditional" social units. This policy is also destined to fail with disastrous consequences because it suppresses diversity.

THE NATURE OF FAMILY HEALTH, A NEW DEFINITION?

Chaos and complexity theory, with their emphasis on diversity and dynamics, also suggest that the notion of a "healthy" family which has a dynamic quality that certainly is changeable and may not be the same for every social unit. Presently, therapists often view families (though we do not realize it) through the lens of sociological functionalism (Parsons & Bales, 1955). This was a dominant theory in behavioral sciences at the time that cybernetics first became popular. In functionalism (or any of its academic sociological descendants), families exist primarily to meet certain needs. Families are then judged to be "normal" if they meet these needs; for example, if they are able to provide food, shelter, socialization, and protection for their young. From a functionalism perspective, family impairment is judged by how much a family fails to meet these functions.

These new theories argue that "healthy behavior" is not an absolute, but depends on the demand characteristics placed on the family by various social system and internal attractors. Furthermore, the "health" in healthy families is not necessarily in any attributes that the family possesses, but in the way they negotiate the pull of internal and external attractors. Health is largely *patterns and processes,* not a set of narrow attributes. Therefore, family health may be much more transitory than we originally thought, based on the idea that adaptation may be rapid, slow, or somewhere in between. Also, behaviors that may be functional for families in one situation may be dysfunctional in others. This suggests very strongly that family therapists will need to learn much more about the cultural factors that influence family functioning (Bütz, 1995b), an important issue to be discussed in this chapter.

Does this mean that we allow any type of dysfunction, and simply leave it alone because it is usually less healthy to intervene in complex systems? Not at all, as we will demonstrate in our discussion of ethics. What it does suggest, however, is that apart from meeting the instrumental needs of specific members, higher levels of family functioning will probably be associated with encouraging diversity of functioning and personal growth of members through a variety of life experiences. A similar belief was advocated by Murray Bowen (1978). With still other families, it may imply limiting diversity and directing a family's energy into more adaptive pursuits. These notions suggest that therapists do a better job of differentiating between family competence to meet instrumental needs on one hand (L'Abate & Wagner, 1988), and developmental bifurcation points that influence aspects of family functioning on the other. A number of family competence skills may be necessary, but they are not sufficient for family health. Beyond this notion of sufficient complexity and adaptation, however, maximal family health will probably be found in a continual process of self-organization that may be idiosyncratic for every family unit.

FAMILY THERAPY IS OBLIGED TO BECOME LESS INVASIVE: JUST SIT THERE!

A principle from chaos and complexity theory's applications to family therapy that we have reiterated is that the therapist usually should intervene as little as possible. In the long run, we believe that chaos theory will make it more likely that therapists will do less. This is not an ironclad rule, but a useful suggestion—a recommendation that is richly grounded in the new science of nonlinear dynamical systems.

We have attempted to illustrate that, too often, family therapists are simply too active in the session. Family therapy is hard work and it will continue to be so in the future. Practitioners who routinely work with both individuals and families can attest that family therapy is usually more complex and mentally taxing, because the therapist must simultaneously consider the interactions of multiple systems. Yet family therapy has been made even more difficult by a common clinical sentiment that the therapist must usually act decisively and resolutely, often at the very beginning of treatment. Practitioners trained in the traditions of structural

and strategic therapy, particularly, are likely to embrace these sentiments. While the intentions of these therapists are admirable, their actions may be countertherapeutic since the therapist can do little that
surpasses the family's natural ability to heal itself, once brief systemic
perturbations have been successfully negotiated.

On the other hand, many family therapists recognize that the family
has a profound potential for adaptation and self-organization (Keeney,
1983; Ray & Keeney, 1993). In the past few years, there has been an impassioned discussion in the therapeutic community about the need to recognize that family therapy has too often acted as an instrument of power
and control (Cecchin, Lane, & Ray, 1994). Particularly in the narrative and
collaborative approaches that are gaining popularity (e.g., Gergen, 1991;
Hoffman, 1993), there is an emphasis that the therapist substitute power
and control for family collaboration (Ray & Keeney, 1993). Yet most of the
discussion about this important sentiment has not produced a definitive
statement why therapists should avoid exerting power and control as well
as the aggressive interventions that are popular in some circles. Many objections seem political, moral, or even aesthetic.

Chaos theory presents a stronger rationale. Families follow their own
internal dynamical processes that will unfold through time, in ways that
the therapist cannot predict. The dysfunctional behavior of families is
often the result of issues acting as attractors, pulling the family into
seemingly bizarre, inconsistent behavioral patterns. Interfering with
these processes is only necessary if the family becomes "stuck" in repetitive dysfunctional behaviors. Invasive interventions, as discussed in
Chapter 8, (or actually any interventions) may have untoward effects. Invasive interventions are not the treatment of choice. Sometimes they are
necessary, *but they are always risky*. If we are to be active, our activity
needs to be inward, where we consider numerous treatment options and
their contingencies as we follow the metaphors families provide us with.

Minimal intervention is advantageous because of the danger involved
in therapy. No systemic therapy, nor any therapy for that matter, is without risk (Cecchin, Lane, & Ray, 1994). As physicists have long known, the
act of observing a system changes it (Herbert, 1985). And, as behavioral
scientists have long known, the act of treating a system results in change,
even if the "treatment" is intended as a placebo (Parloff, 1992), or consists
of gathering information (Selvini-Palazzoli et al., 1980). Families that
come into treatment are usually there because they have reached a developmental crisis, often one that makes them exquisitely sensitive to
change. The more invasive an intervention is, *the more likely it is to have*

untoward consequences, which cannot be predicted. The art of family therapy, which we believe may be learned through experience and supervision, is to be able to intervene only as much as is necessary.

CHAOS AND COMPLEXITY THEORY SUGGESTS DIFFERENT MODELS OF FAMILY CHANGE

Almost every viable system of psychotherapy, whether individual or family oriented, has a theory of change. For the Freudians, change occurred through the transference process and subsequent insight. For behaviorists, change occurs through the process of reinforcement. For Gestaltists, change occurs through sudden awareness. For structural family therapists, change occurs through an alteration in the family's hierarchy or other structural aspects. For other family therapists, change is often believed to occur through social influence (Cecchin, Lane, & Ray, 1994).

Chaos theory suggests that therapeutic change can occur through any number of mechanisms. Change mechanisms are simply attractors exerting direction in a system. A single theory of change is not necessary or even logical. However, the most successful therapy usually involves a special type of change: self-organization toward a higher level of functioning. For other forms of therapy, we need to remain ecumenical regarding methods and strategies of systemic modification. Like physicists able to think about light as either particles or waves, we believe that no one model can account for the diversity of impact and outcome in family therapy.

However, we believe a model of exchange of energy and information during therapy (Bütz, 1993b; Langs & Badalamenti, 1993) will become more prominent. We can usually surmise that at the point a family enters treatment, the information and energy in the system will have collapsed around an identified problem (Chamberlain, 1995). An important part of the therapist's job is to gently perturb family members to act differently to complete a loop from dysfunctional behavior to new order. Often, this can be accompanied with less, rather than more interventions. And since families in transition are highly sensitive to initial conditions, initial interventions will be perhaps more modest in scope than they often are. By minimally directing energy, though energy which is critically timed, will change the dynamical processes.

When more energy must be transformed into the family, it is usually best if it occurs through time (Langs, 1992). Some degree of disorganizing or discomfort may be necessary to allow families to self-organize to a greater degree of complexity. Therapists who work too "successfully" or quickly may risk having their client families reach a lesser level of change than would be possible if they allowed them to remain on the edge of chaos for a longer period. As we have attempted to demonstrate, families that resolve their crises too quickly do not usually change much. In addition to becoming rapid cycling, they frequently become treatment resistant. Through our best efforts, they often become worse and more dependent on care providers.

FAMILY THERAPY AND THE
LIMITS OF INFLUENCE

Paradoxically, given our concerns about the intensiveness of interventions expressed earlier, chaos theory indicates that the therapist's *immediate* influences may be more minimal than he or she often wishes. Throughout this book, we have indicated exactly how little the therapist is actually able to predict and control. Other theorists have wisely commented on this fact (e.g., Cecchin, Lane & Ray, 1994; Ray & Keeney, 1993). Yet they have lacked a sufficient theoretical paradigm to thoroughly explain these observations. The new paradigm of chaos shows us why our immediate influence may be minimal, but our long-term influence may be unpredictable and much more profound.

We now know that complex systems are governed by their own dynamics. We may prod them, jump-start them, restrain them, or attempt to change their direction. But their behaviors will be punctuated with periods where they are largely unpredictable and often novel. Complex systems are usually slow to change because of the vast amount of feedback the systems receive (Casti, 1992). An exception is systems that are behaving chaotically or beginning to bifurcate, which may be exquisitely sensitive to any outside influences and consequently change very rapidly. But for the most part, systems will change more slowly, ebbing and flowing in complex skeins that often do not make sense to the observer.

This knowledge about complex systems contrasts with some of the prevailing sentiments in classical clinical family practice, such as strategic therapy (e.g., Haley, 1980). A concept popular in these circles is that if a family does not get better (the goals of the family therapist or the referring agency are not met), then it is the fault of the therapist. This in turn, implies that the therapist needs supervision. An entire cottage industry has arisen surrounding the status of supervision in family therapy. However, chaos theory suggests that the therapist simply may not have enough *immediate and predictable* influence in the system to overcome the direction asserted by other attractors. This is especially true for well-developed and maintained symptoms that may have taken years to develop. It has nothing to do with the need for supervision or the therapist's skills, but instead is a simple fact of the behavior of complex systems.

Furthermore, chaos theory disabuses us of the notion that we can quickly "fix" families. This notion, that certain families are "sick" and can be "cured" through radical intervention probably derives from an outdated concept of illness, which does not recognize the role that long-term systemic factors play in promoting and maintaining disease (Engel, 1992). Yet this popular misunderstanding of the medical model is so ingrained in many therapists that it will truly take a paradigm shift to alter it.

For therapists who insist on using the medical model as a metaphor for the family therapy process, a more useful construct might be the chronic disease model. This model may be especially appropriate for families with a long history of severe and apparently intractable problems, such as rapid cycling families. The dysfunctional behaviors of these families, like chronic diseases, are fostered by a number of systemic facets that are difficult to unravel. Cause and effect become blurred. These disorders are usually thought to be "multidetermined" by complex factors acting in unpredictable and idiosyncratic manners. Chronic diseases are not cured, but often may be controlled through treatment for an extended period. Hypertension and diabetes are two examples. Longer term, less invasive treatments are usually necessary.

Therapy for families with chronic and long-standing problems may have to go on longer than some therapists wish because the system may respond better to the presence of the therapist as an attractor over time. Indeed, clinical research suggests that quick change in systems generates an opponent process where resistance forms in an equally rapid fashion (McCown & Johnson, 1993). Quick change of chronic problems generates an insidious hindrance, as practitioners who treat substance-abusing families know. Rapid therapy may cure the client, and yet it may make the rest of the system sicker.

Family therapists will need to face the implications of these realities. We are guilty of both bad science and bad practice if we make claims that we can always treat families both briefly and effectively. Sometimes we can, sometimes we can't. Chaos theory assures us that often we will have no way of knowing until we are in the process of treatment. This is not as trivial a concern as it may seem. We are aware of practitioners who promote family therapy primarily as a briefer alternative to individual treatment.

We need to be honest about what we can and can't do and not be embarrassed that the complexity of nonlinear systems makes it impossible to specify the length of treatment. The position we have advanced here indicates that interventions may be needed at a variety of places in the family's life cycle and the amount of intervention may not be predictable in advance.

CHAOS THEORY INDICATES THAT THERE ARE LIMITS ON PREDICTION

The limits of prediction for the length of therapy are not the only area where we have problems making useful clinical forecasts. Chaos theory is very firm in its recognition that there are many things about behavior that we will not be able to predict. As systems become more complex, patterns may become predictable, but specific behaviors of constituent parts usually become much less so. As Abraham and Shaw (1992) have stated, chaos theory allows us to make better *qualitative* predictions, but less meaningful and accurate *quantitative* predictions. We can, for example, predict that a specific family will behave in a violent or perhaps in an avoiding fashion. We cannot, however, predict when such behaviors will occur. Very frequently, we cannot even predict who in the family system will be most connected with these specific actions.

Chaos theory will free us from the mistaken belief that prediction is the same as understanding (Chamberlain & Bütz, 1997). As we have noted throughout, behavioral science has labored under this outdated model, which was largely derived from science that was popular during the nineteenth century. According to this view, we should be able to make perfect predictions from linear methods, providing the specific model we have developed is both accurate and appropriate to the phenomenon being studied. As we have argued, much of the history of the behavioral sciences in general, and psychology in particular, can be seen as having been the quest for more accurate linear models. For example, when we design a study hoping to find better predictors of violence than in previous research, we are attempting to alter our model to find variables that account for more of the variance than other efforts. Most behavioral science research conducted today reflects this strategy. The overwhelming sentiment is that our models are good, but that we have not been clever enough to use them with optimal results. Only very rarely will behavioral scientists conclude that linear models are inappropriate for the phenomena being studied.

The French mathematician Poincaré was one of the first to show that this view is wrong. A major reason, though not the only one, is that due to the problem of measurement error we will never be able to make many predictions with certainty. Yet things are even more complex than Poincaré realized. Moore (1990), in a provocative application of dynamical systems theory, has shown that there exist complex chaotic systems whose behavior cannot be predicted *even if we know all the initial conditions exactly.* Only trivial statements will be able to be known about such systems. In other words, even with no measurement error, there will be limits on our ability to predict.

Actually, mathematicians have known this for some time, having reached a similar conclusion through a different method of reasoning than Moore's application. The well-known theorem of Kurt Gödel, first published in the early 1930s (Wang, 1987), demonstrated that arithmetic is not completely formalizable. Gödel showed that in any system some truths will be paradoxically unprovable, yet still true (Robertson, 1992). This concept, also called *formal undecidability,* means that there are many things about the future that we cannot in principle predict. For the family therapist, this also means that we will never be able to describe all the important or true characteristics about a family from any particular theoretical viewpoint or paradigm. A theory is never more inclusive than the phenomena it attempts to describe. Novel behaviors will emerge that will remain outside our theories, and hence our ability to predict.

The limits on our ability to predict have serious ethical implications. Behavioral scientists are routinely called on to make predictions about certain occurrences. Therapists, in particular, are asked to predict such behaviors as what their clients will do or which parent may make the best guardian or even how dangerous a person might be. Our inaccuracy in making these predictions is well known. However, this inaccuracy is also inherent and may call for a revision of our conceptualization of some aspects of treatment.

WE WILL NEED TO CHANGE OUR CONCEPTIONS OF PSYCHOTHERAPY OUTCOME

Chaos theory suggests that virtually every psychotherapy outcome study must now be recognized as theoretically inadequate. We actually have very little idea about how influential and effective family and individual psychotherapies really are. There are four reasons for this:

1. We have inappropriately restricted our studies by limiting their longitude.
2. Most of these studies are based on a linear idea of change.
3. We have not included in these studies any discrimination between effective and ineffective therapists, or even unethical therapists.
4. We have failed to assess the impact of therapy on the identified clients' extended social networks.

To fully understand the failure of traditional outcome studies, we should briefly review what we know about psychotherapy outcome. Most of what we know comes from semicontrolled studies, almost exclusively involving individual psychotherapy. The strategy for traditional psychotherapy research, including most family research, is not particularly complex. Symptoms are measured in a particular patient group and then a treatment is given. Symptoms are measured at the end of treatment and perhaps, if the study is sophisticated and well funded, some time in the future. The amount of change is compared with results obtained from another group of interest, often a group receiving a placebo treatment or a therapy to be contrasted with the novel intervention. In very sophisticated studies, family members other than the identified client may also receive some type of assessment to determine whether the treatment affected them as well.

It has been very difficult to find consistent studies that indicate that symptoms change more than one standard deviation (sd) from their previous levels (Brody, 1994). In fact, according to Brody, changes of about .5 sds are within the normal range of spontaneous change in major personality traits. Other meta-analytic work has suggested that psychotherapy can produce a change of approximately .8 sds (Smith, Glass, & Miller, 1980), which seems to be a commonly agreed-on figure for the effects of psychotherapy. Using traditional linear outcome measures (which we will discuss in greater detail later in this chapter), it would be surprising if the aggregate level of symptom change in family therapy were beyond this level, at least as measured in the short term.

Managed mental health care often justifies itself by the notion that there is a strong dose response in psychotherapy (Howard, Kopta, Krauss, & Orlinsky, 1986). This means that change in therapy is modeled to be highly linear, with most of the benefits in therapy occurring in relatively brief periods. Therefore, it is asserted that the impact of therapy occurs relatively quickly and that more "bang for the buck" occurs in the first sessions. Hence, lengthier treatment is not necessary. (Interestingly, most of the data from Howard et al.'s study involves not only individual therapy, but also classic neurotic disorders that seem to follow a linear remission through time even if they are not treated, as Eysenck, 1952, demonstrated in his classic paper.)

Chaos theory suggests that more appropriate data collections will be much more difficult and that studies such as the ones summarized by meta-analytical literature are inappropriately shallow (Bütz, 1997). In the linear model, if change is not seen immediately, it is assumed to be absent. Yet it is not uncommon for clinicians to describe such change. Invariably, it is discussed by clinicians in terms of the metaphor of "planting a seed." It is also not uncommon for therapists to report that poorly recalled patients or clients contact them in the distant future to discuss how helpful psychotherapy was for them. Often such clients will state that particular interventions that the therapist attempted and that seemed like a failure at the time eventually were the cause of extraordinary behavioral change. The therapist is usually stymied to duplicate this intervention with other clients, which would be inappropriate in any case, as each family has within it unique dynamics that call for equally tailored interventions.

A linear model of change assumes that any therapeutic effect will be demonstrated at the time a therapy ends or slightly soon after. A nonlinear model of change assumes that therapeutic effect caused by the therapy may not necessarily be demonstrated at the termination of the therapy and may indeed appear sometime later. Figure 10.1 illustrates the different assumptions of these two models. Note that the nonlinear model hypothesizes that change may occur long after formal treatment ends. Notice also that treatment gains may wane more than those obtained in linear change treatment.

Hawkins (1992) has suggested that brief, psychodynamic psychotherapy may result in a nonlinear change process similar to that shown in Figure 10.1. In this illustration, a change process is started in therapy but is

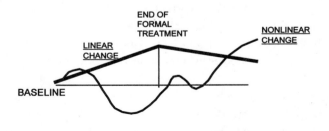

Figure 10.1 Contrasting Assumptions of Linear and Nonlinear Models.

not completed by the time the therapy is terminated. However, the client continues to make self-organizing changes without the presence of a therapist and weekly treatment. A relatively simple test of this hypothesis would be to follow clients who have terminated from brief psychotherapy for a prolonged period, perhaps several years. Change could be assessed on a simple scale and analyzed at many intervals, controlling for the effects of life stressors and predictable developmental problems. While such a project is simple in theory, it may require a massive undertaking of resources to implement on a large scale.

We are not discounting that the linear model may be an appropriate methodology for specific classes of disorders. For example, linear behavioral change may be an appropriate scientific model for problems treated from behavioral and learning theory perspectives as these paradigms are primarily linear. For example, phobias and many other classical neurotic disorders appear to have a very predictable, well-known course of treatment (Eysenck, 1967). It is not surprising that a strong dosage effect has been found for such disorders. Yet the process of change involving apparently more complex mechanisms is less well understood and is almost certainly nonlinear. If this is the case, then many of our outcome measures in traditional psychotherapy are at best inappropriately linear, and more likely, are failing to measure long-term benefits that we are not examining.

Following from the linearization and short-lived nature of these studies, we also run into a massive problem with psychotherapy outcome research—therapist effectiveness. In a recent, widely publicized study, *Consumer Reports* (a magazine that offers evaluations of everything from automobiles to blenders without remuneration for advertisements that might bias them) took on the issue of evaluating psychotherapy (1995). Yet, despite the great rigor with which they undertook this project, there was no estimation of, or even, discrimination between therapists who were effective and those who were not (Seligman, 1995). Furthermore, even if these researchers did discriminate between types of therapists it is unclear how accurate a measure of this type would have been, given our earlier statements about supervision and linear and nonlinear measures of change.

In addition, however, in family therapy, and perhaps also in individual therapy, chaos theory indicates that our outcome evaluation will have to include many other systems than simply the identified client and their therapist. An example will help illuminate why this is true. Consider the following case recently treated by one of the coauthors. A family comes into treatment with nebulous and vaguely defined problems and receives family therapy. As a result of treatment, the wife, who has been rather disenfranchised in the relationship with her overbearing and controlling husband, becomes more assertive. The husband responds by becoming more depressed. The child fluctuates between the parent's two symptoms, as Figure 10.2 illustrates. The question that we want answered is "Has therapy been effective?"

From the perspective of the wife, the answer is probably yes. Measurement of symptoms with a psychometrically valid instrument such as the SS-77 (Johnson, 1992) indicates that the wife is less symptomatic. Self-reports consistently indicate that she is happier and functioning much better. Yet as Figure 10.2 shows, from the perspective of the husband, treatment has been disastrous. His depression, particularly, has markedly increased, and he recently has begun a trial of antidepressant medications. From the perspective of the child, it is impossible to say whether what is occurring is beneficial, since aggregate symptoms seem to change every week. There is no well-accepted methodology for aggregation of the symptoms that have changed in this family system, which would help us determine whether treatment has been effective. Yet from

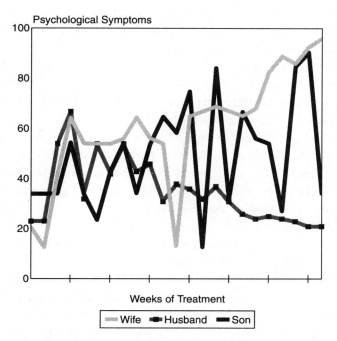

Figure 10.2 Symptom Change in the Family through Time.

our level of analysis thus far, therapy probably can at best be qualified as a mixed success.

But chaos theory suggests that systems are much more connected than the data revealed in this simple triad (Jantsch, 1980). The therapy evaluator must ask about the effects of treatment on other social units. Here the picture may get much more complex. Suppose, in this case, the wife has a midlevel managerial job. Her ability to successfully interact with her husband has boosted her capacity to supervise her employees. Her previous managerial and personal style was one of being explosive and tyrannical. Now that she feels better about herself, she is able to be more cooperative. This in turn has had a very positive effect on the mental health of people who work under her. In at least one case, the change in the boss's attitudes and coping styles has had an indirect, yet positive effect on an employee's marital problems. Because her boss is more reasonable, this worker reports being less preoccupied at home about events at work and is able to respond to her family's needs in ways that she and her husband consider more satisfactory. From that level, treatment appears to have been an undeniable success. The impact of treatment on the wife has spread to others in a positive manner.

But where do we stop measuring changes in behavior following the therapy? Let's make the situation even murkier, as it actually is in real life. The husband, who is a college professor, has become depressed, agitated, and withdrawn following his wife's progress in therapy. Consequently, he no longer is as kind to and as tolerant of his legion of students. Before the treatment, he was often viewed by other faculty members as being pompous and controlling. Yet he was very patient of his students' shortcomings. In fact, despite his aberrant relationship with his wife, the professor was previously an outstanding teacher. He was particularly adept at reaching students with less-than-optimal academic preparation and would spend many long hours helping educationally disadvantaged pupils. This is particularly important because the professor teaches at a university that enrolls many underprivileged and educationally ill-prepared freshmen.

Now, however, he is passive, almost indolent and has lost the spark that he once had for educating difficult students. These students who used to flock to his classes have noted that he is no longer helpful and at times seems downright dull and ordinary. The extra effort he would demonstrate to help people who otherwise might not find academic success is now gone. A large number of students have been affected by this change. Should we consider this change in evaluating the effects of therapy? How about the effects this treatment had on the mental health of the professor's students as well as future students? Where do we stop measuring?

These are questions for future theorists. We know that chaos theory gives us a better grasp of the fact that all systems are interconnected. In this case, a traditional research design may have measured the wife alone or, at most, the husband and the wife. Yet reality is much more complex, as this case illustrates. We are treading on very new ground in even asking these questions. Any type of psychotherapy outcome research will require a great deal more data than we have traditionally collected. It may also require an emphasis on qualitative research (e.g., Denzomn & Lincoln, 1994) that some may find objectionable. Finally, it may require that research practitioners have a greater understanding of nonlinear mathematics, a point we have yet to discuss. Regardless of how much effort we have put forth to answer the question regarding the effectiveness of mental health therapies, we have barely begun to satisfactorily address this problem.

OUR CONCEPTION OF THERAPY ETHICS WILL HAVE TO CHANGE

Concern with applied issues in ethics is characteristic of any new profession grappling with autonomy and rapid change (Starr, 1982). Not surprising, given family therapy's expeditious rise, an inordinate amount of literature has been generated regarding what are considered as "pragmatically based" ethical discussions. These involve practical issues such as the duty to warn, the importance of record keeping, and similar practice-related concerns. However, accent on the development of a pragmatically based code of ethics may obfuscate the meta-ethical problems involved in establishing true normative professional standards (Beauchamp & Childress, 1989). Meta-ethics is the analysis of language, reasoning, and contradiction in ethical statements. Meta-ethical problems of family therapy practice are rarely discussed, perhaps because they are believed by most practitioners to be synonymous with those in other branches of healing arts.

The foremost normative meta-ethical principle of any healing art, including family therapy, is the axiom of nonmaleficence, or *do no harm* (Beauchamp & Childress, 1989). Often proclaimed as the fundamental principle in the Hippocratic tradition, this concept extends at least as far back as the Pythagoreans, and perhaps into the code of Hammurabi (Pellegrino & Thomasma, 1981). The principle of nonmaleficence is recognized by many ethicists as the basis of not only medical conventions but also general social morality. Nonmaleficence has also been endorsed by philosophical theorists as diverse as utilitarians (e.g., Brandt, 1979) and deontological moralists (e.g., Rawls, 1971).

As the ethicist Singer (1979) has commented, however, nonmaleficence in the healing arts is inherently intertwined with a second principle, that of *beneficence*, or of doing good. Ethical dilemmas arise for the helping professional when the principle of *primum non nocere* ("Above all, do no harm") conflicts with the possibility that a potentially necessary or beneficial treatment may be harmful for a particular patient. Since at least the time of the Roman physician Galen, reasonable ethical procedures have involved weighing the risks of potential helping interventions with their likely benefits (Pellegrino & Thomasma, 1981). Even when a treatment may be effective, it is considered unethical if it carries a high probability of substantial iatrogenic harm. Usually this means that ethical decisions necessarily involve assessment of inherent risks of treatment to subpopulations, a so-called risk analysis. In medical settings, an application of risk analysis may be seen when a patient with a serious disease is denied a potentially life-saving treatment because the side effects might prove too precarious.

Various schools of individual psychotherapy have advocated the equivalent of a risk analysis in determining what constitutes an ethical treatment intervention. For example, psychoanalysts and other psychodynamically oriented therapists consider "depth" therapeutic approaches unethical in patients whose ego structures will not tolerate the anxiety associated with such procedures (Freud, 1938). In this case, the treatment of choice is supportive, rather than insight-oriented therapy (Cameron & Rychlak, 1985). Similarly, behaviorists generally do not consider it ethical to provide treatments that have a high probability of making a client worse or that would not generalize beyond the therapist's office (Rycklak, 1973). In each case, ethicalness of the proposed intervention is based on an assessment of potential risks versus potential benefits, with both assessments being grounded in careful diagnosis and consideration of a variety of normative factors.

Risk analysis involves a knowledge and assessment of the potential dangers of the proposed treatment. In other words, a preliminary stage in ethical treatment is *risk assessment*. A few observers have recognized the difficulty in family therapy of adequately assessing appropriate risk of family treatment (e.g., Worthington, 1987). Dell (1980, 1982) has eloquently commented on the characteristic ethical problems involved in the potentially countertherapeutic and disruptive aspects of family intervention. Dell's analysis expresses an apprehension that systems therapists cannot always accurately anticipate the effects of their interventions on family systems. Unlike medicine, where interventions generally have a relatively predictable linear dosage effect, the results of systemic intervention may be highly unpredictable. This has long been noted by humanistic family therapists who emphasize the potential uniqueness of family intervention and the impossibility (as well as undesirability) of a priori assumptions regarding a given course of therapy (Satir, 1967; Ray & Keeney, 1993).

The principle of nonmaleficence may be impossible to maintain for the practicing family therapist, simply because it may not be feasible to specify if a particular intervention will be helpful or harmful to a family or to specific members. The only way in which it can be consistently guaranteed is to not intervene, which, of course, violates the ethical principle of beneficence. Often, as they consider the treatment of a family, even the most competent therapists find themselves in this dilemma. More alarming are therapists who do not. We do not know how to address these issues, but they will warrant further attention in the literature.

A similar argument occurs regarding targeting the person in the family system who will be helped. A specific intervention or series of interventions may be beneficial to some family members, yet detrimental to others. Reviewing the preceding example, a family reorganization designed to increase a wife's autonomy might enhance the self-esteem of the depressed wife but lower the well-being and life satisfaction of her narcissistic and controlling husband. Nonmaleficence also becomes hard to justify as an overriding ethical principle when a treatment may result in the superior functioning of most family members, at a trade-off of increased symptomatology of a smaller subset of the family unit. The decision whether to concentrate therapeutic efforts on the more "salvageable" members of a family unit is a common clinical quandary that the clinician working with multidysfunctional systems often faces (McCown & Johnson, 1993). It soon becomes apparent that family therapists may need to reexamine the meta-ethical assumptions of their interventions. In the meantime, what do therapists interested in chaos theory do to handle these ethical issues?

Perhaps anecdotal experiences of the previous decades may be helpful until meta-ethical statements can be identified. Some readers may remember the regrettable situation that occurred when structural and strategic therapies first became popular. At that time, many poorly trained therapists performed interventions with disastrous results, which they attempted to justify by arguments regarding their "success with the system." For example, therapists may have allowed incest or severe substance abuse to continue because it was "good for the system." As we look back, these statements make us bristle but they were once uttered by well-meaning therapists. Lest these assertions seem far-fetched, we often hear practitioners at various professional talks disclose to us quite belatedly that they tolerated inappropriate family behavior, such as physical violence, because they are afraid that if they intervene into the system there may be unpredictable consequences. This is appalling, and it leads to a therapy that is amorphous and without substance.

We have no immediate solutions. At times, very necessary interventions have had untoward consequences, such as when a domestic partner has been separated from an abusive partner who later kills himself in despair. This is rare, but it does happen. Our best approach is a commonsense pragmatism, based on the instrumental/perceptual distinctions advocated in Chapters 7 and 8. As much as is possible, the nonlinear dynamical therapist must attempt to avoid furthering of instrumental harm to any family member. This will usually require implementation of linear or commonsense models of prediction, which, as we have seen, do not do well. However, psychometric predictions based on the linear model only do slightly better, as behavioral science literature indicates. As much as possible, we must try to eliminate harm. This means that obvious instrumental dangers—incest, child abuse, substance abuse, parental neglect, profound depression—deserve the same seriousness that they receive in other forms of therapy.

TRAINING NEEDS WILL CHANGE

A change that chaos theory may evoke is that it will require an expansion of traditional family therapy training curriculum. Recently, one of the coauthors reviewed some typical family systems syllabi with a systemically oriented life scientist. Most of the syllabi came from doctoral programs in family therapy or doctoral tracks in psychology programs. It was embarrassing to see what is taught and passed off as new thinking. Concepts that are equivalent in currency to a Ptolomic view of the universe are being promoted as "innovative." Present on practically every syllabus were such elementary concepts as cybernetics and homeostasis. Absent were introductions to concepts as commonplace and important as catastrophe theory, control theory, entropy, fuzzy logic, Gödel's theorem, optimal processes, set theory, undecidability, universal computation, and general systems theory, to say nothing of chaos theory and complexity. The life science reviewer noted quite seriously that it looked as though family therapy's understanding of systems "stopped at about 1942." More distressing still is that, by and large, family therapy draws on more contemporary scientific research than many of its sister disciplines.

The reason for this is that family therapists, as well as others, lack the mathematical training to understand contemporary systems theories. Our understanding is limited to a few very simple models, such as cybernetics, which do not require hard work to understand. Casti (1992) discusses the background for understanding contemporary systems theories. He concludes the following is probably necessary: exposure to and assimilation of material found in calculus, linear algebra and matrix theory, ordinary differential equations, and probability theory. Moreover, as Casti notes, it is necessary to be competent in the basic vocabulary and techniques of mathematics. In other words, a mastery of undergraduate mathematics is necessary. It is impossible for family therapists to fully participate in the revolution in systems theory unless we become better prepared.

Courses in physics and life sciences will be also indispensable. If our trainees lack such backgrounds, then we may have to provide remedial training in these areas. Family therapy of the twenty-first century can no longer be the place of habitation for students who have avoided the "difficult" courses of mathematics and harder sciences. Indeed, as Crutchfield noted in response to a question at a recent lecture (1996), family therapists are attempting to not only measure static systems that exhibit chaos, but dynamic systems that exhibit chaos. Such measurement requires more, not less expertise.

For now, understanding the analogies we have made here may be enough, as the basics of establishing the existence of chaos and complexity are being hammered out. But, innovation in systemic therapy will only be common when therapists are comfortable visitors, if not at home, discussing the mathematical assumptions of nonlinear systems the way our students now are able to discuss the assumptions of linear models.

WE WILL HAVE TO MAKE THERAPY MORE CULTURALLY CONGRUENT

Another issue related to training is that chaos theory suggests we are deficient in training practitioners to meet the variety of families that come for treatment. The scientific theories we have discussed suggest that effective therapy will be primarily an effort of continued and congruent effort. For years, many of us believed that once we understood certain universals about family systems, we did not need to know specifics about the cultural contexts of families. For example, shared worldviews, stressors, and assumptions that are common to specific religious, ethnic, racial, or national groups may have been viewed as irrelevant or not important compared with "important" concepts such as the identified patient, symbiosis, family structure, and other constructs.

This is not the case. The relationship of the family to the therapist will probably always be tenuous, capable of being disrupted by systemic forces that the therapist can only approximate and cannot control. The therapist can no longer relax with the knowledge that he or she is technically competent. Cultural competence is equally important (Bütz, 1995a, 1997; Bütz, Duran, & Tong, 1995).

To provide the transforming energy, the butterflies that can occur in "phrase space," we may have to learn more about each family's worldview. To this extent, we actively need to recruit therapists from disadvantaged and culturally diverse backgrounds. We must go beyond our present methods of redressing (which haven't been successful) easily identified numerical minorities, to recruit persons to the ranks of training who have had diverse life experiences. Consider the treatment of religious fundamentalists, a growing body of patients that we have illustrated through several case studies. Failure to understand the worldviews and assumptions of this group may result in the generation of systemic forces that will encourage noncompliance or termination. Cross-cultural training does not mean an overview of stereotypes about different racial groups such as African Americans, Asian Americans and Native Americans. Nor does it mean that racial matching will assure understanding (Sue, 1992). Matching colors is no more cross-cultural than stereotyping different ethnicities, since a fourth-generation Asian American may be no better prepared to understand a first-generation Samoan American than an individual of European decent. We must come to understand our own cultural blinders, as being an "American" not only can be offensive to other "Americans," but also seems to sum up to silly slogans involving apple pie and purchasing a particular automobile (Chamberlain & Bütz, 1997). Have ethnic identities here in the United States come down to which TV commercial one supports? Knowing and understanding our own frame of reference, comprehending the impact of colonization on Native American people in the United States (Duran & Duran, 1995), fathoming the disappointed plans gone sour to come to the United States and return home rich as in some portions of the Asian American experience (Tong, 1994; Takaki, 1989), and grasping the politics of violence within these families (Carrillo, 1995) all are starts on this journey. Since the 1930s or so, we have known that our observation of an event changes it, and in the cross-cultural world this is no less the case. Our presence, our frame of reference, our understanding of the dynamics within these systems alter the course of therapy and its ability to be effective. For now, at the very least, graduate training programs in cross-cultural issues must go beyond mere educational approaches and allow students the opportunity to gain information about the culturally different families they will be treating and experience that lifestyle to some degree (McGoldrick et al., 1982).

THE FUTURE: A CAUSE FOR OPTIMISM?

Chaos theory, or nonlinear dynamical systems theory, as it is more formally known, is designed to investigate complex behavior and to look for an underlying determinism in data that were previously considered random or the result of error variance. As we have shown, in a very short period, chaos theory has gone from a fringe movement in the physical and life sciences to become mainstream orthodoxy. Other related theories, such as complexity and the new physics have also risen with the tide. There are many implications of chaos theory, but among the most important is the apparent paradox of phenomena that are simultaneously completely deterministic, but essentially, still unpredictable.

Chaos, complexity, and the assumptions of the new physics are everywhere. It has now been discovered at many levels of measurement, from the macrolevel of movements of bodies in the solar system, to the microlevel of the movement of wave particles in the quantum world. Chaos theory and related theories are rapidly proving to be the third major revolution in the physics of the twentieth century. Despite many clever analogies, it is not clear that the first, relativity, directly involves family therapy. Nonlinear systems theory described here, on the other hand, has many implications.

Neither chaos or complexity in our world, nor chaos, complexity, and the new physics in science will go away. These sets of theories when applied to family therapy do what new paradigms are supposed to do. Together, they answer previously unanswered questions and make us revise how we think and feel about the world. Complex problems become understandable, while simpler, often inadequate explanations melt away. Still other questions, which we didn't even have the conceptual framework to pose, now become paramount. Many will prove unanswerable, yet this is the price we pay for progress.

Thinking about families in terms of this group of theories is not easy. The assumptions are complex and sometimes counterintuitive. The mathematics are formidable. Yet the possibilities are dramatically fruitful. Despite the difficulties involved, most of the concepts in chaos, complexity, and the new physics are well known to family therapists, though our language may lack the elegance to describe them fully. We will forever alter families and family therapy once we learn about chaos, complexity, and the new physics; align these ideas with traditional ideas that have been elaborated from observation; and begin to create new conceptualizations. With discipline and creativity, we should be able to develop an environment that not only nurtures the astounding capacity for adaptation families have, but also see to it that effective family treatment will remain a viable option well into the next century.

CHAPTER 11

Epigram: Measuring Change in Chaotic Systems, Problems with Modeling, and the Need for Case Studies

Mathematics, like life in general, is not going to give you something for nothing.

Biological systems are constantly changing. This is the major difference between biological studies of chaos and investigations examining stable physical systems like electronic circuits. This is why rigorous demonstration of chaotic behavior is so much more difficult for biologists.

— Paul Rapp (1993, pp. 92–93)

A S WE MENTIONED in Chapter 2, the majority of the work done involving chaos theory is quite technical and filled with confusing jargon for those unfamiliar with the territory. In this chapter, we are going to push a little deeper into this territory to explain scientifically why we present the majority of our ideas in a theoretical single case study format.

In science, there is a nice little formula that directs researchers in how to go about their studies. It is called the scientific method, and while we mentioned it briefly in Chapter 2, it seems worth revisiting here. Roughly, it follows these steps:[1]

1. We have a recognized problem.
2. We have a formulation, an idea of how to solve the problem that is generally titled a theory.
3. Theories that makes sense are pursued, and other, silly theories are discarded.
4. Theories have hypotheses about the problem and how to solve it.
5. Hypotheses are tested after they have been operationalized.
6. Once the hypotheses have been operationalized, a method of analysis is chosen.
7. Data are collected to be analyzed.
8. The analysis occurs and each hypothesis is either supported, not supported, or merits further research.
9. If the hypotheses are supported, then the theory to a degree is given credence, and in time may be elaborated as a law.
10. If the hypotheses are not supported, then the theory is weak and not worthy of serious study—or a theorist who is particularly clever might claim that current methods of analysis are too crude for the complexities of the theory.

So, there we have it, the scientific method in a nutshell. Now, as stated earlier, many of the ideas that had been previously shelved as "too complex to study" have been dusted off and revisited with the methods of analysis used in chaos theory. And, in a number of cases, these theories with the requisite hypotheses have been supported. But, as Rapp points out, biological systems are a trifle more difficult to test as they are "constantly changing."

In the study of chaos theory's application to modes of therapy, generally two approaches have been employed. One group, the "theorists," develop theory to elucidate testable hypotheses, while the second group, the "modelers," take certain data and plug them into methods of analysis to detect the presence or absence of chaos. The theorist method is more cautious than the other. The modelers are close cousins to the empiricists in behav-

---

[1] We were amazed that it was difficult, if not impossible, to find the definition for the scientific method in contemporary texts. They simply do not mention it, or like Kuhn (1962/1970, 1977), mention it only in passing without fully defining it. It seems as though the old paradigm of empiricism is to some extent housed in mysticism when one cannot even find a proper definition for its method. We used Webster's (1989) as the basis for our statements.

ioral science, since they have a propensity to believe that chaos only exists if you are able to model it (Barton, 1994). In chaos theory, as we have described briefly in Chapter 2, chaos is found through modeling data on the planes of a phase portrait to detect the presence or absence of a strange attractor or other such phenomenon. If one of these portraits does emerge, the theorist in the crowd might be compelled to ask, "What is it that you are modeling, what does it mean?" The answer back might well be "chaos," but is our friend the modeler actually finding chaos? Paul Rapp (1993, 1995), and others, might question the quality of the modeling techniques being used. Rapp, a recognized expert on modeling chaos in biological systems, has even asserted: "Is there any evidence for chaos in the human nervous system? The body of evidence in support of this conclusion continues to decrease as analytic methods improve" (Rapp, 1995, p. 99).

So, caution in modeling chaotic phenomena is called for, especially in constantly changing biological systems. Therefore, we have chosen to use modeling techniques only sparingly as we develop our theory focusing more on single-case examples with what appear to be comparable dynamics found in more stable physical systems. As we will describe in detail, it appears premature to "put all our eggs in one basket" using modeling techniques (Elkaïm, 1990) that prove difficult to validate in biological organisms, much less systems as complex as families.

THE HEURISTIC POTENTIAL OF MODELING AT THIS POINT

At this time, data are weak, and methodologies for modeling family functioning, chaos, self-organization, and theories of complexity are quite crude.[2] The complicated nature of the subject, along with other difficulties,

---

[2]The reader should not confuse the extraordinary difficulty in successfully modeling chaotic structures with the less difficult task of developing mathematical models of discrete, but stable, dynamic change. Discrete nonlinear phenomena—that is, events produced by fixed dynamic structures, may be very difficult to model, but are often "solvable" by difference equations (Huckfeldt, Kohfeld, & Likens, 1982). Indeed, very useful social science models have been generated under the assumption that stability exists in underlying nonlinear change. However, diachronic change, where there is underlying dynamic structure, is not stable, and these problems are not made stable by difference equations—usually they require use of nonlinear differential equations. There is no general or well accepted method of solving even first order nondifferential equations. As equations become more complex, they often become technically and mathematically unsolvable. Approximations generated by such methods, as more easily solvable difference equations, lack the global stability to be useful for describing continuous dynamical systems. Simply put, most complex systems *cannot* be successfully modeled in mathematical terms.

have limited our research primarily to single case studies and to very small samples. There are several reasons for our slow progress and for the largely speculative and theoretical nature of major contributions (e.g., Kaplan & Kaplan, 1991; Langs, 1992).

A serious problem limiting the usefulness of this approach to date is that of obtaining "enough data" to determine that chaotic processes actually exist (Burlingame & Bloch, 1996; Burlingame & Hope, 1996; Langs & Badalamenti, 1993; Rapp, 1993). Compared with the probability of simply finding randomness or noise, it takes hundreds, and usually thousands of measured points to adequately demonstrate the existence of chaos. Because of this, much more work has been theoretical rather than empirical, a first and necessary step, but one that will eventually prove insufficient if this new approach to changing families is ever to have a "scientific" underpinning. As stated, our goal here is to explore the territory qualitatively and share with you what we have found.

FINDING CHAOS, AND SEARCHING FOR IT IN FAMILIES

Other researchers, feeling more established in their theorizing, have moved on to submit their hypotheses to the scrutiny of numbers and modeling. In the following pages, we will review a number of quasi-experimental attempts to find chaos in human experience. Still, we will also point out the problems in extrapolating these models to family therapy, offering some of our own research as an example of the inherent difficulties clinicians encounter as they go "searching" for chaos in a family.

One group of researchers, led by the mathematician Anthony Badalamenti and the psychoanalyst Robert Langs, have investigated the role of entropy—which is essentially the expected and unexpected patterns of energy flow—in individual psychotherapy communications (Badalamenti, 1992; Badalamenti & Langs, 1992; Badalamenti, Langs, & Ferguson, 1992). Again, the advantage of sampling large numbers of data from a single-subject design is the ability to perform time series research, necessary for establishing the existence of complex and chaotic patterns. The advantage of studying a single patient/therapist interaction is that it reduces data complexity. Badalamenti and Langs (1992) discuss a five-dimension representation of psychotherapeutic communication in the patient-analyst dialogue. Assuming the dimensions are additive, a similar representation for communications between all family members would lead to an extraordinarily unwieldy set of data, impossible to visualize in any meaningful manner and probably beyond the computing abilities of most of us.

Another outstanding area of exception regarding empirical work and the need to transcend theory has been in the area of motor development, where Kelso and Fogel (1987) have shown a number of very clever methods of obtaining repeated measures in a brief time. Smith and Thelen (1993) summarize contemporary research in motor and cognitive development, based on nonlinear and dynamic systems theories, and illustrate how repeated measures can be obtained from human subjects (mostly infants) using objective criteria.

Infants, however, are not adolescents nor adults. There is certainly less motivation among bigger people to sit in a laboratory several hours at a time, where hundreds of measures are taken. Apart from some early research by Hannah (1991) involving the extraordinarily demanding task of having subjects reporting their mood states at 15- or 30-minute intervals for two weeks, there is very little longitudinal data on human behavior or comparisons of degrees of chaos with more specific and traditional psychological constructs.

Reidbord and Redington (1992; Redington & Reidbord, 1992) have provided an interesting example in studying the role of anxiety (Bütz, 1990, August) in the therapeutic process. They examined chaotic dynamics in autonomic nervous system activity of a single patient during a psychotherapy session, where hundreds of measures could be relatively unobtrusively obtained. They discovered:

> First, as shown by others, heart rate evidenced nonlinear dynamics. Second, the phase space of heart rate exhibited interesting structure. There were fairly well-defined clusters of data in the phase space, some of which differed modestly in size of orbit. Each cluster may represent a psychophysiological attractor, which in turn might correspond to stability—or, more negatively, incarceration—within a psychological state. Third, types II and III trajectories, which may represent chaotic bifurcations, appear to be related in time to psychologically meaningful events. Fourth, a type IV or "wandering" trajectory may represent highly nonlinear behavior resulting from complex chaotic attractors in the phase space, and may be related to relatively healthier psychological functioning. (Redington & Reidbord, 1992, p. 1004)

What they are describing is that chaotic attractors may be related to insights in the therapy session, where these attractors seem to "coincide with therapist interventions" (Reidbord & Redington, 1992, p. 656). Despite the degree of detail demonstrated in the preceding, rather lengthy quote, Reidbord and Redington describe their work as preliminary.

The problem with sampling limitations, is one of the reasons that seminal work regarding chaos in human behavior has been done in the area of brain waves. This is seen in the work of Skarda and Freeman (1987), Freeman (1991), Rapp (1987; Rapp et al., 1989) and many other researchers.

To the family therapist, the essence of the problem is how to obtain large data sets. Raymond Cattell (1982) has noted that it takes approximately 10 to 100 times as long to get behavioral variables as it does to get physical variables, such as saliva or serum samples. Psychophysical variables, such as brain waves or skin conductance, for all their unreliability, are obtainable at probably 10,000 times the frequency of behavioral variables. This suggests that someday we may want to wire families into monitors while we examine family processes. In the meantime, we will be forced to analyze whatever limited data we have.

WHAT DO WE DO WITH THE DATA?

Once we have data about systems that we suspect behave chaotically, the next set of problems involves what to do with these data. Disagreement regarding appropriateness of data analysis plagues the field, as it does any new field (Casti, 1992). Some authors, such as Abraham, Abraham, and Shaw (1990) have recommended avoidance of mathematical presentation altogether and instead have suggested that researchers concentrate on visual displays. Methods of complex data display have been reiterated in a more general volume by R. Abraham and Shaw (1992).

However, as Cattell (1982) has noted, social science in general, and psychology in particular, is wrongly, but almost inherently enamored with the concept of "significance" and the use of rather simple tests to describe differences in complex behavior. These roots are deeply embedded in United States psychology, though actually are somewhat paradoxical, inasmuch as the behavioral tradition often favored graphical representation of data rather than numerical analysis (Roback, 1952). Therefore, a discussion of numerical methods and ways to "determine the presence" of chaos in a system seems appropriate.

There are numerous ways of analyzing data to demonstrate an underlying deterministic nonlinearity, that is, chaos. As discussed earlier, some researchers consider it appropriate simply to show phase portraits of complex systems, and aside from generating hypotheses based on theory this is a likely first step for any researcher. Other empirically oriented persons calculate Lyapunov exponents, which are a measure of sensitivity to initial conditions. Technically, the Lyapunov exponent is a measure of the rate at which nearby trajectories in phase space diverge. Chaotic orbits have at least one positive Lyapunov exponent and in general, there are as many exponents as there are dynamical equations driving the system (Moon, 1992).

The Lyapunov exponent is itself unstable, however; it is incredibly sensitive to initial conditions and sample size, and random data can produce a spurious positive Lyapunov exponent (Devaney, 1992). This can naturally add to the difficulty the researcher faces. We can also calculate a capacity dimension D, or the Hausdorf dimension (Sprott & Rowlands, 1992), which is another index of the degree of chaos found in data. Once this step is completed, one plots the log of the fraction of hypercubes that are occupied with data points versus the log of the normalized linear dimension of hypercubes. The average slope of the line for the two middle segments is the capacity dimension (Moon, 1992). There is little agreement in the literature under what circumstances D represents true randomness compared with chaos. Therefore, the advantage of using this statistic is as yet unclear. At this time a somewhat lively debate exists among social scientists regarding appropriate statistical summation and examination of data expected to be "chaotic."

Now how do we test the significance of between-group differences, as is traditionally done in psychological or other scientific research? No one knows. Our own earlier work in this area (McCown & Johnson, 1993) used singular value decompensation, which is a method of generating an orthogonal set of functions, similar to factor analysis (Casti, 1992). This technique was initially designed to study turbulence. Yet the mathematical assumptions are not well worked out. Is it necessary to remove linear terms first? What does it mean when we find 6 versus 4 functions in time series data? It took psychological theorists practicing factor analysis 50 years to solve these problems with linear models, and controversy still is endemic. Since the mathematics involved in the study of nonlinear systems is so much more complex, we might well anticipate slower progress.

Measurement Error

Another problem with the understanding or the determination of chaos in complex systems is the inherency of measurement error (Badalamenti, Langs, & Ferguson, 1992). When we measure a behavioral science construct, such as depression, or anxiety, we frequently use psychometric instruments or inventories (Kline, 1984). The theory behind such instruments is that their use involves summation of two components:

$$Score = ST + SE$$

Score is a person's position on a test or measure of interest, ST is the person's "true" score and SE is error introduced from an infinite number of sources (Cattell, 1982).

It is also assumed that error is uncorrelated with true score and is itself randomly distributed.

Traditional test construction theory assumes that it is possible to reduce error to about 10% to 20% of a total test variance, but generally no more. Measurement error is problematic in any social science field or any time we attempt to do human research (Cook & Campbell, 1977; Searle, 1987) and maybe even more so in research regarding family therapy (Todd & Stanton, 1983). For traits that are relatively stable, such as extroversion or general scholastic ability, we may make relatively accurate predictions regarding individual behavior, despite measurement error (Eysenck & Eysenck, 1985). Over the short run, we may even be able to match individuals or families to specific treatments, based on measurement that is fraught with error. For example, L'Abate, Farrar, and Serritella (1992) believe that a history of different addictive behavior justifies a different modality of treatment, a commonsense approach that has been all but ignored by many practitioners.

Yet, when we are dealing with systems that are sensitive to initial conditions (e.g., chaotic), traditional measurement error is devastating in its impact on our ability to predict the future. Keep in mind the butterfly effect, discussed in Chapter 2, where one to three decimals may have influential effects on the direction a system will take. Imagine how much worse off we are when our measurement error may equal 20% of the variance! This problem has not gone unnoticed by chaoticians. As Ruelle (1991) has noted, chaos has most easily been demonstrated in social sciences where measurement error is less problematic. An example is in economics, where dependent measures of relatively error-free terms exist such as those involving commodity prices or precious metal futures. Furthermore, our constructs themselves may need reification. As noted, chaos theory was advanced in areas where the constructs were extraordinarily well defined, such as fluid dynamics, meteorology, and eventually, particle physics. Casti (1990), a well-known dynamical systems theorist, notes further that chaos became applicable in fields where strong mathematical models already existed. Where constructs were less well defined such as in biology, sociology, or psychology, there has been less success. Family therapy, where even fewer such models exist, may provide very difficult data to analyze.

In chaotic systems, such error is both extremely important and also, paradoxically, quite irrelevant (Ruelle, 1991). Because of sensitivity to initial conditions, the behavior of chaotic systems can only be predicted for short periods. Measurement error compounds this problem tremendously, as Lorenz found out in the 1960s while calculating the weather.

Measurement error limits our ability to make predictions much more than in linear models. On the other hand, measurement error does not influence recognition of any of the characteristics of nonlinear systems, providing that enough data points are sampled. If measurement error is truly random, then it is merely white noise and will not influence the dynamical system's characteristics. Furthermore, if measurement error itself reflects a chaotic, systematic variance, then it too is part of the system and is actually of interest. This is a complex question with no presently clear answers.

AN APPLICATION OF CHAOS: CRISIS-PRONE AND TREATMENT-RESISTANT FAMILIES

Most of our empirical work to date has involved the study of chaos in families recognized by clinicians as having a history of extensive or constant turmoil. We have also examined the treatment patterns associated with families who resist outside intervention, including family and individual psychotherapy. These groups are not mutually exclusive, as Figure 11.1 illustrates. Families can be both crisis-prone and treatment-resistant, two systemic characteristics that make it difficult to receive appropriate help. We have labeled this third group of families as "high risk."

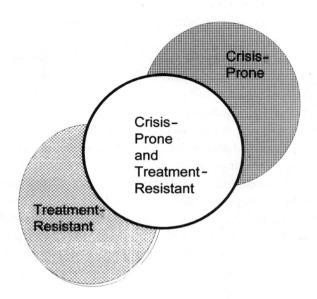

Figure 11.1 Overlap between Crisis-Proneness and Treatment-Resistance.

McCown and Johnson (1993) have studied the diagnoses, behavioral characteristics, service utilization patterns, and socioeconomic variables of crisis-prone, treatment-resistant, and high-risk families. Families were defined as treatment-resistant if they met at least one of the following criteria: (a) families who missed one third of scheduled sessions; (b) families who terminated against therapist advice; (c) families who terminated abruptly; and (d) families who terminated before treatment began (during the intake session or immediately after). Families that dropped out while on a waiting list or who changed to another therapist in a different agency or in the private sector were not included in these categories or in this study, since their status could not be determined.

Families were defined as crisis-prone if any members of the immediate family (IP, parents, sibling, or other cohabiting relatives) performed any of the following behaviors more than three times in the subsequent year, as indicated by chart record: (a) called during nonscheduled hours, requesting to speak with either a therapist or an emergency worker (not including calls to clarify appointment times), (b) requested an unscheduled appointment between sessions or regular appointment times, (c) contacted another community mental health resource in crisis (such as a hospital, another therapist, a crisis line, etc., as indicated by client report or chart note). Since it was hypothesized that most families are especially crisis-prone during the first few weeks of therapy, crisis calls or services provided during the first month of treatment were excluded from this count.

Our hypothesis was that we would find more chaos in crisis-prone, rather than treatment-resistant families. As will be discussed, fractal dimensionality is a tool for recognizing the degree of chaos in a system with comparatively limited points.

Ten transcripts each for crisis-prone and treatment-resistant families were obtained from the preceding study and coded for components of response to therapist injunctives.

For treatment-resistant families, the mean fractal dimension was 1.221, whereas for the crisis-prone families, the dimension was 3.624. These results are interpreted as meaning that treatment-resistant families are much less likely to respond by acting in synchronicity with the therapist, while crisis-prone families are much more likely to overreact to whatever the therapist is saying. Chaos exists in both types of systems; however, crisis-prone clients are more chaotic.

We have also determined the fractal dimensionality of high-risk families, where variability of symptomatology is the rule, rather than the exception. The fractal dimensionality was 3.80, much closer to that of the crisis-prone families than the treatment-resistant families.

DIMENSIONALITY AND SYMPTOMS

A tenet of family systems theory is that systems frequently have a dynamic quality. Displacement of symptoms from one person to another is possible, though not always probable, as the rigid hydraulic model of nineteenth-century physics would suggest. How stable are symptoms in families? The answer probably depends on what we mean by "symptoms" and the manner in which we measure them.

One method useful for measuring symptomatology in families has been an adaptation of Johnson's (1992) Symptom Survey-77 (SS-77). This is a measure of a client's symptomatology within the previous week, with a modification making it useful to measure current state behavior. The SS-77 is a measure of major affective problems identified in the clinical and scientific literature as typically associated with mental health, psychiatric, and medical patients. The SS-77 was designed to reflect specific symptom changes by including only symptom items suggested as being capable of modification by psychotherapy or neuropharmacology. Because of this quality, the SS-77 has rather minimal sensitivity to changes in personality structure and long-standing traits, but very good sensitivity to changes from psychotherapy. Scales of the SS-77 include items measured in Table 11.1.

Table 11.1
SS-77 Scales

1. Somatic Complaints (Items = 8)
2. Depression (Items = 10)
3. Alcohol and Other Drug Abuse (Items = 8)
4. Anxiety (Items = 10)
5. Obsessive-Compulsive Symptoms (Items = 9)
6. Panic Disorder Without (Items = 9) and With Agoraphobia (Items = 11)*
7. Traumatic Stress (Items = 9)
8. Minimization of Symptoms (Items = 8)
9. Magnification of Symptoms (Items = 8)

*These items are the same for both scales except that two additional items are added for agoraphobia.

In one study of crisis-prone families, five families, each with three members, were administered the SS-77 daily for 300 days. In each case, as in the case of all the families, a high degree of dimensionality (>3) was obtained, suggesting evidence of probable chaos, at least when data is sampled at daily intervals. Positive Lyapunov exponents were also obtained for all of the families.

This contrasts with more "normal families" (those not in treatment) where evidence gathered to date indicates more linearity in symptoms and less variability. The Lyapunov exponent in these families are *not* positive, indicative of the absence of chaos.

SINGLE CASE STUDIES OF CHANGE

Only additional data and longer sampling will determine whether symptoms have dynamic qualities that family therapists have claimed. Yet it may be useful to follow individual cases to determine whether specific interventions can reduce aggregate symptomatology, a method analogous to the single case study design in experimental psychology.

Here, we have more data, though again, this is research limited to single family case studies. SS-77 data were used on a number of families receiving treatment. Aggregate levels of symptoms were summed, as in the preceding study. Results are pertinent to an understanding of the manner in which nonlinear dynamics affects family change.

A first finding is that families change in an individual and idiosyncratic style. Clinical experience suggests that there are two different patterns of family change. Two types of patterns of family changes are common. One pattern change is linear and "dose dependent," almost like the effect of medications. However, not all change occurs in a linear fashion, a fact that is becoming increasingly recognized by psychologists (Collins & Horn, 1991; Haynes, 1992).

The study of nonlinear change is highly problematic in the behavioral sciences, where most of our models are built on the assumption of strong linearity. Haynes (1992) has noted specifically that nonlinear change is inappropriately modeled by statistics with strong normal distribution assumptions, such as meta-analytically derived effect sizes (Bangert-Drowns, 1986). Complex or curvilinear relations, as well as an absence of "dose dependence" may explain the comparative low efficacy of family therapy, as measured in traditional meta-analytic methods.

A third pattern of family change needs commentary. Figure 11.2 shows aggregate symptom levels of a family in treatment for depression and

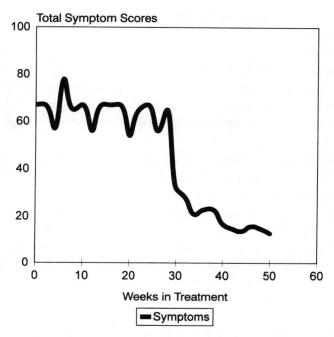

Figure 11.2 Total Symptom Scores of Family in Treatment (Note the Dramatic Drop after 31 Weeks).

acting out behavior of their teenage daughter. Note that for 30 sessions there was no major reduction in symptomatology, however on session 31 the family began a pattern of extraordinary progress. It is clear that the family obtained some type of behavioral change; the therapist attributes the change to "insight" and session notes do not reflect any differences in external family stressors or a new type of therapeutic approach. As the therapist noted, "The family was just getting ready to boil for so long, storing up heat. Finally they did." This metaphor conveys the dramatic process of nonlinear change that sometimes occurs.

An advantage to using the terminology from theories of chaos and complexity is that they enable us to refine our terms and to find similarities between what can occur in therapy and what occurs in other complex systems. This is not an attempt to draw faulty analogies, but instead to use the findings from chaos theory to justify as well as improve what we do in the clinic, with actual clients. According to the often cited work of Kuhn (1962/1970), this is exactly what happens when we replace one paradigm with another. We enhance our ability to make sense of previously baffling phenomena, and usually we find sharper and more precise terminology to replace the patchwork of solutions generated in an attempt to save the previous paradigm.

In this chapter, we have described the inherent problems with measuring change in family therapy. In noting ideas in chaos theory, and the required familiarity with mathematical computation, we stress that the theory requires greater caution, not less, in attributing significance (Burlingame & Hope, 1996; Burlingame & Bloch, 1996). For these reasons, and others listed throughout the text, we have kept our expositions theoretical and focused on single case studies. While we will continue to experiment with certain promising ideas in our research (Proskauer & Bütz, 1996), here, in our first full treatment of the topic, our thrust is to outline similarities between patterns in family therapy and to compare these patterns with those found in chaos theory. Theory, along with reasoning by analogy, seems more sensible to us than pushing into territory so ill defined. Any sort of race that would have us do so is merely an index of the degree to which we are suffering from physics envy. As Walter Freeman reminds chaoticians:

> Scientific experiments come in two flavors: exploratory and confirmatory. Schoolchildren are taught the rigors of replication, statistical validation, and double-blind controls. These techniques have their uses when we know what hypothesis we are trying to falsify, but they are premature if we don't yet know the right questions, let alone the right answers. At present we are in the joyous phase of children let out of school, who are free to wander in a garden of delights just to see what is there. The hard work of proof will come soon enough, but it should not be required before our imaginations have taken wing. (1995, p. xi)

Family therapy is an established field, with discrete and well-understood concepts. We do not feel it is necessary to turn it into a subfield of physics. Rather, some ideas from physics and other such sciences may further some ideas, support others, and ask us to examine certain tenets to clarify family therapy as a discipline. Our use of ideas in chaos theory is in this vein, and we would encourage others who want to study physics to do so, not to pursue family therapy.

References

Abraham, F. D., Abraham, R. H., & Shaw, C. D. (1990). *A visual introduction to dynamical systems theory for psychology.* Santa Cruz, CA: Aerial.

Abraham, R. H., & Shaw, C. D. (1992). *Dynamics: The geometry of behavior* (2nd ed.). Redwood City, CA: Addison-Wesley.

Ackerman, N. W. (1938). The unity of the family. *Archives of Pediatrics, 55,* 51–62.

Ackerman, N. W. (1962). Family psychotherapy and psychoanalysis: The implications of difference. *Family Process, 1*(1), 30–43.

Ackerman, N. W. (1967). Prejudice and scapegoating in the family. In G. Zuk Boszormenyi-Nagy, I. (Ed.), *Family therapy and disturbed families.* Palo Alto, CA: Science and Behavioral Books.

Ackerman, N. W. (1972). The growing edge of family therapy. In H. S. Kaplan (Ed.), *Progress in group and family therapy.* New York: Brunner/Mazel.

Albert, M. (1990). *Chaos: A new order.* Unpublished manuscript.

American Psychiatric Association. (1994). *Diagnostic and statistical manual—IV.* Washington, DC: American Psychiatric Association.

Appelbaum, P., & Gutheil, T. (1991). *Clinical handbook of psychiatry and the law* (2nd ed.). Baltimore: Williams & Wilkins.

Appleyard, B. (1993). *Understanding the present: Science and the soul of modern man.* New York: Doubleday.

Aradi, N. S., & Kaslow, F. W. (1987). Theory integration in family therapy: Definition, rationale, content and process. *Psychotherapy, 24*(3), 595–608.

Aronson, E. (1965). *The social animal* (5th ed.). New York: Freeman.

Auerswald, E. H. (1985). Thinking about thinking in family therapy. *Family Process, 24*(1), 1–12.

Auerswald, E. H. (1987). Epistemological confusion in family therapy and research. *Family Process, 26*(3), 317–330.

Badalamenti, A. F. (1992). Language and the intuition of meaning. *Systems Research, 8*(4), 43–66.

Badalamenti, A. F., & Langs, R. J. (1992). The progression of the entropy of a 5-dimensional psychotherapy system. *Systems Research, 9*(3), 3–28.

Badalamenti, A. F., & Langs, R. J. (1992). Stochastic analysis of the duration of the speaker role in the psychotherapy of an AIDS patient. *American Journal of Psychotherapy, XLVI*(2), 207–225.

Badalamenti, A. F., Langs, R. J., & Ferguson, R. (1992). Work and force in psychotherapy. *Mathematical and Computer Modeling, 16*(12), 3–17.

233

Bagarozzi, D. A. (1982). The family therapist's role in treating families in rural communities: A general systems approach. *Journal of Marital and Family Therapy, 8*(2), 51–58.

Baker, G. L., & Gollub, J. P. (1990). *Chaotic dynamics and introduction.* New York: Cambridge University Press.

Bangert-Drowns, R. L. (1986). Review of developments in meta-analytic method. *Psychological Bulletin, 99,* 388–399.

Barnsley, M. (1993). *Fractals everywhere (2nd ed.).* Boston: Academic Press Professional.

Barry, M. P. (1972). Feedback concepts in family therapy. *Perspectives in Psychiatric Care, 10*(4), 183–189.

Barton, S. (1994). Chaos, self-organization and psychology. *American Psychologist, 49*(1), 5–14.

Bateson, G. (1955). A theory of play and fantasy. *Approaches to the Study of Human Personality, 2,* 39–51.

Bateson, G. (1972). *Steps to an ecology of mind.* New York: Ballantine.

Bateson, G. (1979). *Mind and nature: A necessary unity.* New York: Dutton.

Bateson, G., Jackson, D. D., Haley, J., & Weakland, J. H. (1956). Toward a theory of schizophrenia. *Behavioral Science, 1*(4), 251–264.

Batten, M. (1988). Charting life's unpredictable pathways: Stephen Jay Gould. *The Cousteau Society Calypso Log, 15*(4), 14–17.

Beauchamp, T., & Childress, J. (1989). *Principles of biomedical ethics* (3rd ed.). New York: Oxford Press.

Beltrami, E. (1993). *Mathematical models in the social and biological sciences.* Boston, MA: Jones and Bartlett.

Bendar, R., Bendar, S., Lambert, M., & Waite, D. (1991). *Psychotherapy with high risk clients: Legal and professional standards.* Pacific Grove, CA: Brooks/Cole.

Bergman, J. S. (1985). *Fishing for barracuda: Pragmatics of brief systemic therapy.* New York: W. W. Norton.

Bertalanffy, L. (1968). *General system theory, foundations, development, applications.* New York: Braziller.

Blalock, H. M. (1971). *Causal models in the social sciences.* Chicago: Aldine-Atherton.

Boerop, J. L. D. B. (1975). General systems theory and family therapy in practice. *Family Therapy, 2*(1), 69–77.

Bohm, D. (1980). *Wholeness and the implicate order.* New York: Ark.

Bohm, D., & Peat, F. D. (1987). *Science, order and creativity.* New York: Bantam.

Bongar, B. (1991). *The suicidal patient, clinical and legal standards of care.* Washington, DC: American Psychological Association.

Boscolo, L., & Bertrando, P. (1992). The reflexive loop of past, present and future in systemic therapy and consultation. *Family Process, 34,* 119–130.

Bowen, M. (1960). A family concept of schizophrenia. In D. D. Jackson (Ed.), *The etiology of schizophrenia.* New York: Basic Books.

Bowen, M. (1978). *Family therapy in clinical practice.* New York: Aronson.

Brandt, R. (1979). Towards a credible form of utilitarianism. In E. Bayles (Ed.), *Contemporary utilitarianism.* Oxford: Clarendon Press.

Brendler, J., Silver, M., Haber, M., & Sargent, J. (1991). *Madness, chaos and violence.* New York: Basic Books.

Breunlin, D. (1989). Clinical implications of oscillation theory: Family development and the process of change. In C. N. Ramsey (Ed.), *Family systems in medicine.* New York: Guilford.

Bridgman, P. (1927). *The logic of modern physics.* New York: Macmillan.

Briggs, J., & Peat, F. D. (1984). *Looking glass universe, the emerging science of wholeness.* New York: Simon & Schuster.

Briggs, J., & Peat, F. D. (1989). *Turbulent mirror.* New York: Harper & Row.

Broderick, C. B., & Schrader, S. S. (1981). The history of professional marriage and family therapy. In A. S. Gurman Kniskern, D. P. (Ed.), *Handbook of family therapy.* New York: Brunner/Mazel.

Brody, N. (1994). .5+ or −.5: Continuity and change in personal dispositions. In T. Heatherton & J. Weinberger (Eds.), *Can personality change?* Washington, DC: American Psychological Association.

Burke, W. W. (1982). *Organizational development, principles and practices.* Boston: Scott, Foresman.

Burlingame, G., & Hope, C. (1996). Dynamical systems theory and social psychology: The promise and pitfalls. *Psychological Inquiry, in press.*

Burlingame, G. M., & Bloch, G. J. (1996). Complexity theory: A new direction for psychoneuroimmunology. *ADVANCES: The Journal of Mind-Body Health, 12*(1), 16–20.

Bütz, M. R. (1990, August). Chaos, an omen of transcendence in the psychotherapy process. In L. Vandervert (Chair), *A chaotic/fractal dynamical unification model for psychology,* a symposium presented at the American Psychological Association National Convention, Boston, MA.

Bütz, M. R. (1992a). Chaos, an omen of transcendence in the psychotherapy process. *Psychological Reports, 71,* 827–843.

Bütz, M. R. (1992b). Looking for unification? Remember chaos theory? *The Social Dynamicist, 4*(1), 8–10.

Bütz, M. R. (1993a). A model of developmental transformation: Process, perspective and symöbia—A view of symbols in chaos. *Studies in Psychoanalytic Theory, 2*(2), 3–18.

Bütz, M. R. (1993b). Practical applications from chaos theory to the psychotherapeutic process, a basic consideration of dynamics. *Psychological Reports, 73,* 543–554.

Bütz, M. R. (1995a). Chaos theory, philosophically old, scientifically new. *Counseling and Values, 39*(2), 84–98.

Bütz, M. R. (1995b). Hegemonic therapy, not recognizing the symbol: A case study of a Russian family's attempt to self-organize. *Journal of Family Psychotherapy, 6*(2).

Bütz, M. R. (1997). *Chaos and complexity: Implications for psychological theory and therapy.* Washington, DC: Taylor & Francis.

Bütz, M. R., Duran, E., & Tong, D. B. (1995). Cross-cultural approaches to chaos and chaos theory: An ancient idea with new meaning in science. In R. Robertson & A. Combs (Eds.), *Chaos theory in psychology and the life sciences.* Hillsdale, NJ: Erlbaum.

Bütz, M. R., Duran, E., Tong, D. B., & Tung, M. (1991). Older civilizations and chaos theory: concern about horses, tigers and their relation to Heraclitus. *The Social Dynamicist, 2*(4), commentary section.

Cahan, E. D., & White, S. H. (1992). Proposals for a second psychology. *American Psychologist, 47*(2), 224–235.

Çambel, A. B. (1992). *Applied chaos theory: A paradigm for complexity.* San Diego, CA: Academic Press.

Cameron, N., & Rychlak, J. (1985). *Personality development and psychopathology: A dynamic approach.* Boston, MA: Houghton Mifflin.

Cannon, W. B. (1929). Organization for physiological homeostasis. *Physiological Review, 9,* 399–431.

Capra, F. (1983). *The turning point; Science, society, and the rising culture.* New York: Bantam.

Carrillo, R. (1995). *Family violence and men of color.* New York: Springer.

Carter, B., & McGoldrick, M. (1988). *The changing family life cycle* (2nd ed.). New York: Gardner.

Case, E. M., & Robinson, N. S. (1990). Toward integration: The changing world of family therapy. *The American Journal of Family Therapy, 18*(2), 153–160.

Casti, J. (1990). *Searching for certainty: What scientists can know about the future.* New York: William Morrow.

Casti, W. (1992). *Reality rules.* (Vol. I). New York: Pergammon.

Cattell, R. B. (1982). *Psychotherapy by structured learning.* New York: Springer.

Cecchin, G., Lane, G., & Ray, W. (1994). Influence, effect and emerging systems. *Journal of Systemic Therapies, 13,* 13–21.

Chaitin, G. J. (1988). Randomness in arithmetic. *Scientific American, 259*(1), 80–85.

Chamberlain, L. L. (1993, August). Strange attractors in patterns of family inter-action. In M. R. Bütz (Ed.), *Chaos theory and the family: Practical application-research and practice.* Symposium conducted at the American Psychological Association National Convention, Toronto, Ontario, Canada.

Chamberlain, L. L. (1995). Strange attractors in patterns of family interaction. In R. Robertson & A. Combs (Eds.), *Chaos theory in psychology and the life sciences.* Hillsdale, NJ: Erlbaum.

Chamberlain, L. L., & Bütz, M. R. (1997). *Clinical chaos: A therapist's guide to non-linear dynamics and therapeutic change.* Washington, DC: Taylor & Francis.

Chubb, H. (1990). Looking at systems as process. *Family Process, 29*(2), 169–175.

Cohen, R., Swerdlik, M., & Smith, D. (1992). *Psychological testing and assessment: Introduction to tests and measurement* (2nd ed.). Mountain View, CA: Mayfield Publishing Company.

Coleman, S. (1985). *Failure in family therapy.* New York: Guilford.

Collin, L., & Horn, J. (1991). (Eds.). *Best methods for the analysis of change: Recent advances, unanswered questions, future directions.* Washington, DC: American Psychological Association.

Cook, T., & Campbell, D. (1977). *Quasi-experimentation: Design and analysis issues for field settings.* Boston, MA: Houghton Mifflin.

Constantine, L. L. (1989). Furniture for firewood—Blaming the systems paradigm. *Journal of Marital and Family Therapy, 15*(2), 111–113.

Consumer Reports. (1995). Mental health: Does therapy help, 734–739.

Corcoran, E. (1992). The edge of chaos. *Scientific American, 267*(4), 17–22.

Coveney, P., & Highfield, R. (1990). *The arrow of time, a voyage through science to solve time's greatest mystery.* New York: Fawcett Columbine.

Coyne, J. C. (1982). A brief introduction to epistobabble. *Family Therapy Networker, 6*(4), 27–28.

Crutchfield, J. P. (1996). *Invited Address,* given at the Sixth Annual International Conference of The Society of Chaos Theory in Psychology and the Life Sciences, Berkeley, CA.

Crutchfield, J. P., Farmer, J. D., Packard, N. H., & Shaw, R. S. (1986, December). Chaos. *Scientific American,* (257), 46–57.

Csanyi, V. (1989). *Evolutionary systems and society: A general theory of life, mind and culture.* Durham, NC: Duke University Press.

Cvitanovic, C. (1984). *Introduction to universality in chaos.* Bristol, England: Adam Hilger.

Davies, P. (1988). *The cosmic blueprint.* New York: Simon & Schuster.

Davies, P. (1989). *The new physics.* New York: Cambridge University Press.

Davies, P. (1992). *The mind of God: The scientific basis for a rational world.* New York: Simon and Schuster.

De Angelis, T. (1993). Chaos, chaos everywhere is what the theorists think. *APA Monitor, 24*(1), 1, 41.

Dell, P. F. (1980). Researching the family theories of schizophrenia: An exercise in epistemological confusion. *Family Process, 19,* 321–335.

Dell, P. F. (1982). Beyond homeostasis. Towards a concept of coherence. *Family Process, 21,* 21–41.

Dell, P. F. (1985). Understanding Bateson and Maturana: Toward a biological foundation for the social sciences. *Journal of Marital and Family Therapy, 11*(1), 1–20.

Dell, P. F. (1986). In defense of "lineal causality." *Family Process, 25,* 513–521.

Dell, P. F. (1987). Maturana's constitutive ontology of the observer. *Psychotherapy, 24*(3), 462–466.

Dell, P. F., & Goolishian, H. A. (1981). Order through fluctuation, an evolutionary epistemology for human systems. *Australian Journal of Family Therapy, 21,* 175–184.

Denzomn, N., & Lincoln, Y. (1994). *Handbook of qualitative research.* Thousand Oaks, CA: Sage.

Devaney, R. (1992). *A first course in chaotic dynamical systems: Theory and experiment.* Redwood City, CA: Addison-Wesley.

Ditto, W. I., Rauseo, S., & Spano, M. L. (1990). Experimental control of chaos. *Physical Review Letters, 65,* 3211–3213.

Ditto, W. L., & Pecora, L. M. (1993). Mastering chaos. *Scientific American, 269*(2), 78–84.

Duran, E. (1990). *Transforming the soul wound, a theoretical/clinical approach to American Indian psychology.* Berkeley, CA: Folklore Institute.

Duran, E., & Duran, B. (1995). *Native American postcolonial psychology.* Albany, NY: University of New York Press.

Edelman, G. M. (1992). *Bright air, brilliant fire.* New York: Basic.

Einstein, A. (1954). *Ideas and opinions.* New York: Bonanza Books.

Elkaïm, M. (1981). Non-equilibrium, chance and change in family therapy. *Journal of Marital and Family Therapy, 7,* 291–297.

Elkaïm, M. (1990). *If you love me, don't love me.* New York: Basic Books.

Elkaïm, M., Goldbeter, A., & Goldbeter-Merinfeld, E. (1987). Analysis of the dynamics of a family system in terms of bifurcations. *Journal of Social and Biological Structures, 10,* 21–36.

Elkaïm, M., Prigogine, I., Stengers, I., & Denenbourg, J.-L. (1982). Openness: A round-table discussion. *Family Process, 21,* 57–70.

Engel, G. (1992). How much longer must medicine's science be bound by a seventeenth century world view? *Family Systems Medicine, 10,* 333–346.

Erickson, G. D. (1988). Against the grain: Decentering family therapy. *Journal of Marital and Family Therapy, 14*(3), 225–236.

Everstine, D. S., & Everstine, L. (1983). *People in crisis: Strategic therapeutic interventions.* New York: Brunner/Mazel.

Eysenck, H. J. (1952). The effects of psychotherapy: An evaluation. *Journal of Consulting Psychology, 16,* 319–324.

Eysenck, H. J. (1967). *The biological basis of personality.* Springfield, IL: Charles C. Thomas.

Eysenck, H., & Eysenck, M. (1985). *Personality and individual differences: A natural science approach.* New York: Plenum.

Farber, M. L. (1977). Factors determining the incidence of suicide within families. *Suicide and Life-Threatening Behavior, 7*(1), 3–6.

Farberow, N. L. (1981). Assessment of suicide. In P. McReynolds (Ed.), *Advances in psychological assessment* (Vol. 5). San Francisco: Jossey-Bass.

Fedanzo, A. J. (1983). Autopoiesis, dissipative structures and spontaneous social orders and a systems view of man [Review of same two titles]. *Journal of Social and Biological Structures, 6*(2), 173–175.

Feigenbaum, M. (1978). Quantitative universality for a class of nonlinear transformations. *Journal of Statistical Physics, 19,* 25–52.

Feigenbaum, M. (1979). The universal metric properties of nonlinear transformations. *Journal of Statistical Physics, 21,* 669–706.

Fisch, R., Weakland, J., & Segal, L. (1983). *The tactics of change: Doing therapy briefly.* San Francisco: Jossey Bass.

Ford, J. (1989). What is chaos, that we should be mindful of it? In P. Davies (Ed.), *The new physics.* New York: Cambridge University Press.

Framo, J. (1982). *Explorations in marital and family therapy: Selected papers of James L. Framo, Ph.D.* New York: Springer.

Freeman, W. (1991, February). The physiology of perception. *Scientific American,* (264), 78–85.

Freeman, W. J. (1995). Forward. In R. Robertson & A. Combs (Eds.), *Chaos theory in psychology and the life sciences* (pp. ix–xi). Mahwah, NJ: Erlbaum.

Freud, S. (1938). *The basic writings of Sigmund Freud.* New York: Modern Library.

Gample, D. (1991, August). *Fractal selves, the fragility of relationships and chaos theory.* Paper presented at the Inaugural Conference of the Society for Chaos Theory in Psychology, San Francisco, CA.

Garfinkel, A. (1983). A mathematics for physiology. *American Journal of Physiology, 245,* 455–466.

Garfinkel, A. (1987). The virtues of chaos. *Behavioral and Brain Sciences, 10,* 178–179.

Gergen, K. (1991). *The saturated self.* New York: Basic Books.

Gibney, P. (1987). Co-evolving with anorectic families, difference is a singular moment. *Australian and New Zealand Journal of Family Therapy, 8*(2), 71–80.

Glass, L., & Mackey, M. C. (1988). *From clocks to chaos: The rhythms of life.* Princeton, NJ: Princeton University Press.

Gleick, J. (1987). *Chaos making a new science.* New York: Viking-Penguin.

Goerner, S. (1993). *Chaos and the evolving ecological universe: A study in the science and human implications of a new world hypothesis.* New York: Gordon & Breech.

Goerner, S. J. (1992). *The evolving ecological universe: a study in the science and human implications of a new world hypothesis.* Dissertation, Saybrook Institute, San Francisco, CA.

Goldberger, A. L. (1990, August). The fractal dynamical model of impulse regulation in living systems. In L. Vandervert (Ed.), *A chaotic/fractal dynamical unification model for psychology.* Symposium conducted at the American Psychological Association National Convention, Boston, MA.

Goldberger, A. L., Rigney, D. R., & West, B. J. (1990). Chaos and fractals in human physiology. *Scientific American, 262*(2), 42–49.

Goldstein, J. (1993–94). Linguistic ambiguity in nonlinear dynamics. *Society for Chaos Theory in Psychology and the Life Sciences—Newsletter, 2*(1), 2–3.

Goldstein, J. (1995). The tower of Babel in nonlinear dynamics: Toward the clarification of terms. In R. Robertson & A. Combs (Eds.), *Chaos theory in psychology and the life sciences.* Mahwah, NJ: Erlbaum.

Goldstein, S. (1986). Bye bye Brady Bunch. *Family Therapy Networker, 10*(1), 31–32, 76–78.

Goolishian, H., & Anderson, H. (1987). Language systems and therapy: An evolving idea. *Psychotherapy, 24*(3), 529–538.

Gould, S. J. (1980). *The panda's thumb: More reflections in natural history.* New York: W. W. Norton.

Gray, W., & Rizzo, N. (1969). History and development of general systems theory. In W. Gray, F. Duhl, & N. Rizzo (Eds.), *General systems theory and psychiatry.* Boston, MA: Little Brown.

Gurman, A., & Kinskern, D. (1978). Deterioration in marital and family therapy: Empirical, clinical and conceptual issues. *Family Process, 17,* 3–20.

Haley, J. (1959). The family of the schizophrenic: A model system. *Journal of Neuroses and Mental Diseases, 129,* 357–374.

Haley, J. (1962). Introduction to family process. *Family Process, 1*(1), 1–4.

Haley, J. (1973). *Uncommon therapy: The psychiatric techniques of Milton H. Erickson, M.D.* New York: W. W. Norton.

Haley, J. (1976). *Problem-solving therapy.* San Francisco: Jossey-Bass.

Haley, J. (1980). *Leaving home: The therapy of disturbed young people.* New York: McGraw-Hill.

Haley, J. (1987). The disappearance of the individual. *The Family Therapy Networker, 11*, 39–40.

Hall, N. (1991). *Exploring chaos: A guide to the new science of disorder.* New York: W. W. Norton.

Halpern, H. A., Canale, J. R., Bant, B. L., & Bellamy, C. (1979). A systems-crisis approach to family treatment. *Journal of Marital and Family Therapy, 5*(2), 87–94.

Hannah, T. (1990, Fall). Does chaos theory have application to psychology? The example of daily mood fluctuations. *Network,* 13–14.

Hannah, T. (1991, August). *Mood, anxiety and relation to life events.* Paper presented at the Inaugural Meeting of the Society for Chaos Theory in Psychology, San Francisco, CA.

Hao, B. L. (1984). *Chaos.* Singapore: World Scientific.

Hawkins, R. C. (1992). Solution oriented brief therapy: Facilitating "healthy chaos" in managed care settings. *The Social Dynamicist, 3*(3), 6–7.

Haynes, S. (1992). *Models of causality in psychopathology: Toward dynamic, synthetic and nonlinear models of behavior disorders.* New York: MacMillan Publishing Company.

Heisenberg, W. (1958). *Physics and philosophy.* New York: Harper & Brothers.

Held, B. S., & Pols, E. (1987a). Dell on Maturana: A real foundation for family therapy? *Psychotherapy, 24*(3), 455–461.

Held, B. S., & Pols, E. (1987b). The philosophy of Dell and Maturana. *Psychotherapy, 24*(3), 466–468.

Herbert, N. (1985). *Quantum reality: Beyond the new physics.* New York: Anchor Press.

Hill, R. (1949). *Families under stress.* New York: Harper & Row.

Hoffman, L. (1981). *Foundations of family therapy, a conceptual framework for systems change.* New York: Basic Books.

Hoffman, L. (1993). *Exchanging voices: A collaborative approach to family therapy.* London: Karnac Books.

Hornstein, G. A. (1992). The return of the repressed: Psychology's problematic relations with psychoanalysis. *American Psychologist, 47*(2), 254–263.

Howard, K., Kopta, S., Krause, M., & Orlisky, D. (1986). The dose effect relationship in psychotherapy. *American Psychologist, 41*, 159–164.

Hsu, F. L. K. (1985). The self in cross-cultural perspective. In A. J. Marsella, G. De Vos, & F. L. K. Hsu (Eds.), *Culture and self: Asian and Western perspectives.* New York: Tavistock.

Huckfeldt, R., Kohfeld, C. H., & Likens, T. (1982). *Dynamic models: An introduction.* Beverly Hills, CA: Sage.

Hunter, D. E. K., Hoffnung, R. J., & Ferhold, J. B. (1988). Family therapy in trouble: Psychoeducation as a solution and as a problem. *Family Process, 27*(3), 327–338.

Hutchinson, M. P., & Draguns, J. G. (1987). Chronic, early exposure to suicidal ideation in a parental figure: A pattern for presuicidal characteristics. *Suicide and Life Threatening Behavior, 17*(4), 288–298.

Hyler, L. (1994). *Trauma victim: Theoretical issues and practical suggestions.* Muncie, Indiana: Accelerated Development Inc.

Jackson, D. (1957). The question of family homeostasis. *Psychiatric Quarterly Supplement, 31,* 79–90.

Jackson, D. (1965). Family rules: Marital quid pro quo. *Archives of General Psychiatry, 12,* 589–594.

Jantsch, E. (1980). *The self-organizing universe, scientific and human implications of the emerging paradigm of evolution.* New York: Pergamon.

Johnson, J. (1992). *The comprehensive survey of symptoms (SS-77)* (2.01 ed.). San Antonio, TX: Psychological Corporation.

Johnson, J. (1994). *What managed care can learn from behavioral sciences.* New Orleans: Northshore Press.

Johnson, J., & McCown, W. G. (1996). *Family therapy of neurobehavioral disorders.* New York: Hayworth.

Jordan, J. R. (1985). Paradox and polarity: The Tao of family therapy. *Family Process, 24*(2), 165–174.

Jurek, A. W., Maier, M. E., Sandgren, A. K., Tall, K. M., & Searight, H. R. (1989). Challenging the uniformity myth in family therapy: Toward prescriptive intervention. *Family Therapy, 16*(3), 271–281.

Kaplan, M. L., & Kaplan, N. R. (1991). The self-organization of human psychological functioning. *Behavioral Science, 36,* 161–178.

Kaplan, N. R., & Kaplan, M. L. (1987). Process of experiential organization in individual and family systems. *Psychotherapy, 24*(3), 561–569.

Kaslow, F. (1986). Theories of marital and family therapy. In M. Sussman & S. Steinmetz (Eds.), *Handbook on marriage and the family.* New York: Plenum.

Kassen, D., & O'Connor, W. (1988). A prospective study of predictors of violence in adult male mental patients. *Law and Behavior, 112,* 174–181.

Kauffman, S. A. (1991). Antichaos and adaptation. *Scientific American, 265*(2), 78–84.

Kauffman, S. A. (1993). *The origins of order: Self-organization and selection in evolution.* New York: Oxford University Press.

Kauffman, S. A. (1995). *At home in the universe.* London: Oxford.

Keeney, B. P. (1983). *Aesthetics of change.* New York: Guilford.

Keeney, B. P., & Ross, J. M. (1985). *Mind in therapy.* New York: Basic Books.

Kelly, J. L. (1986). A new interpretation of information rates, pp. 121–129. In R. Hellman, *Information and exchange in parimutuel wagering.* New York: David MacKay. (Original work published 1955)

Kelso, J. A., & Fogel, A. (1987). Self-organizing systems and infant motor development. *Developmental Review, 7*(1), 39–65.

Kerlinger, F. (1986). *Foundations of behavioral research.* New York: Holt, Rinehart and Winston.

Kline, P. (1984). *Handbook of test construction.* London: Methuen.

Korzybski, A. (1948). On structure. In A. Korzybski (Ed.), *Science and sanity.* Lakeville, CT: International Non-Aristotelian Library.

Kuhn, T. S. (1970). *The structure of scientific revolutions* (2nd ed.). Chicago: University of Chicago Press. (Original work published 1962)

Kuhn, T. S. (1977). *The essential tension, selected studies in scientific tradition and change.* Chicago: University of Chicago Press.

Kuhn, T. S. (1991, November). The problem with the historical philosophy of science. In The Robert and Maurine Rothchild Distinguished Lecture. Address delivered at Harvard University, History of Science Department, Cambridge, MA.

L'Abate, L. (1986). *Systemic family therapy.* New York: Brunner/Mazel.

L'Abate, L. (1992). *Programmed writing: A self-administered approach for interventions with individuals, couples and families.* Pacific Grove, CA: Brooks/Cole.

L'Abate, L. (1994). *A theory of personality development.* New York: Wiley.

L'Abate, L., & Cox, R. (1992). *Programmed writing: A self-administered approach for interventions with individuals, couples and families.* Pacific Grove, CA: Brooks/Cole.

L'Abate, L., Farrar, J., & Serritella, D. (1992). *Handbook of differential treatments for addictions.* Needham Heights, MA: Allyn & Bacon.

L'Abate, L., & Wagner, V. (1988). Testing a theory of development competence in the family. *American Journal of Family Psychology, 16,* 23–35.

Laing, R. D. (1969). *The divided self.* New York: Pantheon.

Landau-Stanton, J., Griffiths, J., & Mason, J. (1982). The extended family in transition. Clinical implications. In F. Kaslow (Ed.). *The international book of family therapy.* New York: Brunner/Mazel.

Langsley, D., & Kaplan, D. (1968). *The treatment of families in crisis.* New York: Grune and Stratton.

Langsley, D., Pittman, F., Machotka, P., & Flomenhaft, K. (1968). Family crisis therapy: Results and implications. *Family Process, 7,* 145–148.

Langsley, D., Pittman, F., & Swank, G. (1969). Family crisis in schizophrenics and other mental patients. *Journal of Nervous and Mental Diseases, 149,* 270–276.

Langs, R. J. (1992). *Science, systems and psychoanalysis.* London: Karnac.

Langs, R. J., & Badalamenti, A. (1993). *The physics of mind.* New York: Ballantine.

Leahey, T. H. (1987). *A history of psychology: Main currents in psychological thought* (2nd ed.). Upper Saddle River, NJ: Prentice-Hall.

Leahey, T. H. (1992). The mythical revolutions of American psychology. *American Psychologist, 47*(2), 308–318.

Lebow, J. L. (1987). Integrative family therapy: An overview of major issues. *Psychotherapy, 24*(3), 584–594.

Levy, S. (1992). *Artificial life, the quest for a new creation.* New York: Pantheon.

Levy, J., & McCown, W. G. (1983). *Family therapy as a crisis intervention.* Symposium presented at the First Prince William County Family Therapy Conference, Manassas, Virginia.

Lidz, T. (1963). *The Family and Human Adaptation.* New York: International Universities Press.

Lidz, T., Cornelison, A., Fleck, S., & Terry, D. (1957). The intrafamilial environment of schizophrenic patients: II. Marital schism and marital skew. *American Journal of Psychiatry, 114,* 241–248.

Lidz, T., Fleck, S., & Cornelison, A. (1965). *Schizophrenia and the Family.* New York: International Universities Press.

Lonie, I. E. (1995). The princess and the swineherd: Applications of chaos theory to psychodynamics. In R. Robertson & A. Combs (Eds.), *Chaos theory in psychology and the life sciences* (pp. 253–265). Mahwah, NJ: Erlbaum.

Lorenz, E. N. (1963). Deterministic nonperiodic flow. *Journal of Atmospheric Sciences, 20,* 130–141.

Loye, D. (1995). How predictable is the future? The conflict between traditional chaos theory and the psychology of prediction, and the challenge for chaos psychology. In R. Robertson & A. Combs (Eds.), *Chaos theory in psychology and the life sciences.* Mahwah, NJ: Erlbaum.

Loye, D., & Eisler, R. (1987). Chaos and transformation: Implications of nonequilibrium theory for social science and society. *Behavioral Science, 32,* 53–65.

MacKinnon, L., & Miller, D. (1985). The sexual component in family therapy: A feminist critique. *Feminist Perspectives on Social Work and Human Sexuality, 3*(2–3), 81–101.

Mahoney, M. J. (1991). *Human change processes, the scientific foundations of psychotherapy.* New York: Basic.

Mandelbrot, B. B. (1977). *Fractals: From, chance, and dimension.* San Francisco: W. H. Freeman.

Maturana, H. R. (1980). Autopoiesis: Reproduction, heredity and evolution. In M. Zeleny (Ed.), *Autopoiesis, dissipative structures and spontaneous social orders.* Boulder, CO: Westview.

Maturana, H. R., & Varela, F. J. (1987). *The tree of knowledge, biological roots of human understanding* (2nd ed.). Boston, MA: Shambhala.

May, R. M. (1976). Simple mathematical models with very complicated dynamics. *Nature, 261,* 459–462.

McCown, W. (1992, August). Chaos theory and family therapy: A new unifying paradigm? In W. M. Cown (Ed.), *Chaos theory and family therapy: A new unifying paradigm?* Symposium conducted at the American Psychological Association National Convention, Washington, DC.

McCown, W. (1993, August). Crisis proness, treatment resistance, and ideodynamics of impulsive family systems. In M. R. Bütz (Ed.), *Chaos theory and the family: Practical application-research and practice.* Symposium conducted at the American Psychological Association National Convention, Toronto, Ontario, Canada.

McCown, W. G., & Johnson, J. (1991). *Empirical characteristics of crisis-prone families.* Paper presented at the annual meeting of the American Psychological Association, San Francisco, CA.

McCown, W. G., & Johnson, J. (1993). *Therapy with treatment resistant families, a consultation-crisis intervention model.* New York: Haworth.

McCubbin, H., & Patterson, J. (1983). The family stress process: The double ABCX model of family adjustment and adaptation. In H. McCubbin, M. Sussman, and H. Patterson (Eds.), *Social stress and the family: Advances and developments in family stress theory and research.* New York: Haworth.

McGoldrick, M., & Gerson, R. (1988). Genograms and the family life cycle. In B. Carter & M. McGoldrick (Eds.), *The changing family life cycle, a framework for family therapy.* New York: Garder Press.

McGoldrick, M., Pearce, J. K., & Giordan, J. (1982). *Ethnicity and family therapy.* New York: Guilford.

McLeod, W. R. (1988). Epistemology and constructivism, some implications for therapy. *Australian and New Zealand Journal of Family Therapy, 9*(1), 9–16.

McNally, R. J. (1992). Disunity in psychology: Chaos or speciation? *American Psychologist, 47*(8), 1054.

Mead, G. H. (1933). *Mind self and society.* Chicago: University of Chicago Press.

Middleton, C., & DiBello, R. (1990). Personality as a strange attractor. *The Social Dynamicist, 1*(2), 1–3.

Middleton, C., Fireman, G., & DiBello, R. (1991, August). *Personality traits as strange attractors.* Paper presented at the Inaugural Conference of the Society for Chaos Theory in Psychology, San Francisco, CA.

Minuchin, S. (1974). *Families and family therapy.* Cambridge, MA: Harvard University Press.

Minuchin, S., Baker, L., Rosman, B. L., Liebman, R., Milman, L., & Todd, T. C. (1975). A conceptual model of psychosomatic illness in children. *Archives of General Psychiatry, 32,* 1031–1038.

Minuchin, S., & Fishman, H. C. (1981). *Family therapy techniques.* Cambridge, MA: Harvard University Press.

Monahan, J. (1977). Strategies for an empirical analysis of the prediction of violence in emergency civil commitment. *Law and Human Behavior, 1,* 363–371.

Monahan, J. (1984). The prediction of violent behavior, toward a second generation of theory and policy. *American Journal of Psychiatry, 141,* 10–15.

Monahan, J. (1992). Mental disorder and violent behavior, perceptions and evidence. *American Psychologist, 47*(4), 511–521.

Monahan, J., & Stedman, J. (1994). *Violence and mental disorders: Developments in risk assessment.* Chicago: University of Chicago Press.

Moon, F. (1992). *Chaotic and fractal dynamics: An introduction for applied scientists and engineers.* New York: Wiley.

Moore, C. (1990). Unpredictability and undecidability in dynamical systems. *Physical Review Letters, 64,* 2354–2357.

Morawetz, A., & Walker, G. (1984). *Brief therapy with single-parent families.* New York: Brunner/Mazel.

Morgan, R. F. (1983). *The iatrogenics handbook.* Toronto, Ontario: IPI.

Mostwin, D. (1974). Multidimensional model of working with the family. *Social Casework, 55*(4), 209–215.

Murray, M. E. (1975). A model for family therapy integrating system and subsystem dynamics. *Family Therapy, 2*(2), 187–197.

Neff, J., & Carroll, T. L. (1993). Circuits that get chaos in sync. *Scientific American, 269*(2), 120–122.

Nagel, E. (1961). *The structure of scientific problems in the logic of scientific explanation.* New York: Harcourt, Brace & World.

Norcross, J., & Prochaska, J. (1982). A national survey of clinical psychologists: Affiliations and orientations. *Clinical Psychologist, 35*(1), 4–6.

Olson, D., Russell, C., & Sprenkle, D. (1983). Circumplex model VI: Theoretical update. *Family Process, 22,* 69–83.

Olson, D. H., Sprenkle, D. H., & Russell, C. S. (1979). Circumplex model of marital and family systems: Cohesion and adaptability dimensions, family types, and clinical applications. *Family Process, 18,* 2–28.

Ott, E., Grebogi, C., & Yorke, J. (1990). Controlling chaos. *Physical Review Letters,* *64*(11), 1196–1199.

Papp, P. (1983). *The process of change.* New York: Guilford.

Parloff, M. (1992). Placebo controls in psychotherapy research: A sine qua non or a placebo for research problems. In A. Kazdin (Ed.), *Methodological issues and strategies in clinical research* (pp. 585–606). Washington, DC: American Psychological Association.

Parry, A., & Doan, R. E. (1994). *Story re-visions.* New York: Guilford.

Parsons, T., & Bales, R. (1955). *Family socialization and interaction processes.* Glencoe, IL: Free Press.

Pearsall, P. (1992). *Ten laws of lasting love.* New York: Simon & Schuster.

Peat, F. D. (1995). Chaos: The geometrization of thought. In R. Robertson & A. Combs (Eds.), *Chaos theory in psychology and the life sciences* (pp. 359–372). Mahwah, NJ: Erlbaum.

Pellegrino, E., & Thomasma, D. (1981). *A philosophical basis of medical practice.* New York: Oxford University Press.

Pendick, D. (1993). Chaos of the mind. *Science News, 143,* 138–139.

Percival, I. (1993). Chaos: A science for the real world. In N. Hall (Ed.), *Exploring chaos: A guide to the new science of disorder* (pp. 11–21). New York: W. W. Norton and Company.

Perna, P. A. (1995). Regression as chaotic uncertainty and transformation. In R. Robertson & A. Combs (Eds.), *Chaos theory in psychology and the life sciences* (pp. 253–265). Mahwah, NJ: Erlbaum.

Pfeffer, C. R. (1981). The family system of suicidal children. *American Journal of Psychotherapy, 35*(3), 330–341.

Pittman, F. S. (1973). Managing acute psychiatric emergencies: Defining the family crisis. In D. Bloch (Ed.), *Techniques of family psychotherapy, seminars in psychiatry* (Vol. 5 (2), pp. 219–227). New York: Grune & Stratton.

Pittman, F. (1988). Family crisis: Expectable and unexpectable. In C. Falicov (Ed.), *Family transitions.* New York: Guilford.

Platt, J. (1970, November). Hierarchical growth. *Bulletin of the Atomic Scientists,* 2–4, 46–48.

Prigogine, I. (1971). Interpretations of life and mind. In R. Greene (Ed.), *Essays around the problem of reduction.* New York: Humanities Press.

Prigogine, I. (1980). *From being to becoming—time and complexity in the physical sciences.* San Francisco: W.H. Freeman & Sons.

Prigogine, I. (1982). Dialogue with Piaget concerning the irreversible. *Archives de Psychologie, 50*(192), 7–16.

Prigogine, I. (1986). Editorial. *Brain Mind Bulletin, 11,* 15.

Prigogine, I., & Stengers, I. (1984). *Order out of chaos.* New York: Bantam.

Proskauer, S. (1996). *Shannon's entropy as a measure of chaos and constraint in couples and family communication.* Paper presented at the Sixth Annual International Conference of the Society for Chaos Theory in Psychology and the Life Sciences: Berkeley, CA.

Proskauer, S., & Bütz, M. R. (1996). *Chaotic and constrained communication in family therapy* (B-Start Grant No. National Institute of Mental Health).

Rabkin, R. (1972). On books. *Family Process 2*, 12.

Rapp, P. E. (1986). Oscillations and chaos in cellular metabolism and physiological systems. In A. V. Holden (Ed.), *Chaos*. Manchester, England: Manchester University Press.

Rapp, P. E. (1987). Why are so many biological systems periodic? *Progress in Neurobiology, 29*, 261–273.

Rapp, P. E. (1993). Chaos in the neurosciences, cautionary tales from the frontier. *Biologist, 40*(2), 89–94.

Rapp, P. E. (1995). Is there evidence for chaos in the human central nervous system? In R. Robertson & A. Combs (Eds.), *Chaos theory in psychology and the life sciences* (pp. 89–100). Mahwah, NJ: Erlbaum.

Rapp, P. E., Bashore, T. R., Martinerie, J. M., Albano, A. M., Zimmerman, I. D., & Mees, A. I. (1989). Dynamics of brain electrical activity. *Brain Topography, 21*(1/2), 99–118.

Rapp, P. E., Jiménez-Montano, M. A., Langs, R. J., Thomson, L., & Mees, A. I. (1991). Toward a quantitative characterization of patient-therapist communication. *Mathematical Biosciences, 105*, 207–227.

Rasband, S. N. (1990). *Chaotic dynamics of onlinear systems*. New York: Wiley.

Rawls, J. (1971). *A theory of justice*. Cambridge, MA: Harvard University Press.

Ray, W., & Keeney, B. (1993). *Resource focused therapy*. London: Karnac Books.

Redington, D. J., & Reidbord, S. P. (1992). Chaotic dynamics in autonomic nervous system activity of a patient during a psychotherapy session. *Biological Psychiatry, 31*, 993–1007.

Reidbord, S. P., & Redington, D. J. (1992). Psychophysiological processes during insight-oriented therapy, further investigations into nonlinear psychodynamics. *The Journal of Nervous and Mental Disease, 180*, 649–657.

Reik, T. (1948). *Listening with the third ear*. New York: Grove Press.

Richardson, H. B. (1948). *Patients have families*. New York: Commonwealth Fund.

Richman, J. (1979, June). The family therapy of attempted suicide. *Family Process, 18*, 131–142.

Richman, J. (1986). *Family therapy for suicidal people*. New York: Springer.

Roback, A. A. (1952). *History of American psychology*. New York: Modern Library Press.

Robertson, R. (1992). Gödel, Jung and the continuum hypothesis. *Unpublished manuscript*.

Robinson, G. (1994, May). *The circumplex model and chaotic attractors*. Paper presented at the annual meeting of the Montana Psychological Association, Great Falls, MT.

Ruelle, D. (1980). Strange attractors. *Mathematical Intelligencer, 2*, 126–137.

Ruelle, D. (1991). *Chance and chaos*. Princeton: Princeton University Press.

Ruelle, D., & Takens, F. (1971). On the nature of turbulence. *Communications in Mathematical Physics, 23*, 343–344.

Russell, C. S., Olson, D. H., Sprenkle, D. H., & Atilano, R. B. (1983). From family symptom to family system: Review of family therapy research. *The American Journal of Family Therapy, 11*(3), 3–14.

Russell, R., & Candyce, S. (1979). Circumplex model of marital and family systems. III. Empirical evaluation with families. *Family Process, 18*, 29–45.

Rychlak, J. (1973). *Introduction to personality and psychotherapy: A theory construction approach.* Boston, MA: Houghton Mifflin.

Sands, R. G., & Dixon, S. L. (1986). Adolescent crisis and suicidal behavior: Dynamics and treatment. *Child and Adolescent Social Work, 3*(2), 109–122.

Satir, V. (1967). *Conjoint family therapy: A guide to theory and technique.* Palo Alto, CA: Science and Behavioral Books.

Searle, S. (1987). *Linear models for unbalanced data.* New York: Wiley.

Seligman, M. E. P. (1995). The effectiveness of psychotherapy, the *Consumer Reports* study. *American Psychologist, 50*(12), 965–974.

Selvini-Palazzoli, M. (1970). The families of patients with anorexia nervosa. In E. J. Anthony & C. Koupernik (Eds.), *The child in his family.* New York: Krieger.

Selvini-Palazzoli, M., Boscolo, L., Cecchin, G., & Prata, G. (1978). *Paradox and counterparadox, a new model in the therapy of the family in schizophrenic transaction.* New Jersey: Aronson.

Selvini–Palazzoli, M., Boscolo, L., Cecchin, G., & Prata, G. (1980). Hypothesizing-circularity-neutrality: Three guidelines for the conductor of the session. *Family Process, 19*(1), 3–12.

Shinbrot, T., Ott, E., Grebogi, C., & Yorke, J. (1990). Using chaos to direct trajectories to targets. *Physical Review Letters, 65,* 3215–3218.

Singer, J. (1990). *Seeing through the visible world: Jung, Gnosis and Chaos.* New York: Harper & Row.

Singer, P. (1979). *Practical ethics.* Cambridge: Cambridge University Press.

Skarda, A., & Freeman, W. J. (1987). How brains make chaos into order to make sense of the world. *Behavioral and Brain Sciences, 10,* 161–195.

Small, M. (1992, August). Logic of chaos theory. In W. G. McCown (Ed.), *Chaos theory and family therapy: A new and unifying paradigm?* Symposium conducted at the American Psychological Association National Convention, Washington, DC.

Smith, M., Glass, G., & Miller, T. (1980). *The benefits of psychotherapy.* Baltimore: Johns Hopkins University Press.

Smith, L., & Thelen, E. (1993). *A dynamic systems approach to development: Applications.* Cambridge, MA: The MIT Press.

Smolensky, P. (1988). On the proper treatment of connectionism. *Behavioral and Brain Sciences, 11*(1), 1–74.

Sperry, R. (1988). Psychology's mentalist paradigm and the religion/science tension. *American Psychologist, 43*(8), 607–613.

Sprott, J. C. (1993). *Strange attractors, creating patterns in chaos.* New York: M&T Books.

Sprott, J. C., & Rowlands, G. (1992). *Chaos data analyzer.* New York: American Institute of Physics.

Staff. (1989, February). Terminal chaos. *Discover,* 12.

Staff. (1992). Professor Ilya Prigogine, the interview. *The Chaos Network, 4*(3), 1–4.

Starr, P. (1982). *The social transformation of American medicine.* New York: Basic Books.

Steinglass, P. (1984). Family systems theory and therapy: A clinical application of general systems theory. *Psychiatric Annals, 14*(8), 582–586.

Stevens, B. A. (1991). Chaos: A challenge to refine systems theory. *Australian and New Zealand Journal of Family Therapy, 12*(1), 23–26.

Stevens, W. (1982). *Wallace Stevens: The collected poems.* New York: Vintage.

Stoppard, T. (1993). *Arcadia.* Boston: Farber and Farber.

Strogatz, S. H., & Stewart, I. (1994). Coupled oscillators and biological synchronization. *Scientific American, 269*(6), 102–109.

Sue, S. (1992). Changing demographics: Old and new issues for psychology. In S. Schneider (Chair), *Second century group symposium: Effect of changing demography on the second century of psychology,* given at the American Psychological Association's National Convention, Washington, DC.

Sulis, W. (1995). Naturally occurring computational systems. In R. Roberston & A. Combs (Eds.), *Chaos theory in psychology and the life sciences.* Mahwah, NJ: Erlbaum.

Swanson, J. W., Holzer, C. E., Ganju, V. K., & Jono, R. T. (1990). Violence and psychiatric disorder in the community: Evidence from epidemiologic catchment areas surveys. *Hospital and Community Psychiatry, 41*(7), 761–770.

Takaki, R. (1989). *Strangers from a different shore, a history of Asian Americans.* Boston, MA: Little, Brown.

Terano, T., Asai, K., & Sugeno, M. (1994). *Applied fuzzy systems* (C. Aschmann, Trans.). Boston, MA: AP Professional Books.

Todd, T., & Stanton, M. D. (1983). Research on marital and family therapy: Answers, issues and recommendations for the future. In B. Wolman & G. Stricker (Eds.) *Handbook of family and marital therapy.* New York: Plenum.

Tolstoy, L. (1982). *War and peace* (R. Edmonds, Trans.). New York: Greenwich House. (Original work published 1869)

Tong, D. B. (1994). Chinese American culture: Still paradigmaticly crazy after all these years. In K. Monteiro (Ed.), *Ethnicity and psychology.* Debuque, IA: Kendall/Hunt.

Trepper, T., & Barrett, M. (1986). Introduction to the multiple systems perspective for the treatment of intrafamily child sexual abuse. *Journal of Psychotherapy and the Family, 2,* 5–12.

Tufillaro, N., Abbott, T., & Reilly, J. (1992). *An experimental approach to nonlinear dynamics and chaos.* Redwood City, CA: Addison Wesley.

Vallacher, R. R., & Wegner, D. M. (1987). What do people think they're doing? Action identification and human behavior. *Psychological Review, 94* 3–15.

Vandervert, L. (1992, August). Why bother with chaos theory? In L. Vandervert (Ed.), *Chaos theory in a historical philosophical perspective-initial translation.* Symposium conducted at the American Psychological Association National Convention, Washington, DC.

Vandervert, L. (in press). Introduction. *Journal of Mind and Behavior.*

Varela, F. (1989). Reflections on the circulation of concepts between a biology of cognition and systemic family therapy. *Family Process, 28*(1), 15–24.

Waldrop, M. M. (1992). *Complexity, the emerging science at the edge of order and chaos.* New York: Simon & Schuster.

Wang, H. (1987). *Reflections of Kurt Gödel.* Cambridge, MA: MIT Press.

Watzlawick, P. (1976). *How real is real: Confusion, disinformation, communication.* New York: Vintage.

Watzlawick, P. (1984). *The invented reality: How do we know what we believe we know?* New York: W. W. Norton.

Watzlawick, P., Beavin, J., & Jackson, D. D. (1967). *Pragmatics of human communication.* New York: W. W. Norton.

Webster's ninth new collegiate dictionary. (1989). Springfield, MA: Merriam-Webster.

Wekstein, L. (1979). *Handbook of suicidology: Principles, problems, and practice.* New York: Brunner/Mazel.

Whitaker, C. A. (1958). Psychotherapy with couples. *American Journal of Psychotherapy, 12,* 18–23.

Whitaker, C. A. (1975). Psychotherapy of the absurd: With a special emphasis on the psychotherapy of aggression. *Family Process, 14*(1), 397–409.

Whitaker, C. A. (1989). *Midnight musings of a family therapist.* New York: W. W. Norton.

White, M. (1986). Negative explanation, restraint, and double description: A template for family therapy. *Family Process, 25*(2), 169–184.

Whitehead, A. N., & Russell, B. (1964). *Principia mathematica* (2nd ed.). New York: Cambridge University Press. (Original work published 1910)

Wiener, N. (1961). *Cybernetics, or control and communication in the animal and the machine* (2nd ed.). New York: Wiley.

Worthington, E. (1987). Treatment of families during life transitions: Matching treatment to family response. *Family Process, 26,* 295–308.

Yorke, J. (1975). Period three implies chaos. *American Mathematical Monthly, 82,* 985–992.

Author Index

Abbott, T., 33, 123
Abraham, F. D., 26, 51, 164, 224
Abraham, R. H., 26, 51, 122, 132, 163, 164, 204, 224
Ackerman, N. W., 7, 15, 123, 160
Albano, A. M., 61, 65, 224
Albert, M., 70
Allgood, 23
Anderson, H., 18
Appelbaum, P., 181
Appleyard, B., 35, 41, 86
Aradi, N. S., x
Aronson, E., 88
Asai, K., 196
Atilano, R. B., x
Auerswald, E. H., 14, 50–51

Badalamenti, A., 201, 222, 225
Bagarozzi, D. A., 15
Baker, G. L., 23, 25
Baker, L., 14
Bales, R., 127, 198
Bangert-Drowns, R. L., 230
Bant, B. L., 17
Barnsley, M., 94, 107
Barrett, M., 120
Barry, M. P., 14
Barton, S., 66, 221
Bashore, T. R., 61, 65, 224
Bateson, G., 7, 8, 9, 10, 11, 15, 18, 42, 122
Batten, M., 48
Beauchamp, T., 211
Beavin, J., 11, 14, 122, 180
Bellamy, C., 17
Beltrami, E., 21
Bendar, R., 181
Bendar, S., 181

Bergman, J. S., 91, 123, 181, 182
Bertalanffy, L., 12, 14, 46, 55
Bertrando, P., 195
Blalock, H. M., 234
Bloch, G. J., 222, 232
Boerop, J. L. D. B., 15
Bohm, D., 5, 22, 47, 48
Bongar, B., 181
Boscolo, L., 8, 11, 12, 13, 57, 62, 122, 150, 195, 200
Bowen, M., 7, 14, 102, 107, 123, 197, 199
Brandt, R., 212
Brendler, J., 72
Breunlin, D., 168
Bridgman, P., 235
Briggs, J., x, 18, 19, 22, 23, 25, 48, 67, 172, 173, 174
Broderick, C. B., 7, 11
Brody, N., 206
Burke, W. W., 88
Burlingame, G., 222, 232
Bütz, M. R., x, 20, 35, 56, 65, 112, 142, 169, 177, 178, 187, 193, 195, 199, 201, 204, 207, 216, 223, 232

Cahan, E. D., 35
Çambel, A. B., 142, 146, 147
Cameron, N., 140, 212
Campbell, D., 226
Canale, J. R., 17
Candyce, S., 57
Cannon, W. B., 118
Capra, F., 22
Carrillo, R., 216
Carroll, T. L., 177
Carter, B., 58
Case, E. M., x

Casti, J., 226
Casti, W., 94, 164, 202, 215, 224, 225
Cattell, R. B., 122, 224, 225
Cecchin, G., 8, 11, 12, 13, 57, 62, 122, 150, 200, 201, 202
Chaitin, G. J., 33
Chamberlain, L. L., 59, 64, 201, 204, 216
Childress, J., 211
Chubb, H., 25, 59, 73, 78
Cohen, R., 37, 236
Coleman, S., 160
Collin, L., 230
Constantine, L. L., 16
Cook, T., 226
Corcoran, E., 44
Cornelison, A., 7
Coveney, P., 25
Cox, R., 110, 114, 158, 162
Coyne, J. C., 15
Crutchfield, J. P., 33, 215
Csanyi, V., 237
Cvitanovic, C., 31

Davies, P., 22, 23, 25, 42, 44, 58, 60, 133
De Angelis, T., 237
Dell, P. F., x, 10, 15, 17, 60, 77, 212
Denenbourg, J. -L., 33, 65
Denzomn, N., 211
Devaney, R., 24, 123, 131, 132, 225
DiBello, R., 71
Ditto, W. I., 143
Ditto, W. L., 62, 177
Dixon, S. L., 180
Doan, R. E., 113
Draguns, J. G., 180
Duran, B., 58, 65
Duran, E., x, 58, 65, 216

Edelman, G. M., 86, 216
Einstein, A., 5
Eisler, R., 26, 32, 132
Elkaïm, M., xi, 17, 18, 33, 64, 65, 88, 221
Engel, G., 203
Erickson, G. D., 16
Everstine, D. S., 123
Everstine, L., 123
Eysenck, H., 105, 207, 208, 226
Eysenck, M., 105, 226

Farber, M. L., 180
Farberow, N. L., 181
Farmer, J. D., 33
Farrar, J., 226
Fedanzo, A. J., 15
Feigenbaum, M., 32
Ferguson, R., 222, 225
Ferhold, J. B., 39
Fireman, G., 71
Fisch, R., 117
Fishman, H. C., xi, 17
Fleck, S., 7
Flomenhaft, K., 124
Fogel, A., 223
Ford, J., 49, 195
Framo, J., 123, 150
Freeman, W. J., 61, 65, 96, 169, 224
Freud, S., 212

Gample, D., 72
Ganju, V. K., 181
Garfinkel, A., 34, 96, 170
Gergen, K., 200
Gerson, R., 173
Gibney, P., 18, 19, 20, 60, 64, 77, 174
Giordan, J., 58, 217
Glass, G., 206
Glass, L., 34, 96
Gleick, J., ix, x, 4, 22, 32, 35, 47, 50, 70, 86, 96, 132, 173
Goerner, S. J., 63, 122
Goldbeter, A., xi, 18, 65, 96, 239
Goldbeter-Merinfeld, E., xi, 18, 65
Goldstein, J., ix, 22, 63
Goldstein, S., 58
Gollub, J. P., 23, 25
Goolishian, H. A., x, 17, 18, 60, 77
Gould, S. J., 34, 48, 49, 197
Gray, W., 119
Grebogi, C., 146
Griffiths, J., 123
Gurman, A., 150
Gutheil, T., 181

Haber, M., 72
Haley, J., x, 7, 8, 10, 55, 57, 91, 122, 123, 150, 160, 165, 202
Hall, N., 34
Halpern, H. A., 17
Hannah, T., 71, 223

Hao, B. L., 96
Hawkins, R. C., 207
Haynes, S., 230
Heisenberg, W., 40
Held, B. S., 16
Herbert, N., 5, 200
Highfield, R., 25
Hill, R., 124
Hoffman, L., xi, 17, 55, 88, 91, 193, 200
Hoffnung, R. J., 39
Holzer, C. E., 181
Hope, C., 222, 232
Horn, J., 230
Hornstein, G. A., 35
Howard, K., 206
Hsu, F. L. K., 240
Huckfeldt, R., 221
Hunter, D. E. K., 39
Hutchinson, M. P., 180
Hyler, L., 120

Jackson, D. D., 7, 10, 11, 14, 119, 122, 126, 129, 149, 165, 180
Jantsch, E., 6, 23, 49, 172, 210
Jiménez-Montano, M. A., 65
Johnson, J., 87, 105, 107, 119, 120, 121, 124, 126, 133, 134, 139, 146, 147, 151, 161, 163, 203, 209, 213, 228, 229
Jono, R. T., 181
Jordan, J. R., 17
Jurek, A. W., x

Kaplan, D., 124
Kaplan, M. L., 18, 222
Kaplan, N. R., 18, 222
Kaslow, F. W., x
Kassen, D., 182
Kauffman, S. A., x, 44, 45, 133, 134, 162, 171, 172, 197
Keeney, B., 41, 187, 189, 200, 202, 213
Kelly, J. L., 141
Kelso, J. A., 223
Kerlinger, F., 41
Kinskern, D., 150
Kline, P., 122, 225
Kohfeld, C. H., 221
Kopta, S., 206
Korzybski, A., ix, 7, 9, 59

Krause, M., 206
Kuhn, T. S., 34, 35, 187, 220, 231

L'Abate, L., 110, 114, 117, 121, 123, 150, 158, 162, 170, 199, 226
Laing, R. D., 63
Lambert, M., 181
Landau-Stanton, J., 123
Lane, G., 200, 201, 202
Langs, R. J., 65, 170, 201, 222, 225
Langsley, D., 124
Leahey, T. H., 4, 35
Lebow, J. L., x
Levy, J., 126
Levy, S., xii, 13, 22, 23, 64
Lidz, T., 7
Liebman, R., 14
Likens, T., 221
Lincoln, Y., 211
Lonie, I. E., 71
Lorenz, E. N., x, xi, 47, 172
Loye, D., 26, 32, 132, 195

Machotka, P., 124
Mackey, M. C., 34, 96
MacKinnon, L., 11
Mahoney, M. J., 16, 122, 124
Maier, M. E., x
Mandelbrot, B. B., 33, 94
Martinerie, J. M., 61, 65, 224
Mason, J., 123
Maturana, H. R., 15, 42
May, R. M., 33, 34
McCown, W. G., 20, 57, 87, 105, 107, 119, 120, 121, 124, 126, 133, 134, 139, 146, 147, 151, 161, 163, 203, 213, 228
McCubbin, H., 124, 131
McGoldrick, M., 58, 173, 217
McLeod, W. R., 18, 19, 58
McNally, R. J., 35
Mead, G. H., 114
Mees, A. I., 61, 65, 224
Middelton, C., 71
Miller, D., 11
Miller, T., 206
Milman, L., 14
Minuchin, S., xi, 14, 17, 124, 150, 151
Monahan, J., 181, 182

Moon, F., 21, 34, 97, 105, 123, 131, 139, 164, 224, 225
Moore, C., 205
Morawetz, A., 58
Morgan, R. F., 163
Mostwin, D., 15
Murray, M. E., 15

Neff, J., 177
Norcross, J., x

O'Connor, W., 182
Olson, D. H., x, 57, 103
Orlisky, D., 206
Ott, E., 146

Packard, N. H., 33
Papp, P., 78, 87
Parloff, M., 200
Parry, A., 113
Parsons, T., 127, 198
Patterson, J., 124, 131
Pearce, J. K., 58, 217
Pearsall, P., 71
Peat, F. D., x, 5, 18, 19, 22, 23, 25, 47, 48, 67, 85, 172, 173, 174
Pecora, L. M., 62, 177
Pellegrino, E., 211, 212
Pendick, D., 71
Percival, I., 31
Perna, P. A., 71
Pfeffer, C. R., 180
Pittman, F., 124
Platt, J., 44, 48, 50
Pols, E., 16
Prata, G., 8, 11, 12, 13, 57, 62, 122, 150, 200
Prigogine, I., 6, 13, 19, 20, 33, 40, 42, 43, 48, 49, 56, 65, 133, 172, 196
Prochaska, J., x
Proskauer, S., 142, 232

Rabkin, R., 11
Rapp, P. E., 34, 61, 65, 132, 219, 221, 222, 224
Rasband, S. N., 246
Rauseo, S., 143
Rawls, J., 212
Ray, W., 200, 201, 202, 213
Redington, D. J., 61, 65, 223

Reidbord, S. P., 61, 65, 223
Reik, T., 63
Reilly, J., 33, 123
Richardson, H. B., xi, 7
Richman, J., 180, 188
Rigney, D. R., 96
Rizzo, N., 119
Roback, A. A., 224
Robertson, R., 205
Robinson, G., 104
Robinson, N. S., x
Rosman, B. L., 14
Ross, J. M., 200
Rowlands, G., 105, 225
Ruelle, D., 33, 69, 172, 226
Russell, B., 7, 9, 10, 55
Russell, C. S., x, 57, 103
Russell, R., 57
Rychlak, J., 140, 212

Sandgren, A. K., x
Sands, R. G., 180
Sargent, J., 72
Satir, V., 121, 149, 171, 213
Schrader, S. S., 7, 11
Searight, H. R., x
Searle, S., 226
Segal, L., 117
Seligman, M. E. P., 208
Selvini-Palazzoli, M., 8, 11, 12, 13, 57, 62, 122, 150, 200
Serritella, D., 226
Shaw, C. D., 26, 51, 122, 132, 163, 164, 204, 224
Shaw, R. S., 33
Shinbrot, T., 146
Silver, M., 72
Singer, J., 247
Singer, P., 212
Skarda, A., 61, 65, 96, 224
Small, M., 247
Smith, D., 236
Smith, L., 223
Smith, M., 206
Smolensky, P., 124
Spano, M. L., 143
Sperry, R., 40
Sprenkle, D. H., x, 57, 103
Sprott, J. C., 68, 105, 225
Stanton, M. D., 226

Starr, P., 211
Stedman, J., 181
Steinglass, P., 10
Stengers, I., 6, 13, 20, 33, 40, 42, 43, 48, 49, 56, 65, 172, 196
Stevens, B. A., 18, 19, 20, 67
Stevens, W., 3
Stewart, I., 177
Stoppard, T., 93
Strogatz, S. H., 177
Sue, S., 216
Sugeno, M., 196
Sulis, W., 45
Swank, G., 124
Swanson, J. W., 181
Swerdlik, M., 236

Takaki, R., 216
Takens, F., 172
Tall, K. M., x
Terano, T., 196
Terry, D., 7
Thelen, E., 223
Thomasma, D., 211, 212
Thomson, L., 65
Todd, T. C., 14, 226
Tolstoy, L., 38
Tong, D. B., x, 216
Trepper, T., 120

Tufillaro, N., 33, 123
Tufurilla, N., 22
Tung, M., x

Vallacher, R. R., 114
Vandervert, L., 22, 195
Varela, F. J., 15, 42

Wagner, V., 199
Waite, D., 181
Waldrop, M. M., 5, 22, 24, 44, 164
Walker, G., 58
Wang, H., 205
Watzlawick, P., 11, 14, 42, 122, 180
Weakland, J. H., 7, 10, 117, 122
Wegner, D. M., 114
Wekstein, L., 181
West, B. J., 96
Whitaker, C. A., 7, 63, 146
White, M., 10, 113
White, S. H., 35
Whitehead, A. N., 7, 9, 10, 55
Wiener, N., 8, 10, 55, 57, 196
Worthington, E., 124, 212

Yorke, J., x, 23, 33, 146, 195

Zimmerman, I. D., 61, 65, 224

Subject Index

ABC-X model, 124, 128
Action Identification theory, 114
Adaptability (in Circumplex Model), 103, 104
  rigid/flexible, 104
Adaptation (phase in FAAR model), 124–125
Addictive behavior, and modality of treatment, 226
ADEPT method, 162
Adjustment (phase in FAAR model), 124–125
Al-Anon, 112
Al-Ateen, 112
Alcoholics Anonymous (AA), 112
Ambiguity (set theory), 9
Animism, 39
Anorexia, 18, 19, 60
Anthropomorphism, 56
Antichaos, 44
Anxiety, 56, 62
  role of, in therapeutic process, 223
Arithmetic, not completely formalizable, 205
Assumptions:
  contrasting, of linear and nonlinear models of change (Figure 10.1), 207
  of energy, 194
  of family systems theory, 121
  of linear model, 122
  of scientific enterprise, 39
Attractor(s):
  cyclic, or limit cycle (Figure 2.2), 28
  definition, 25
  issues acting as, in dysfunctional family behavior, 200
  point attractor, 25, 26, 27

definition, 25
fixed (Figure 2.1), 27
strange, see Strange attractors
Autocorrective capacity, 10–12, 20
  paradigm two ("a totality that autocorrects"), 10–12
Autopoiesis, 15–16

Balanced family types, 104
Behavioral rehearsal, 110
Behavioral science, 36–39
Behaviorism/ists, 5, 35, 85, 109, 201, 212
Being/becoming, 58
Benchmarks, 18
Beneficence, principle of, 212
Betting analogy, 141
Bifurcation, 20, 27, 51, 56, 58, 88, 89, 108, 133, 169, 173, 194
  cascade, 56
  critical developmental, 88, 164–169, 170, 199
  and risk assessment, 164–169
  and/or critical moments (theoretical construct 6), 48
  definition, 25
  indicator of family's history, 172–175
  and stability (Figure 2.4), 30
  with complexity (Figure 2.5), 45
Bilingual families, 74–75
Biology/biologists/biological systems, 33, 219, 226
Booster sessions, 143
Boundaries, 58, 69, 194
  fluidity of, 59–61
  identity-defining, 74
  information, 60, 65, 75, 173

Boundaries *(Continued)*
   language/communication, 74
   movement, 59, 61, 65, 90, 173
   phenotypic, 59, 69
   therapist/family, 91
   verbal, 60
Brain/computer metaphor, 86
Butterfly effect, 24, 26, 32, 46, 51,
      61–62, 85, 86–87, 88, 186, 194, 216,
      226
   definition, 25
   theoretical construct 5, 47–48

Canyon ("A Walk Through the
      Canyon"; metaphor, big picture of
      chaos theory), 26–31
Capabilities/demand/meanings
      (FAAR model), 124–125
Capacity dimension *D*, 105, 224
Cardiac rhythms, 65
Case studies:
   Blevins family (John/Jeremy/June)
      (crisis-prone families;
      Satanism), 134–135
   Brown family (undifferentiated;
      five sisters), 113–114
   "Collage" family
      (Sue/Chris/Joe/Peggy/Barbara
      ), 175–180
   Cruise family (Jon/Bill/Ted)
      (undifferentiated; macro
      system involvement), 110–111
   Fineman family
      (Robert/Anita/Nathan)
      (destabilization), 154–155
   Glenn family
      (Alan/Vicki/Todd/Mark/Kend
      ra) (undifferentiated), 99–101,
      104, 108
   Green family
      (Helen/Cyndi/Donna/Susan)
      (undifferentiated), 98–99, 104
   Hughes family (Janet/Roger)
      (destabilization), 146–147
   Imal/J'wan/Shonda
      (destabilization), 151–153
   Jenkins family (Jerry/Cleo/Oscar)
      (destabilization), 155–158
   Jennifer, Tom, Laura (crisis-prone
      families; Satanism), 135–137

Jewish family
      (David/Alan/mother/father)
      (destabilization dangers;
      cultural insensitivity of
      therapist), 167–169
   Jim and Eric (gay couple;
      destabilization dangers;
      unrecognized instrumental
      crisis), 165–167
   Joe/Martha/Lucy/Susan (suicidal
      behavior), 183–188
   Kathy/Sabrina (undifferentiated
      families), 115
   Kurtz family (John/Mary/John, Jr.)
      (destabilization dangers;
      spectacular treatment failure),
      159–160
   McKeen family (perceptual crisis),
      129–130
   Mark/Ellen (far-from-equilibrium),
      78–81
   Smith family (instrumental crisis),
      127–129
   Tiffany/Sean/Steven (white noise
      therapy), 144–146
Catastrophe theory, 214
Caterpillars, 13
Causality/cause-and-effect, concept
      of, 4–5, 38, 78
CFS (Critical Feedback Stabilization),
      142–143, 144
Change, family:
   how much is enough?, 64–65, 180
   inherent in complex systems, 132
   measuring, 65–66
   mechanisms for therapeutic, 201
   models of, suggested by
      chaos/complexity theory,
      201–202
   patterns of, 230–231
   single case studies of, 230–232
   theory of, 201
Chaos/chaos theory
   big picture ("a walk through the
      canyon"), 26–31
   chaotic systems:
      applying chaos to, 146–147
      and destabilization ("beyond
         linear predictions"), 163–164
      examples of, 33–34

definitions, 21, 22–23, 24, 25
    associated terms, 25–26
history/applications, 3, 22, 31–34, 226
    revolution (third major) in physics
        of twentieth century, 217
and human behavior, 56
    family dynamics, 55–66, 121,
        222–224
    models of family change, 201–202
    suicidal behavior (descriptive not
        predictive model), 181
mathematics of, 31
modeling chaotic structure, 221
mythological construct, ix–x
and systems in crisis, 131
theorists, 22
and therapy, 85
    and crisis-prone/treatment-
        resistant families, 227–229
    and future of, 195–196
    guidelines concerning crisis
        induction, 169–171
    modes; two approaches
        (theorists/modelers), 220
    and prediction, limits on, 204–205
    training needs, changing, 214–215
and understanding of political
    action failure, 197
Choice of orders, 48
Chronicity, 203
Circular reasoning/thinking, 17, 105
Circumplex Model, 103–105, 138, 174
Clinician's role, 63
Clocklike laws (Newton), 31, 40
Closed systems, 43, 44, 57, 174, 196
Coevolving/coevolution, 18, 64, 174
Cognitive behavioral intervention, 109
Cognitive coping, 110
Cohesion (in Circumplex Model),
    103–104
    four levels
        (disengaged/separated/connect
        ed/enmeshed), 104
Collage family (case study), 175–180
Collapse in system, 77, 78, 80, 201
Collective mind, 48
Commonsense pragmatism, 214
Communication, 6, 74
    and facilitation (in Circumplex
        Model), 103, 104

family, 10
patterns, 193
psychotherapeutic (five-dimension
    representation of), 222–223
theorists, 118
Complexity, 4, 43–46, 66, 76, 217
    and future of family therapy,
        195–196
    and how much change is enough,
        64–65
    increasing within the family
        system, 112–116
    overwhelming system, 35
    and stability/bifurcation (Figure
        2.5), 45
    theoretical construct 3, 43–46
Conditioning, 5
Confinement, 139
Confirmatory/exploratory scientific
    experiments, 232
Confrontation, in-session, 114
Conjoint relaxation, 139
Constructivism, 18, 19
Construct (terminology), 41. *See also*
    Theoretical constructs
Consumer Reports (evaluation of
    psychotherapy), 208
Containing, 62–63, 177
Controllability/invasiveness,
    spectrum of, 138–139
Control theory, 214
Conversations, 105, 106
    fractal dimension of, 106
Coping, 125
    cognitive, 110
Coupled, 62–63
Craziness, 63, 146
Creativity, 174
Crisis/crises:
    case studies (instrumental *vs.*
        perceptual), 127–129, 129–130
    and chaos theory, 131–138
    induction of, 117, 149. *See also*
        Destabilization, therapeutic
    guidelines from chaos theory,
        169–171
    intervention, 117–118
    and pathological families,
        125–126
    self-limiting, 132

Crisis/crises *(Continued)*
 techniques (novel) of controlling,
  142–147
  applying chaos to chaotic
   systems, 146–147
  Critical Feedback Stabilization
   (CFS), 142–143
  increasing family stress, 147
  structured crisis, 147
  white noise therapy, 143–146
 theories, contemporary, 123–126
  stress/buffering models, 123–125
 as threat/opportunity, 121
 treatment, rationale for, 120–121
 and treatment-resistant families,
  227–229
 types of (critical distinction),
  126–131
  instrumental, 126, 128–129, 131,
   133, 139, 169
  perceptual, 126, 129, 131, 133, 137,
   139, 169, 170
 underlying attractor, 131
Crisis-prone families, 101, 120, 134,
 138, 140, 147, 230
Critical developmental bifurcation, *see*
 Bifurcation, critical
 developmental
Critical Feedback Stabilization (CFS),
 142–143
Critical moment, 172–189, 194
 conclusion, 188–189
 theoretical construct 6, 48
Critical points, 164. *See also*
 Bifurcation
Cross-cultural training, 216–217
Cuckoo clocks, and
 coupling/synchronization, 63
Cultural:
 congruence, need for, 215–217
 definitions of family, 58
 insensitivity of therapist, 167
 norms (as organizing principles), 71
Cybernetics, 8, 10, 11, 12, 13, 14, 20,
 55, 57, 118, 149, 196, 214, 215
Cyclic, or limit cycle attractor (Figure
 2.2), 28

Dance metaphor for relationships,
 75–76

Data:
 bad, 38
 display/use of, 224–227
 obtaining, problem of, 222–224
D capacity dimension, 105, 224
Death, 23, 43, 72
Demand/capabilities/meanings
 (FAAR model), 124–125
Dementia, 147
Desensitization, 110
Destabilization, therapeutic, 90,
 149–171
 case studies, 151–153, 154–155,
  155–158, 159–160
 chaotic systems and (beyond linear
  predictions), 163–164
 dangers of, 151, 158–161, 165–166
 guidelines from chaos theory,
  169–171
 prediction when
  countertherapeutic, 161–163
 successful approaches, 150–158
 and sudden appearance of
  symptoms, 165–166
 using chaos theory in
  understanding appropriateness
  of, 164
Determinism/deterministic
 paradigm, 48, 50, 96, 217
Developmental bifurcation points, *see*
 Bifurcation, critical
 developmental
Developmental level/stage, of family,
 20, 57
Differential equations, 122–123
Differentiation, 102–105
 Circumplex Model, 103–105
 dysfunction, family (Murray
  Bowen's theory of), 102–103
 and fractals/chaos, 105–109
 undifferentiated ego mass, 102
 undifferentiated families, treatment
  options, 109–116
 undifferentiated response, 108
Dimension, *see* Capacity dimension *D*;
 Fractal dimension
Disaster/rescue situation, 109
Disowned self, 72
Dissipative structure, 19, 58, 173, 174,
 196

Distance/closeness, need for, 72, 73, 74
Diversity, 197–198, 199
Divine intervention, 137
Dosage effect, 208, 230
Double ABC-X model, 124, 128
Double-bind (first paradigm), 7, 8–10
Dualism, 51
Duty to warn, 211
Dysfunction, family:
  Bowen's theory of, 102–103
  result of issues acting as attractors, 200
  safety valve behavior, 149

Early treatment termination, 160–161, 162–163, 170
Ecologists, 33
Edge of chaos, 44, 170, 172, 194, 202
EEG patterns, brain, 65
Ego lending, 103, 139
Ego mass, undifferentiated, 102
Ego weakness, in schizophrenia, 9
Elephant proverb, 121
Emotional cutoff, 8, 107, 197
Emotional/intellectual boundary of information, 60–61
Empiricism, 35, 36
  dramatic shift from, 187
Energy, 80, 195, 196
  assumption of, 194
  flow, 222
  and information, exchange of, 201
  transforming, 216
Enmeshment, 104, 105, 106, 107, 177
  fractal theory of, 108
Entropy, 42, 43, 44, 141, 174, 214, 222
Epistobabble, 15
Equifinality, 14
Equilibrium, 45, 46
Equilibrium thermal chaos, 23
Error in measurement, 225–227
Ethics, 194, 205
  conception of ("will have to change"), 211–214
  and dangers of destabilization, 158–161
Ethnicity, 216
Evolutionary advantage, of undifferentiation, 108

Evolutionary theory, 48
Experimentation:
  exploratory/confirmatory scientific experiments, 232
  traditional paradigm of science, 41
Exponent, *see* Lyapunov exponent
Extroversion, 105, 226

FAAR, *see* Family Adjustment and Adaptation Response Model (FAAR)
Fair fighting techniques, 90
Family(ies):
  change, *see* Change, family
  crises, *see* Crisis/crises; Crisis-prone families
  defining, 58–59, 196–197
  dynamics:
    chaos theory perspective, 55–66
    and differentiation, 102–105
  health, nature of, 198–199
  political right/left on, 197
  theories that change out ideas about, 196–198
  therapy, *see* Therapy, family
  types (Circumplex Model), 104
  undifferentiated, 93, 97–101
    case studies (two), 98–101
Family Adjustment and Adaptation Response Model (FAAR), 124, 131
Family Crisis Therapy (FCT), 124, 126
Family Process journal, 8
Far-from-equilibrium, 43, 76, 173, 182, 186
FCT, *see* Family Crisis Therapy (FCT)
Fear/love, 73–74
Feedback, 11, 14, 33, 55, 57, 118, 132
  positive/negative, 118–119, 181, 182, 188, 195
Fish behavior, 69–70
Fit, concept of, 17
Fixed-point attractor (Figure 2.1), 27
Fluid communication, paradigm of, 6
Fluid dynamics analogy, 32–33, 143
Foot massage therapy, 90–91
Forks in the road, *see* Bifurcation
Formal undecidability, 205
Fractal(s), 70, 93, 94–97, 101

Fractal dimension, 96–97
  of conversations, 106
  and differentiation, 105–109
  means for crisis-prone families, 228
  tool for recognizing degree of chaos, 228
Freudians, 201
Functionalism, sociological, 198
Future of family therapy, 40, 195–196, 214–215, 217–218
Fuzzy logic, 196, 214

Gay couple (case study), 165–167
General to specific, and prediction, 187
General systems theory, see Systems theory, general
Genetic information, and fractals, 97
Genograms, 173, 175
Gestaltists, 201
Gödel's theorem, 214
Grand theory, 41
Grand Unifying Theory in psychology (search for), 50
Group(s), self-help, 110, 111–112
Group relaxation, 110

Halley's Comet, 37
Hausdorf dimension, 105, 224
Healthy family (nature of), 64, 198–199
Heart rate, in phase space, 223
Heat equation, 193
High monogamy, 71
Homeostasis, 12, 13, 14, 18, 46, 55, 118, 124, 196, 214
  negative aspects of, 150
Horse handicapping, 141
Hurricanes:
  in case studies/vignettes, 108–109, 127–128
  prediction of, 132, 187
Hypertension, 203

Identified patient (IP), 126, 216, 228
Identified problem, 201
Imagination, as butterfly, 87
Incest, 120, 214
Individual therapy, 112

Information:
  boundaries, 60, 65, 75, 173
  and energy, 80
  flow/exchange of, 173, 174, 201
  gathering, as intervention, 61
  providing (benign intervention), 139, 140–141
  theory, 141
Insight-oriented therapy vs. supportive, 212
Instability, 18
  concept of (key to chaos theory), 26
  transitional phase of, 164
Instrumental crises, 126–127, 128
Intervention:
  control (variable of), 138–142
  family:
    based on developmental level of functioning, 57
    mechanistic and organic systems, 57
  invasive/noninvasive, 199–200
  levels of, 138–142
  nonverbal interactions, 90
Intimacy/solitude conflict, 72, 73
Invariance of scale, 94
Invasiveness/controllability, spectrum of, 138–139
IP, see Identified patient (IP)
Irreversibility (theoretical construct 2), 42–43, 187

Journal (Family Process), 8

Kelly Criteria, 141
Koch snowflake, 94, 95

Language, 74
  analysis, meta-ethics, 211
  as a map, 9
Leaps/jumps/spontaneity, 49
Linear approximation, 38
Linear model/paradigm, 3, 122, 207
Linear/nonlinear (real/non-real), 34
Linguistic map, 9
Listening with the Third Ear, 63
Logical positivism, 35, 85
Logical types, 9, 55
Lost self, 72

Love, 71, 72
  vs. fear, 74
Lyapunov exponent, 31, 105, 224–225, 230

Machines, theory of, 196. *See also* Cybernetics
Madness/chaos/violence (phases in patterns of violence), 72
Managed mental health care, 109, 120, 151, 206
Mandelbrot set (Figure 6.2), 95
Manipulating behavior by changing roles, 140
Map territory, 7, 55, 59, 65
  ambiguities, 10
Mathematics, 219
  and fractals, 94
  need for training in, 215
Maximal adaptation/diversity, 197
Meanings/demand/capabilities (FAAR model), 124–125
Measurement error, 205, 225–227
Mechanistic language *vs.* organic language, 13
Mechanistic systems, 46, 55, 57, 69
Medical disorders, chaos found in, 34
Medical model, 203
Mentalist paradigm, 40
Message-identifying signal, 10
Metacommunicative messages, 8
Metacommunicative tangles, 8, 9
Metacommunicative wholes (family), 12
Meta-ethics, 211
Metalinguistic messages, 8
Microlevel measurements, 34
Milan Group, 8, 11, 12, 14, 57, 61, 91, 150
Military training, 109
Mirror, one-way, use of, 11, 91
Mississippi River (as fractal), 96, 97
Model(s):
  ABC-X model, 124, 128
  Circumplex Model, 103–105, 138, 174
  Double ABC-X model, 124, 128
  Family Adjustment and Adaptation Response Model (FAAR), 124–125, 131

family change, 201–202
linear model/paradigm, 3, 122, 207
  contrasted with nonlinear model of change (Figure 10.1), 207
  medical, 203
  stress/buffering, 123–125, 131
Modeling:
  boundary changes, 65
  chaotic structure, 221
  heuristic potential of, at this point, 221–222
  techniques, 221–222
Monkeys at play illustration, 8–9
Monogamy, high, 71
Movement, balance of, 80
Movement boundary, 59, 61, 65, 90, 173
Multigenerational transmission process, 102
Music, and fractals, 97
Mythology, 195
Myths, family, 112–113
  as organizing principles, 71

Narrative therapy technique, 113
Negative feedback, *see* Feedback, positive/negative
Negotiation, 140
Neurotic disorders, classic, 208
Newtonian paradigm, 3, 5, 31, 40, 43, 122, 193
  challenge to, 5
Noise, 222
  white noise therapy, 143–146
Noninvasive interventions, 137
Nonlinearity, 3–4, 22, 27, 31
  contrasting assumptions (linear/nonlinear models of change; Figure 10.1), 207
  definition, 25
Nonmaleficence, principle of, 211–212, 213
Nonsummativity, 14
Novelty, pure, 23
Null hypothesis, 37

Objectivity (theoretical construct 1), 41–42, 194
Observation effect, 4, 41, 88, 217

Open systems, 61, 196
  properties of, 14
  with transformative states
      (paradigm 3), 13–15
Optimal processes, 214
Orbits, chaotic, 105
Organisms are not machines
    (theoretical construct 4), 46
Organizing principles, 71
  most basic, 74
Outcome assessment, 205–211
Overlearned behaviors, 114

Paradigm(s):
  Paradigm 1 (double bind), 8–10
  Paradigm 2 (a totality that
      autocorrects), 10–12
  Paradigm 3 (an open system with
      transformative states), 13–15
  Paradigm 4 (autopoiesis), 15–16
  Paradigm 5 (self-organization and
      chaos theory), 16–20, 194
  shifts, 3, 6, 40–51, 196, 203, 217, 231
  of systemic family therapy, 119
  of things/pattern, 41
Paradoxes, 150
Parent advocate groups vs. family
    therapists, 126
Parsimony, law of, 37
Participant manager, 18
Particle physics, 226
"Peace at any price," 8
Perceptions/stressors/resources
    (ABC-X model), 124
Perceptual crises, 126–127, 129
Period-doubling route to chaos, 27, 32,
    56, 169
  definition, 25
Personality dynamics, and strange
    attractors, 71
Perturbation, 19, 27, 30, 78, 169
  definition, 25
Phase portrait, 29, 65, 221
Phase space, 60, 68, 70, 105, 223, 224
Phenotypic boundary, 59, 69
Phobias, 208
Photocopy fractal, 107
Phrase space, 55, 60, 66, 74–76, 173,
    194, 216
  mapping, 75
  "a walk in," 74–76

Physicists, 32
Physics envy, 4
Placebo, 200
Point attractor, 25, 26, 27
  definition, 25
Police, and ego lending, 139
Political groups, 110
Political right and left, on families,
    197
Population biology, 122
Positive connotation, 12
Positive/negative feedback loops, see
    Feedback, positive/negative
Posttraumatic stress disorders,
    120
Prediction:
  concept of (in traditional science),
      39
  enhanced, 163–164
  limits on, 204–205
  qualitative/quantitative, 204
Problems, identified, 77
Professional standards, 211
Psychotherapy, outcome studies,
    205–211
Punctuated equilibria (theoretical
    construct 8), 49–50, 187

Qualitative/quantitative predictions,
    204
Quantum physics/mechanics/theory,
    4, 5, 22, 34, 35, 217
Questioning, as intervention, 61

Race, 216
Racetrack analogy, 141
Randomness, 94, 222
  and D, 105
Rapid cycling family system, 138, 170,
    189, 203
Rapid therapy, 203
Reality, 34–35
Record keeping, importance of, 211
Reductionistic science, 36, 37, 39–40,
    41
Reframing, 87, 140, 150, 163, 185
Rehearsal, behavioral, 110
Reinforcement, 201
  schedules of, 38
Relationships, dance metaphor for,
    75–76

Relativity, Einstein's theory of, 21, 22, 217

Relaxation techniques, 110, 139

Religious beliefs (as organizing principles), 71

Religious fundamentalists, treatment of, 216

Religious organizations, as family support, 110, 111

Rescue situations, 109

Resistance, 18

Resources/stressors/perceptions (ABC-X model), 124

Risk/risk analysis/assessment, 200, 212
  and critical developmental bifurcations, 164–169

Rituals, family, 112–113

Rules, universal, 36

Safety valve, dysfunctional behavior as, 119, 149

Sampling limitations, 222–224

Satanism (in two case studies), 134–137

Schizophrenia/schizophrenogenic family, 7, 9, 10, 102, 120, 126

Scientific method, traditional, 6, 37, 38, 219
  exploratory/confirmatory experiments, 232
  steps (ten), 220

Scientific revolutions (three), 21–22

Score = ST + SE, 225

Seed, planting a (metaphor), 207

Self, disowned/lost, 72

Self-aware transformation, 13

Self-help groups, 110, 111–112, 162

Self-organizing/self-organization, 20, 30, 44, 51, 56, 65, 133, 172, 199
  and chaos theory (paradigm 5), 16–20
  complex, at edge of chaos, 194
  definition, 26
  feedback, 33
  and level of intervention, 138–142
  modeling, 221
  most successful type of change, 201
  and noninvasive interventions, 137
  out of chaos (theoretical construct 7), 48–49, 186

research regarding capacity for, 133
  and stability, 56–57
  states, five main, 56
  system's attempt to adapt, 56–57
  time needed for, 201

Self-similarity, 93, 94, 96, 106, 107

Sensitivity to initial conditions, 24, 25, 26, 32, 47, 61, 74, 87, 122, 169, 172, 194, 226
  definition, 25

Set theory, 9, 196, 214

Shannon Entropy, 141

Significance, concept of, 224, 232

Slow cyclers, 138, 189

Social policies, 197–198

Social service agencies, 177, 180

Social unrest, scientific analysis of, 38

Sociological functionalism, 198

Sociology, 226

Solar system, 33, 34, 217

Solitude/intimacy conflict, 72, 73

Space, in mathematics, 70

Spaghetti metaphor, 68

Spontaneity, 81

SS-77, *see* Symptom Survey-77 (SS-77)

Stability, 14, 27, 61, 118–119
  and bifurcation (Figure 2.4), 30
  with complexity (Figure 2.5), 45

Stabilizing families in crisis, 123

Stagnation, 23, 91–92

Standard deviation (*sd*), 206

Steady state, 14, 46, 55, 56, 57, 196
  and family stability, 118–119

Stereotypes, 216

Strange attractors, 20, 67–81, 172, 221
  case study, far-from-equilibrium conditions, 78–81
  contradictory effects, combining two, 69
  definitions, 25–26, 67–68, 70
  esthetic appeal ("eerie beauty of"), 67, 69
  figures:
    particularly beautiful example of (Figure 4.1), 68
    well-known strange (Figure 2.3), 29
  and human behavior, 71–74
  introduction to, 67–71
  mapping, 73
  in family therapy, 76–81

Strange attractors (Continued)
  in patterns of family interaction,
      59–60
  and phase space (territory in which
      they live), 70
  stretching and folding, 74
  usefulness of metaphor, 28–29
Strategic therapy, 87, 163, 200, 202
Stress/buffering models, 123–125, 131
Stressors/resources/perceptions
      (ABC-X model), 124
Stress vulnerability, theory of, 103
Stretching and folding, 74
Structural family therapists, 199–200,
      201
Structural rearrangement, 163
Structure, defining, 9
"Stuck" families, 76, 117, 182
"Sucked in" (therapist's avoiding
      being), 64, 91, 194
Sudden appearance of symptoms, and
      risk assessment, 165–167, 169
Sudden behavioral shift, 129
Suicidal behavior, and chaos in family,
      180–183
  case study, 183–188
  suicide watch, 182
Supervision in family therapy,
      202–203, 208
Supportive vs. insight-oriented
      therapy, 212
Suspension bridge, 39
Symbolic client, 178
Symbolic interactionism, 114
Symptom(s):
  change in family through time
      (graph; Figure 10.2), 209
  and dimensionality, 229–230
  measurement, 209, 229–230
Symptom Survey-77 (SS-77), 209, 229,
      230
Synchronized chaos, 62
System, three fundamental
      characteristics, 12
  autocorrective capacity, 12
  capacity for transformation, 12
  totality, 12
Systemic therapy, 6, 57, 193
Systems theory, general, 13, 55, 119,
      214

Taoists, 17
Team approach, Milan group, 11
Tension reduction, 139
Test construction theory, 226
Theoretical constructs:
  no. 1 (objectivity), 41–42, 185
  no. 2 (irreversibility), 42–43, 187
  no. 3 (complexity), 43–46, 174
  no. 4 (organisms are not machines),
      46, 57, 188
  no. 5 (the butterfly effect), 47–48,
      186
  no. 6 (critical moments and/or
      bifurcations), 48, 186
  no. 7 (self-organization out of
      chaos), 48–49, 186
  no. 8 (punctuated equilibria), 49–50,
      187
  no. 9 (unpredictability), 50–51, 186
Theoretical construct (terminology),
      41
Theory, life of a, 41
Therapist:
  clinician's role, 63
  containing, 62–63
  ego lending, 139
  influence of, 61–63
  redirecting turbulence, 81
  as stress buffer, 103
Therapy, family, 6
  butterfly in, 87–89
    "be the butterfly, not the storm,"
      91–92
    "flapping the butterfly's wings,"
      89–91
  and cultural congruence (need for),
      215–217
  future of, 195–196
  history, 7–8
  invasive (need to become less),
      199–201
  limits of, 202–204
  modalities/traditions (three
      primary), 6, 57
    strategic, 6
    structural, 6
    systemic, 6, 7, 8
  and nonlinear dynamics
      (contrasting tenets of), 121–123
  outcome assessment, 205–211

pioneers in, 7
stabilization *vs.* destabilization, 117
Thermodynamics, 133
Third-party payers, 120
Thought laws/natural laws, 41
Three-body problem (behavior of three planets in motion), 31
Time, irreversibility of, 43, 193
Topological theory, 105
Training needs, future, 214–215
Traits, 105
Transformative states, 55, 56, 57
open system (paradigm 3), 13–15
Transitional phase of instability, 164
Transitional points, family, 164
Transitional states, 170
Traumatic brain injury, 147
Treatment, 109–116
complexity, increasing, 112–116
experimental interventions today/tomorrow's orthodox treatments, 148
failure to stay in, risk of, 160–161
macro system involvement, 110–112
Treatment-resistant and crisis prone families, 227–229

Turbulence, 224
of fluids, 38
redirecting (in family therapy), 81

Uncertainty principle, 40
Undecidability, 214
Undifferentiated families, *see* Differentiation
Universal computation, 214
Unpredictability, 72, 76, 186, 195
theoretical construct 9, 50–51
Utilization specialists, 120

Ventilation, 128, 140, 144
Verbal boundary, 60
Vicious-circle principle, 9, 10
Violence, 71, 72, 120, 216

Warn, duty to, 211
White noise therapy, 143–146
case study, 144–146
Whole of family functioning larger than sum of its individuals, 121
Writing assignments, therapeutic, 110, 114, 162